The Modern in Spain

The Modern in Spain
Architecture after 1948

Gabriel Ruiz Cabrero

The MIT Press
Cambridge, Massachusetts
London, England

Edited in Spanish by *Raúl Rispa*
Edited in English by *Erica Witschey* and *Matthew Abbate*
Translated into English by *Hawys Pritchard, Claire Godfrey,* and *Gavin Powell*

© Gabriel Ruiz Cabrero
© Tanais Ediciones, s.a., 2001

This book was set in Optima by Monterreina, s.a., and was printed and bound in Spain.

Library of Congress Cataloging-in-Publication Data

Ruiz Cabrero, Gabriel.
    The modern in Spain : architecture after 1948 / Gabriel Ruiz Cabrero.
        p. cm.
    Simultaneously published in Spanish as : El moderno en España.
    Includes bibliographical references and index.
    ISBN: 0-262-53172-0 (pbk.: alk. paper)
    1. Architecture—Spain. 2. Architecture, Modern—20th century—Spain.
    NA1308 .R84 2000
    720'.946'09045—dc21

                                                                    00-056223
                                                                    CIP

Printing: Monterreina, Madrid
D.L.: M-6683-2001

Printed in Spain

CONTENTS

Researched and developed with the support of the
Fundación Antonio Camuñas, Alameda 14, 28014 Madrid

EDITOR'S NOTE

"The greatest achievement of this book," writes Rafael Moneo of *The Modern in Spain: Architecture after 1948*, "is to provide a thorough and synthetic history of recent Spanish architecture throughout very agitated years."

As the definitive critical study of postwar Spanish architecture in English, this book looks at the works, projects, trends, landmarks, architects, and engineers of the period. It is both a descriptive history and a new critical evaluation by one of Spain's most important architectural critics and historians, who has used over 200 plans and photographs provided by the architects of the works, their heirs or their Trusts to illustrate his thesis. The advances made by modern Spanish architecture from the 1940s, when it lay in silence and obscurity, to the 1990s, when it recieved worldwide acclaim, make a dramatic story, probably the most remarkable case of postwar architectural progress in Europe.

The protagonists of this story—both the main characters and the most outstanding buildings—are portrayed through the sharp and critical eye of Gabriel Ruiz Cabrero, practicing architect and professor at the Madrid School of Architecture.

Original drawing,
Trade Union building
(now the Ministry of Health),
Madrid, 1948–1949,
Cabrero.

The purpose of this book is to give an account of Spanish architecture in the second half of the twentieth century.

Before we begin, it must first be established that a Spanish architecture as such does exist: that it has identifiable and identifying traits that distinguish it from the architecture produced in other countries during the same period. It then remains to determine precisely the period of time to be studied, when this architecture had its beginnings, and whether it can now be considered as over.

This book sets out to demonstrate that it is indeed possible to identify a "Spanish way" of executing modern architecture, that it lasted from 1950 to the end of the twentieth century, and that stylistically it can be identified as "Spanish modern."

The global nature of the processes involved in designing, producing, and selling any product or idea in our own end-of-the-century period tends to create a uniform environment in both our cultural and physical surroundings. Architecture enjoys a wealth of information—sometimes too much so, to the point of obscuring what is important—and, given that it is a universally understood mode of expression or language, its spread is both wide and rapid. In consequence, similarities and coincidences occur among architects in countries far apart, thus justifying worldwide interpretive approaches that study architecture by style classifications: organicism, modernism, brutalism, postmodernism, neomodernism, deconstructivism . . .

None of this challenges our stated objective, however, and the following study will attempt, by showing exactly what architecture was built in Spain, to establish what its differentiating features are, what constitutes its identity.

We take the following hypothesis as our point of departure: that awareness of Spain's retarded scientific development, and the resulting frustration that dominated Spanish culture from the beginning of the twentieth century, generated an intense, passionate appetite for modernity.

The concept of modernity,[1] which had been the motivating force behind European thought throughout the nineteenth century and was linked with the concept of internationalism—remember Hitchcock and Johnson's 1932 book, *The International Style*—in all of the dominant ideological approaches before the Second World War, came to be viewed critically both in Europe and in America in the light of the failure that the war represented. The exception was Spain, which had not been involved in either of the world wars and where modernity retained all its fascination, even among those who rejected it with a violence born of frustration. There, it was the Civil War, in everyone's opinion, that had interrupted the road to modernity—a road that had to be continued without delay and without the need for self-criticism. Perhaps this is why, when international criticism started in the eighties to become fascinated by contemporary Spanish architecture, unknown until then, it was doing no more than discovering a chapter in international modern architecture itself. Modern Spanish architecture showed a faith in modernist principles and a desire to put them into practice, and these principles were then not very common beyond Spain's borders, where postmodern and other stylistic doubts flourished.

Rounding off this hypothesis is another conviction: that, as far as architecture was concerned, modernity was achieved in Spain—eventually—in the second half of the twentieth century.

Few stories have one single, clear beginning; beginnings are usually multiple, vague, tentative affairs. Especially if an experience is a collective one, memories and assessments of it are couched in apparently contradictory feelings. Looked at in isolation, successive events seem random, and the narrative seems erratic and haphazard. Yet, at the same time, the simple fact that the events occurred makes them come to seem inescapable, reducing any other possibility to mere fantasy.

That said, however, it is not difficult to ascertain when the objective under consideration here became a clearly stated one. The loss in 1898 of Spain's last overseas territories, Cuba and Puerto Rico in the Caribbean, and the Philippines and other archipelagos in the Pacific, forced Spanish intellectuals to focus their attention on a new objective, a new destiny. This school of thought was expressively labeled *regeneracionismo* (regenerationism), and its reflection in the art world *modernismo*, or *modernisme* in Catalonia.[2]

In architecture, the most consciously exerted and effective efforts to catch up with modernity were made in Barcelona. The rest of Spain was more concerned with recovering its old identity: consider the examples of stylistic movements such as the neomudejar, the neoplateresque, and so many others that only on rare occasions, as in the work of Antonio Palacios, managed happy coexistence with modern structures.

From his Barcelona studio, Josep María Martorell proposed a double objective: Catalan identity and modernity. English industrial architecture, much admired by the Catalans since the time when their own spinning factories began to prosper, had some time earlier found its national model in Gothic art, or at least a model representative of its history that was at the same time structurally direct and efficient (which is to say, modern). By a happy coincidence, the Gothic matched the most brilliant moments of Catalan history, too.

It fell to two of Martorell's disciples—Lluis Domènech i Muntaner and Antoni Gaudí—to forge the way forward, each in his own way. The former, a fervently nationalist and politically committed architect,[3] clearly defined the strategy and consciously developed the proposal. In contrast, Gaudí's work had such a personal cast that, although he lived until 1926 (only three years before Mies van der Rohe's pavilion in Barcelona), his inspired oeuvre skirted the modern debate.[4] Consequently, the influence of his work was limited to his most immediate disciples, particularly Josep María Jujol, a flamboyant architect whose works—by then contemporary with the architecture of the modern movement—found no followers until many years later.[5]

Gaudí's relationship with his patron, Count Güell, is very significant in this respect. The architect is said to have complained to Güell: "My work seems not to be very successful. Only you and I like it." "You're mistaken there," replied the Count. "I don't like it either." The *modernisme* of these architects was succeeded by *noucentisme*,[6] which did little more than provide a reactionary position against which the modernists of the twenties revolted.

The subsequent efforts of the architects associated with GATCPAC to introduce the new tendencies known as rationalism and functionalism into Spain are widely recognized.[7] In both the social and institutional domains, Spain's architects were divided by the same controversial issues as those confronting their European colleagues, of which the debate between Perret and Le Corbusier over the elongated window as paradigm of modernity is one example. While the Republican government commissioned Secundino Zuazo to design Madrid's new ministry buildings, the Nuevos Ministerios, in a traditionalist language, the same Republic chose the architecture of Josep Lluis Sert and Luis Lacasa, both known for their modern approach, to represent it at the Paris International Exposition of 1937.

In other words, modern architecture had already taken root in Spain in the thirties, and certain buildings, such as the Casa Bloc workers' housing complex by Sert, Josep María Torres Clavé, and Joan Bautista Subirana, and the San Sebastián sailing club by José María Aizpurúa and Joaquín Labayen, are worthy of inclusion in an anthology of the best architecture in late-twenties Europe.[8] However, just as these isolated gestures were beginning to gel into recognizable movements, avid for the spirit of modernity—one example was the group in Madrid's Residencia de Estudiantes, whose luminaries included García Lorca, Dalí, and Buñuel—the Civil War broke out. To the war's terrible toll of death and suffering must be added its stifling of the nascent modern movement.

Some disciplines, such as medicine, progress in times of war. The plastic arts tend to become tainted by the requirements of propaganda and, worse still, by the convictions and beliefs of artists who have lost their critical capacities. Architecture in times of war simply disappears, or rather becomes perverted, its skills being used for the purposes of destruction. The Civil War stopped architecture in its tracks, severing traditions both ancient and more recently established. After the war, it had to start all over again.[9] Recovery was to be slow, however, for by this time the Second World War had broken out.

The following work describes and explains the process—a process with its foundations in the dark years of the forties and fifties—of achieving modernity.

Towns and villages having been badly damaged, the lack of housing and public buildings of all kinds made rapid reconstruction a priority. These tragic circumstances provided architects with an excellent opportunity, and it was capitalized on by a very specific sector of the profession: those who, having been students before the war, had fought on the side of the victors and gone on to complete their studies in the early forties.[10]

It was therefore inevitable, even essential, that the first architectonic reaction to the creative silence imposed by the war should occur in Madrid. The many services set up in the capital, obeying a strongly centralist political model, included some whose dreadfully evocative titles such as Regiones Devastadas (Devastated Regions) and the Obra Sindical del Hogar (Trade Union Housing Organization) speak volumes about the state of the country. The departments set up to provide housing brought together many excellent architects from various cities: Rafael Aburto from Bilbao, Ricardo Abaurre from Seville, Francisco Cabrero from Santander, Alejandro de la Sota from Pontevedra, José Antonio Coderch from Barcelona, all drawn there by the centripetal force of a victory to which they had all made their contribution in the trenches.
A very strong link united them: they all belonged to one precise faction among the many that had constituted the self-styled "national" camp. These were the Catholics, who had taken arms to defend their religion, interpreting the war as a crusade, and emerged from it convinced that only on the basis of a Catholic perception of life could society be regenerated. For them, architecture was above all an instrument for building the spaces in which society's ethical necessities could be renewed.

The working methods in the Trade Union Housing Organization offices could, paradoxically, be said to have been communist: no piece of work had one individual author. Given a brief for a group of dwellings, one architect would come up with the basic ideas, another would make the preliminary sketches, a third would outline the project, and this collaborative approach would continue right through to the direction and construction of the required housing. The architects working in these offices were able to evade the regime's most official and political tenets, which demanded a "national" architecture inspired by the Escorial. Instead, fueled by their moral convictions, they engaged in an intense architectonic discourse throughout the arduous reconstruction work to which the forties were dedicated. In consequence, by the start of the fifties, they were in a position to posit an architecture.

The tone of those years is evoked by an anecdote of Aburto's: in the Trade Union Housing Organization offices, located opposite Madrid's Retiro park, the workers felt the beginnings of an earthquake. After the first few tremors, Aburto approached Coderch's desk and, pointing through the window at the employees who had taken refuge in the park, asked him:

Civil Government building,
Tarragona, 1957,
de la Sota.

"Do you think that, as bosses, we ought to stay put?" "Let's go and ask Cabrero—he's higher up than us," answered Coderch. When they got to his drawing board, before they had time to speak, Cabrero said in a worried tone: "I think I must be ill—my pencil's sliding about on the paper."

The decade passed in much the same way in Catalonia, with architects working entirely on reconstruction: a few little fishing villages and local government buildings are the most interesting examples of the period. The fishing villages, such as Rosas, a project designed in 1945 by Enric Giralt and Joan Margarit, tackled issues such as orientation, use, and cir-culation patterns, and on these grounds could be seen as continuing in the urban planning tradition of the modern movement. The local govern-ment buildings—with the exception of Tarragona's Civil Government building—bowed to the classicist orientation imposed by the regime at that time, although this was less rigidly interpreted in Catalonia. Among other reasons, this may have been due to the fact that the prewar classical revival had taken its inspiration from Brunelleschi rather than from the baroque or the plateresque.

Many churches were built throughout Catalonia, while in the busy, middle-class center of Barcelona the tone was set by the modern, restrained, and (perhaps it is redundant to say this) aristocratic team led by Ramón Durán i Reynals: "the silence of the Muntadas house and the wisdom of the house on Avenida de la Victoria."[11]

When Coderch, unhappy living outside his native territory, returned to Catalonia from Madrid—where he had lived and worked with Zuazo and, as we have seen, in the Trade Union Housing Organization—his horizons widened, for the ongoing pursuit of modernity triggered less opposition in Barcelona. Joan Rafols and Gabriel Alomar defended it from the pages of *Cuadernos de Arquitectura.*

Coderch deserves the credit for discovering a fundamental architectonic theme of the fifties: popular architecture. Friends from that period relate how important the effect of Majorcan village architecture was on him; its way of revealing its functional and formal aspects provided the definitive model for that generation, unchallengeable in its national authenticity, and a successful substitute for all other official or foreign models. Coderch is well known to have used photographic montages to explain how inspiration could be sought in popular architecture without mimetic or regionalist effect.

This was what was happening at the start of the fifties, but the most sig-nificant events were yet to come.

Photographic montage of popular architecture, Coderch.

"Hace ya tiempo presenté a u
hice hacer por un no arquitec
de las afueras de Madrid, cuy
todas de una planta; todas ten
na puerta. Aquello me gustal
go, existía una gran variedad
hacemos, y se me ocurrió per
ducimos, en general, en las c
monotonía, resultan falsos; en
arbitrariedad por los que iban
tonces hice recortar (porque
terrelación de unas casas con
resultó una fotografía preciosa
y todos preguntan que dónde e

Discovering Abstraction

In Madrid in the early fifties, there was a small group of architects who, elated at having survived the war and by the feeling that they were starting from scratch, ignored briefs of the Escorial type to capitalize on the frantic reconstruction work, setting in train the sequence of events related here. However, despite close ideological and generational links, no architecture of sufficient homogeneity to be called a school emerged. Juan Daniel Fullaondo designated them the *Equipo de Madrid*—the Madrid Team— consisting of Aburto, Cabrero, Fernández del Amo, Fisac, and de la Sota. Other names must first be mentioned, to provide an accurate picture of the situation at the time. These were the people who had built the city, the successful architects before the Civil War—Aguirre, López Otero, Garrigues, Palacios, Zuazo, Luis Moya, and Luis Gutiérrez Soto—of whom the last two deserve a closer look.

During the thirties and forties, Luis Moya was the authority to whom everyone in Madrid bowed. His constructional skill, his mastery of traditional techniques, especially in ceramic and concrete, and his historical knowledge continued to attract the admiration of students such as Cabrero and Sáenz de Oiza. In the churches of Torrelavega in Santander, and Los Agustinos and El Pilar in Madrid, Moya demonstrated how baroque principles of composition could be attained using modern techniques. But such demonstrations were no longer of interest to a society more concerned with aspirations toward modernity.

After the war Gutiérrez Soto, who had been one of the pioneers who introduced the modern movement, became the most favored architect for the many and varied commissions of which the middle classes—and not just Madrid's—were an abundant source. A possibly apocryphal story is told to explain his transformation from the modern architect he had been before the war into the postwar pragmatist he became: on entering Madrid as a soldier with Franco's troops after years of warfare, he met a colleague whom he promptly asked: "What's fashionable in Madrid at the moment?" Gutiérrez Soto's buildings were always interesting. He created insuperably precise, relevant designs for middle-class housing, but, by their very nature, the commissions that he undertook—luxury housing— distanced him from the architectonic considerations that concern us here.

Critics generally consider the Trade Union building in Madrid, designed by Cabrero and built together with Rafael Aburto, to be the first modern building of the postwar period. As early as 1948, however, Cabrero had already propounded distinctly unacademic ideas in buildings such as the Country Fair pavilion, with Jaime Ruiz, and the Virgen del Pilar apartment block, both in Madrid. In both cases he used a traditional technique, imported from Catalonia and investigated by Luis Moya, to construct partitioned ceramic vaults. In the absence of iron and cement, this cheap and convenient solution made it possible to achieve a morphology that was modern in both its rational and elemental formality and its construction-derived geometry, the use of ceramic providing the inspiration for a distinctive architecture.

Cabrero was the first architect to create buildings that were modern in the full sense of the word, in which Italian and vernacular architectural influences are identifiable.[12] In 1952, he designed and built the Puerta de Hierro house, which shows highly contemporary concepts being applied with a confident, sure touch. By this time, architects had begun to venture across the national frontier, and the influence of Europe, particularly of Scandinavian architects, became evident in their work. This Nordic influence lasted until the end of the decade. Fernández Alba, a specialist in this area, attributes it to two factors: its origin in local architecture, techniques, and materials, and the fact that Scandinavians had not been involved in the Second World War, which allowed them to occupy the sphere of influence in Madrid formerly occupied by Germanic culture. The Puerta de Hierro house is significant for the shift it reveals in an architect characterized by his closeness to construction, who here moves on from partitioned ceramic vaults to reinforced vaults in which the girders of the framework function simultaneously as the radiant heating system. The feeling for economy remains, with iron and heating being hidden from view.

Miguel Fisac, like Cabrero, was self-taught; they were fellow students at a time when there were no teachers of any prestige, no mentors to follow. Fisac taught himself from Letarouilly's *Edifices de Rome moderne* and designed his first buildings on this basis. Their Renaissance-derived composition of symmetrical ground plans and columned facades reveals a superbly ordered and balanced rationalism. In 1948, he was commissioned to design the Cajal Institute of Microbiology in Madrid, which was built in 1951. As research for this project, he traveled around Europe, encountering among other buildings the work of Asplund, which made a vivid impression on him and changed the direction of his work. The Daimiel Institute was built in 1951, and the Arcas Reales Apostolic School in Valladolid, on which he worked with the sculptor Oteiza, in 1952. These were transitional works in which he broke with symmetry to explore free forms, in what he called *arquitectura de mondongo*—"gut architecture"—showing his interest in organic functioning, the primacy of construction, and an open mind in the matter of formal effect.

A student of the same vintage as the previous two, José Luis Fernández del Amo is an artist who is vital to an understanding of this period. The significant characteristics of his oeuvre are a personal interpretation of the

Apostolic School of the Dominican Fathers, Arcas Reales (Valladolid), 1952, Fisac.

Below left:
Country Fair pavilion, Madrid, 1949, Cabrero / Ruiz.

Opposite, above:
Colony-village of Villalba de Calatrava (Ciudad Real), 1955, Fernández del Amo.

Opposite, below:
Basilica of Aránzazu (elevation and model), Oñati (Guipúzcoa), 1949, Sáenz de Oiza / Laorga.

popular, a sense of the ethical and, one might even say, the mystical, and a fruitful relationship with the plastic arts. Hernández Mompó, Feito, Serrano, Sánchez, Canivet, and Millares all found a patron in him during this difficult period. They provided the decoration for villages whose atmosphere was imbued with both an understanding of the new directions in which art was moving and an old awareness of the land. These villages, from Belvís del Jarama in Madrid (1952) to La Vereda in Córdoba (1963), by way of Vegaviana in Cáceres (1954–1958), the best-known and most acclaimed of his urban designs, recipient of several awards, demonstrate the exploration of functional issues—such as separating circulation patterns related to farm work from those related to civic life—and constructional issues—such as using traditional materials in ways that make neoplastically inspired composition possible—that characterized Fernández del Amo's work. Photographs by Joaquín del Palacio, otherwise known as Kindel, succeeded with equal sensitivity in capturing the plastic values of their construction, the play of light and shade in streets set within calm, rhythmic linear patterns.

Of the next generation, born too late to take part in the war, the impressive figure of Francisco Javier Sáenz de Oiza stands out as being ahead of his time. As early as 1946, working with Laorga, he won the design competition for the basilica of La Merced in Madrid, but it was the basilica of Aránzazu that consolidated his reputation definitively. For Sáenz de Oiza, the construction of the church of Aránzazu (which lasted until 1952) provided an intensive apprenticeship in producing complex, large-scale works; starting from a highly conventional symmetrical ground plan, he proceeded to explore its considerable formal potential, as revealed in the treatment of the textured walls and the deeply indented arches and openings. In this building he called on the collaboration of other artists, most of them Basques, such as Pascual de Lara, Chillida, and particularly Oteiza, who played an essential role and with whom, because of the similarity of their names and characters, he would forever be linked from then onward. If a particularly Catholic morality was a prerequisite among the architects mentioned earlier, these artists seemed to stand for another version of religion in which love, blasphemy, and doubt rubbed shoulders, one neatly summed up by an utterance of Oteiza to Sáenz de Oiza, describing his frieze carving depicting the apostles: "There are thirteen apostles rather than twelve: the twelve oarsmen from Orio plus Miguel de Unamuno; pigs with their bellies open."[13]

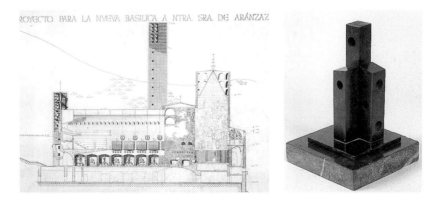

After those early years of the fifties, things progressed quickly. On 1 August 1953, an Abstract Art Course[14] was launched in Santander, with a simultaneous exhibition redundantly titled "Arte Abstracto 1953. Museo de Arte Contemporáneo." Its director was Fernández del Amo, who was also director of the Museum of Contemporary Art founded two years earlier in Madrid.[15] Among other Spaniards taking part were Oteiza, Tharrats, Millares, Aburto, Vázquez Molezún, Gargallo, Cirici i Pellicer, Antonio Saura, and Kindel, while foreign artists included Child, Kelly, Downing, Ionesco, Poliakoff, Franchina, and Matta. These encounters revealed a unanimous interest in so-called abstract art, which was to redirect the work of artists and architects toward stances that would subsequently be given labels such as informalism and structuralism. As director of the museum, Fernández del Amo (who in incorporating different arts and artists into his architecture had revived aspirations toward the *Gesamtkunstwerk*—a concept embraced by the likes of Gropius, heirs of the old romantic tradition of Rousseau and Novalis) provided a launching pad for the new Oteiza of empty box fame, Saura, Chillida, Millares, and Tàpies. These were artists whose works were independent of their environment; more than that, they generated an environment of their own, with its peculiar spaces and times. It was to accommodate these works, which the museum intended to collect, that he drew up a scheme for a building for the Contemporary Art Museum. This was a substantial document, and one whose architectonic consequences were various. A competition to design the museum building was announced in 1953 and won by Vázquez Molezún—a design that, although never built, was highly influential among fellow architects. In the meantime, Fernández del Amo himself remodeled one of the courtyards of Madrid's National Library to provide a temporary hall to exhibit his first acquisitions and to host exhibitions by foreign artists. People old enough to remember the place recall it as the most refreshing, optimistic, and stimulating space in Madrid at that time. Free planes and weightless lines under a timeless light created a fitting space for abstraction.

At about this time, artists began to voice serious disenchantment with the cultural and social situation in which they were living. Beyond the discontent with the policies of the Franco regime that most (though not all) of them felt, their protests were directed against the acquiescence of a society rooted in the false sense of security engendered by a basically autorepressive sense of order. They all spoke of a different order, formulated through the tenets of another kind of art, which could only be

Contemporary Art Museum, Madrid, Fernández del Amo.

Design for the monument to Calvo Sotelo, Madrid, 1955, Cabrero.

abstract. If the existing rules of composition or order were cast aside, a new, different artistic product would inevitably be brought into being that, since it could not be interpreted through the established rules and codes, would by its very nature demand a different sort of philosophy and facilitate discoveries and inventions that would lay the foundations for a new understanding of the arts.

In this sense, 1957 was a very significant year. It saw the founding of the Parpalló group in Valencia; of the Equipo 57 group, led by Oteiza, in Córdoba; and of the El Paso group, whose manifesto presented in February of that year launched what was to prove the most influential group of the period.

The new desire for autonomy in the arts, which coincided with a move away from the abstract at its purest toward informalism and structuralism, was also apparent among architects. Cabrero, for example, while retaining his sense of the monumental and his obsession with the structural, started moving toward the formal simplification that would progressively characterize his oeuvre, which had always been both artistically autonomous and highly disciplined. Buildings of a gentler, more domestic tone, such as the 1956 School of Catering in Madrid, built jointly with Jaime Ruiz, whose composition was neoplastic in its use of materially defined lines and planes, alternated from then on with competition designs such as the monuments to Calvo Sotelo in Madrid and Ali Jinnah in Karachi, both surrealist structures. The Calvo Sotelo monument belonged to the sort of political competition that, frequent in the forties, was now (1955) becoming more and more sporadic. Cabrero proposed a gigantic V for victory in red-colored reinforced concrete, placing a very Max Bill–like geometric gesture in an urban setting. Architecture was held to be capable of interpreting the monument without recourse to other applied arts. The sequence from preliminary drawings showing a group of standard-bearers thrusting their flags dynamically before them, through to the final proposal, simultaneously representative of the letter V, wings, and flags, demonstrates the sort of desire for abstraction that we have noted, and that is observable in many architects.

Fisac, who had also habitually called on other artists, demonstrated with his 1956 church and theological school of the Dominican Fathers, in Madrid, his conviction that architectural forms should be self-sufficient in achieving artistic status.

Church and theological school of the Dominican Fathers, Alcobendas (Madrid), 1955, Fisac.

Alejandro de la Sota's professional career was slower, but much more influential in the long term. For him, the fifties were a period of struggle in which self-doubt played no small part, during which he progressed from early designs in a popular language toward a personal style that he mastered only at the end of the decade. In 1955, he built the village of Esquivel in the province of Seville. Here, he interpreted the clichés of the Andalusian vernacular—grilles, tiles, ornamentation, weather vanes—through a filter of surrealist humor, thereby successfully avoiding a banal reading of popular architecture and achieving the poetic tone that characterizes his entire oeuvre. The house for Dr. Arvesú in Madrid, also built in 1955, reveals how, during that enterprising period, he experimented briefly but successfully with an informalism derived in equal measure from the popular and the surrealist. He, too, was an independent artist who believed in the complete autonomy of architecture. In 1957, approaching a maturity already anticipated in his work, he completed two buildings. Of these, the Civil Government building in Tarragona, whose design competition he had won in 1954 and in which the influ-ence of examples from Como is still evident, seems to distill the essence of its author's personality. This is an exquisitely precise work: even the preliminary sketches, and details such as the stairs, show what de la Sota's fundamental ambition was: to create excitement through the medium of his own imagination. It is one of the finest works of its period. The TABSA aeronautical workshops in Barajas were completed in the same year: here, we see the first appearance of de la Sota's persistent belief in the technical nature of construction as a pure truth.

In the mid-fifties, Sáenz de Oiza was occupied with what was to become another of his specialties: public housing. The overspill neighborhood of Fuencarral A dates from 1955, and the Entrevías housing project from

Colony-village of Esquivel, Seville, 1948–1955, de la Sota.

Opposite page:
Herrera de Pisuerga Institute (detail of the interior and general plan), Palencia, 1955, Corrales / Vázquez Molezún.

1956. Both make use of Dutch models from between the wars, down-scaled to achieve the dramatic effect that this architect loved so much. Mechanically perfect ground plans, another of his characteristics, are in evidence even in these early designs, foreshadowing his mechanics-based approach to achieving formal autonomy in his architecture.

Around this time, José Antonio Corrales and Ramón Vázquez Molezún matured as a team. They were the architects perhaps most widely respected by all their colleagues mentioned so far, and the first Madrid architects to become known outside Spain. De la Sota summed up the regard in which they were held by their colleagues when he described their dedication to architecture. He always remembered how Corrales had left the studio of his uncle, Gutiérrez Soto, where a lucrative and secure future awaited him, to set up an independent practice where he could carry out his own research. Vázquez Molezún, who has already appeared in this narrative, had turned a similarly deaf ear to blandishments being offered from Italy by his admirer Gio Ponti, then at the peak of professional success.

In 1956, they built the Herrera de Pisuerga Institute, a building in which they based the formal and expressionistic power of a Melnikovian idea on a purely functionalist ground plan dictated by orientation and circulation patterns; in which belief in the tectonic potential of its materials creates spaces at once basic and poetic. In 1957, in the Summer Residence in Miraflores, built together with de la Sota, the brave, uncompromising choice of a roof parallel to the ground—as used in local sheepfolds, harmonizing beautifully with the area's granite outcrops—creates space, suspends time, and casts shade on the ground which, contained within glass walls and a Mondrianesque distribution, produces the places, the classrooms and dining rooms to be used by children.

But the work that made a name for Corrales and Vázquez Molezún beyond Spain was the Spanish Pavilion at the 1958 Universal Exposition in Brussels. A structure of hexagonal umbrellas, adaptable to any dimension and any terrain—it accommodated the idiosyncrasies of the Brussels site and incorporated its trees—it not only fitted its brief ideally, allowing maximum flexibility of movement and lighting, but also represented a modern invention, avoiding the idea of the facade in favor of the lattice—a truly part-mineral, part-geometric solution.

This was not the only inter-national prize to be taken by Spanish artists: Cuixart, Tàpies, Saura, Oteiza, and Millares were among those who, as plastic artists, received frequent awards at various biennials.

In 1957, Javier Carvajal and José María García de Paredes won a gold medal at the 11th Milan Triennial. Carvajal, who was later to work in his native Catalonia, and the Cádiz-born García de Paredes set up practice in Madrid. The latter, working with Rafael de la Hoz, built the fine Santo Tomás de Aquino residence hall in Madrid. The lower floors contain a monastery and a secondary school distributed around open and closed cloisters, in the tradition of these scholastic buildings. In this case, however, the buildings are organized in a rectangular geometry emphasized by a 45-degree turn, in which a block with interrupted outer walls containing student accommodations stands out as a significant element. The block stands tall to receive sunlight, and its sharp-edged, dihedral planes create shadows and transparencies, an image at once emphatic and elegant of geometry and light, a highly structured facade by architects who also designed notable buildings of an informalist nature, such as the Chamber of Commerce in Córdoba.

The exploration of structuralist—and, albeit fleetingly, informalist— avenues in Madrid architecture was very useful in establishing a compo-sitional approach to the then frequent commissions for basic housing. Fisac, de la Sota, Cabrero, Sáenz de Oiza, and others designed many low-budget housing complexes, achieving solutions that were restrained and efficient in both functional and formal terms. Rows of houses and slab blocks began appearing on the periphery of Madrid. In the city center, few architects were exploring different avenues, Antonio Lamela being among those that were. The facades of his houses on Paseo de la Castellana and Calle O'Donnell create a play of interrupted planes, and their use of artificial granite and metal balustrades is typical of this period.

Spanish Pavilion at the 1958 Universal Exposition, Brussels, Corrales / Vázquez Molezún.

This sort of work
was reported in two
magazines. One was
Hogar y Arquitectura, an
official publication conscien-
tiously and didactically edited by
Carlos Flores, who gave space to all
good examples of architecture of this type,
along with anything else of quality being produced in Spain. The other
journal, *Arquitectura*—known at one period, when it was backed by the
administration, as the *Revista Nacional de Arquitectura*—belonged to the
Architects' Chamber, and its editor, Carlos de Miguel, was a diligent
channel of communication. Effective at generating cultural interest and
unprejudiced in terms of style, he published information about everything
of any interest, engineered encounters and debate among architects, and
brought in guests such as Alvar Aalto, opening up the discourse, as we
shall see.

R Group

The fifties were a period of unquestionable optimism in both Europe and America: the recovery of the economy after the Second World War encouraged a light, technically confident architecture. Also influenced by this optimism were the Barcelona architects who experienced major changes in the slightly earlier decade from 1948 to 1958, years that saw an uninterrupted sequence of significant events.

Ugalde house,
Caldes d'Estrach
(Barcelona), 1951–1952,
Coderch / Valls.

In 1948, the Dau al Set group was founded. In 1949, lectures given by foreign architects—Gio Ponti, Alberto Sartoris, and Bruno Zevi, to name but a few—triggered controversy and created an awareness of the need for an instrument that would promote progress in architecture. The result was the founding of the R Group in 1951. The status of its members and the belligerent publicity it provided for their opinions turned it into a vital forum. Its founders were Sostres, the group's main motivator, Coderch, Moragas, Valls, Gili, Pratmarsó, Bohigas, and the photographer Català-Roca. They were later joined by Bassó, Balcells, Giráldez, Carvajal, and García de Castro. As we shall see later, the Eucharistic Congress, held in 1952, officially consolidated the status of modern architecture. A year later, in 1953, the FAD (Fomento de las Artes Decorativas) awards were established, which have since provided a continuous and effective measure of the progress of design and its successive movements. And so on until 1958, when Terradas was appointed director of the School of Architecture. He added important teachers to his staff, among them Federico Correa, whose many students would participate in the political mobilization of the sixties and would also create many of the works that occupy the following pages.

But back to the beginning. We have noted Coderch's return to Barcelona, where he triggered another of its many renaissances. In 1951 he designed the Spanish pavilion for the 9th Milan Triennial, winning the gold medal, on the strength of which he became known outside Spain and gained a particular following in Italy. A few years later, students Federico Correa and Alfonso Milà joined his studio staff. This was the beginning of an extremely fruitful collaboration and of a line of influence which later, when figures such as Clotet and Tusquets joined the studio (which Correa and Milà had by then left), was to become central to the architecture of Barcelona.

Following in the footsteps of his mentor, Correa attended the CIAM course held in Venice in 1952, there coming into contact with such figures as Le Corbusier and Ignazio Gardella, and striking up friendships with people of his own generation, among them Vittorio Gregotti.[16] Such international contacts were hugely important not only in creating a profile for Spanish architecture abroad, but also for its own internal dynamic.

Today one can trace the progress of Barcelona's architecture not only through the recollections of the people who were there at the time, but also through two invaluable direct records: the articles published in journals and the photographs taken by Català-Roca. Of the magazines, the most important were *Cuadernos de Arquitectura*, published by the Architects' Chamber of Catalonia and the Balearic Islands, to which Joan Rafols, Gabriel Alomar, Alberto Sartoris, and Antonio Moragas were contributors; *Destino*, for which Oriol Bohigas wrote uninterruptedly from 1945, when he was still a student, until the mid-fifties; *Arquitectura*, published in Madrid; and the *Boletín* of the General Directorate for Architecture and *Serra d'Or*, to which Josep María Sostres contributed frequently. Barcelona architecture was immensely fortunate in Català-Roca.[17] Not only did he depict what was being built with daring vision, but what he chose to focus on was also vital in communicating the way that architecture ought to be. As so often happens, portraitist became designer.

These records highlight certain points. On the one hand, for the Barcelona architects—we have seen the same thing happening in Madrid—reclaiming the modern movement's tenets of functionality and rationality was something that had to be done, and they openly pursued this goal in their architecture and argued for it in publications from the mid-forties on. On the other hand, the need to respond to the demands of place, the homeland, also exerted a strong pull. But while in Madrid this became an ideological issue, in Barcelona it was initially more of an irresistibly sensual pull. Over time, though, the issue became more complicated, with the recurrent theme of popular architecture as its focus—a controversial issue, as we shall see.

The idea that vernacular architecture could be susceptible of contemporary interpretation, and could serve as thematic and compositional material, was launched principally by Coderch. His houses on the Catalan coast and the hills of Gerona served as proof that it was possible to achieve functional and formal symbiosis between the traditional principles manifest in popular architecture's response to place and climate and modern construction and principles. The 1951 Ugalde house in Caldes d'Estrach exemplifies this attitude beautifully. The spaces defined by its ground plan and outer and inner walls merge with pine trees and light and shade to create environments which, considered in the context of contemporary artistic production (Dau al Set, for instance), could be described as informal and surrealist.

In the 1956 Catasús house, the curved shapes of the Ugalde house become rectangular, in response to the different terrain. The experience acquired with this house was developed further in subsequent ones. In the Uriach house in Caldes d'Estrach, built as late as 1961, Coderch again played with the planes of floors and walls. The former sit, almost carpetlike, on platforms set into the site, and the latter orient the spaces according to the light and the landscape offered by rock and sea, within strict parallels like a white village in miniature.

Between 1952 and 1954, Coderch built his La Barceloneta apartment building, which ranks among the finest pieces of Spanish architecture built in this century. The ground plan is an exciting one, its broken planes defining rooms of trapezoidal shapes that are unexpected yet effectively furnished. The functional relationships between the different rooms are

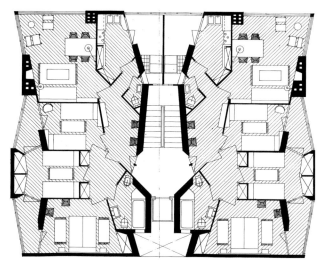

Apartment building in
La Barceloneta,
known as Casa de la Marina,
Barcelona, 1951–1954,
Coderch / Valls.

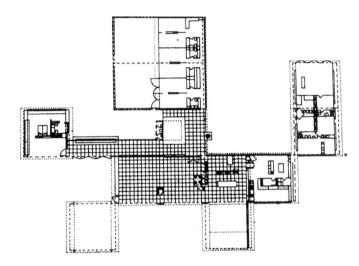

La Ricarda summer house,
El Prat de Llobregat
(Barcelona), 1949–1961,
Bonet Castellana.

Opposite page:
Iranzo house,
Esplugues de Llobregat
(Barcelona), 1957,
Sostres.

perfect. The building is superb in its interface with the outside: terraces and clothes-drying areas, closed off by uniform slats, regulate the relationship between bedrooms and kitchens and the street, successfully creating a private, independent space. The slats and the ceramic cladding on the blind exterior walls wrap the central body of the building in a smooth, continuous skin; this very organic theme, readily appreciated and critically acclaimed, was explored by Coderch at length in subsequent years. Compositionally, the central corpus took its place in its urban context in the classical way: it stands on a plinth (in this case a delicate crisscross of glass and marble) and has an attic floor overhung by modern eaves.

During this period Antoni Bonet, returned from exile, was creating architecture of a very personal kind: he, too, was moving away from the strictly rationalist and designing very expressionist forms. In the La Ricarda summer house, built on the coast near Barcelona, he applied arguments that were very much of their time: the use of a modular scheme based on the square, and distribution determined by areas for daytime and nighttime use. He handled constructional elements such as domes and slatted shutters with ease to create a building that sat lightly on its pine forest site.

Antonio Moragas, like Durán i Reynals and Coderch, was an elitist architect who had already designed modern buildings before the key year of 1952, as the Park Hotel (1950–1953) and the Fémina cinema of the same date attest. The hotel is very clearly described in a text written by Moragas:

> To disguise its narrowness, we added to the main, seven-meter-wide facade all the projecting elements permitted by city regulations. As an additional measure to broaden this facade, projections were delineated not by vertical edges but by interrupted lines, as seen in the photographs. Consequently, when the building is viewed from the side there are no points of reference against which to gauge the exact width of its facade. The fact that the building is located in one of the oldest parts of the city raised the classic dilemma of ancient or modern. It was not, of course, the architect who considered this a dilemma, but the people who think of architecture not as a living thing but as a pretense. Unfortunately, there were a lot of these, and the building caused lively controversy: a father and son are said to have stopped speaking to each other because they held different points of view. But it was really a lot of fuss about nothing: this is an ordinary, unpreten-tious building, as everyday buildings ought to be.[18]

The hotel is decidedly modern in the analytical nature of its elements: an interrupted lateral wall, projections, corbels, and pillars or rounded corners on the ground floor; a thrilling approach to its objectives despite the scarcity of materials and the characteristics of the site, which is long, narrow, and run through longitudinally by a major underground watercourse. It shows no sign of interest in the vernacular model. The Fémina cinema and the slightly later Liceo cinema, built between 1957 and 1959, show a comparable interest in, and successful argument in favor of, the modern. The former reveals an interest in informalist experimentation typical of its period, while the Liceo inclines more toward the geometrical and structuralist.

Josep María Sostres i Maluquer was professor of history at the Barcelona School of Architecture. His best-known buildings are the 1955 MMI house and the 1957 Iranzo house, both in Barcelona's Ciudad Diagonal district.[19] His works apply in practice what he had been preaching in his writings since 1950:

> Some people call the latest modalities of the stylistic development of functionalism "organic" architecture, not realizing that the organic belongs in another category of architectonics. . . . Modern architecture takes its tone not, as used to be the case, from a belief in monumental architecture as an eternal, enduring, definitive value, but from something more elastic and alive, whose modest but no less important purpose is to serve man in both the practical activities of life and in its spiritual and mental aspects.[20]

Words not far removed from Le Corbusier's definition of the house as a "machine for living . . . where it is possible to dream." For Sostres, the principles of the modern movement were still valid and any departure from them was rhetorical, but this was not to say that the forms discovered by the modern movement had to be adhered to like a new catalogue of elements; that would lead to style, which is decadence.

In an inspired critical reassessment of Sostres some time later, *2C* magazine ended its commentary on the MMI house in Ciudad Diagonal thus:

MMI house,
Esplugues de Llobregat
(Barcelona), 1955–1958,
Sostres.

Certain paradigmatic works of modern architecture, such as Le Corbusier's Villa Savoye, Mies's Tugendhat house, and the Barcelona pavilion, seem to have been revised, and they provide the iconographic frame of reference for this building; it becomes one more testimony to the principles that they helped to formulate, and of which they are a product.[21]

The same text also comments on the equilibrium of the MMI house. Equilibrium in its chromatics, dynamics, and the way it relates to its site. Equilibrium, too, in its vindication of the principles adhered to and the examples that support them. The house is an L, folded in on itself, and a square; it obeys the modern archetype—day area, night area—and the *casa patio*, or courtyard house, layout. It is abstract and constructivist in its treatment of planes, volumes, and indoor circulation patterns, and realist in its distribution. Determined to avoid practicing style, Sostres created a building that was highly expressive of its period, in tune with what Eames and Elwood were doing in California and the exiled Breuer in New England. Yet while shunning style, he contributed to the stylistic definition of the architecture of the fifties, not only in Barcelona but in Western culture generally. He made his statement on the question of organic architecture clearly, and his views were still useful, and still had their followers, in the late nineties.

Francisco Mitjans was another propagandist for the modern. His apartment buildings on Calle Vallmayor, built from 1952 to 1954, and on Calle Freixas, built from 1952 to 1958, develop with consummate elegance the approaches to middle-class housing already much explored in suburban Barcelona, tackling the issue of language by calling on the vernacular, a source in which he gradually lost interest in subsequent projects such as the 1957 Tokio building. As we shall see, Mitjans's designs for housing included the low-cost sector, but mention should first be made of the great event of 1952: the Eucharistic Congress.

In this congress, the Vatican provided the Franco regime with an opportunity to present Spain to the outside world. As far as architecture was concerned, the congress demonstrated that the modern had triumphed definitively as the mode of expression, even from the point of view of officialdom, whose concerns, such as technology and basic housing, it was useful in tackling. An altar in Plaza de Pío XII (now destroyed), designed by Soteras i Mauri with a geometrically abstract, constructionally structuralist (forgive the redundancy) canopy, was both symbolist and formal and, praised by Bohigas, was emblematic of this confirmation of the modern. Soteras i Mauri did a great deal of work in this area: with Pineda i Gualba and with Marqués i Maristany, he built the Eucharistic Congress housing which reflected, albeit not brilliantly, the new direction that architecture was taking, even in low-cost housing.

Soteras was exemplary in another area very typical of modern taste: large-scale structures. In 1954, working with Mitjans and García Barbón, he designed the Barcelona Football Club Stadium. Very much altered today, it was in its time a fine example of dynamic, optimistic, functional forms. Again working with García Barbón, Soteras built the Municipal Sports

Stadium in Barcelona in 1955. The structure's finest features are the powerful arches that span the space of the hall, the glass roofs, and the brise-soleils of the main facades.

Mitjans was a central figure in the early fifties, working on the buildings mentioned earlier—and others such as the Monitor building, where he designed the facade of an office block with a glass and aluminum screen wall framed in a wide masonry band—and continuing to explore the question of middle-class housing. The Escorial estate was built between 1955 and 1962. As this occupied an entire urban block, questions such as courtyards giving onto the street were approached using the slab block, with all the formal problems this entailed. Maisonette apartments and galleries, elevators and stair wells, corners, roofs, and ground floors were resolved in ways that adhered strictly to modern tenets. Also involved in the project with Mitjans were Alemany, Ribas i Casas, Ribas i Piera, Bohigas, and Martorell. These same architects built the group of apartment blocks on Paseo Maragall. There, two slab blocks, almost parallel and with a central garden, are organized into a typical solution, each block being divided in two, back to back, to create an open courtyard onto which the apartments' service areas give. Only the stair and elevator wells open off the service courtyard, providing access to four apartments per floor. This solution creates a series of virtually identical apartments, differentiated only by the placing of their balconies, which are arranged either continuously or quincuncially, and provides a compositional potential that is very successfully exploited here.

Such experiments paved the way for the apartment block on Calle Roger de Flor, designed by Martorell and Bohigas and built in 1958. Here they applied the format described above to rationalize an uneven site in suburban Barcelona. The facade, cornice-free in this case, is very simple: it is a brick wall, perforated only by parallel apertures of unequal sizes, on which the shadows cast by the flat-fronted balconies create a very neoplastic play of light and shade.

In this Barcelona-based exploration of how the modern could be interpreted, Barba Corsini played a different role: working within an expressionist informalism, he looked for gentle ways of interpreting and promoting contemporary models. He conducted his most daring formal experiments in 1955, in the attic floor of Gaudí's La Pedrera building,

Football Club Stadium
Barcelona, 1954–1957,
García-Barbón / Mitjans /
Soteras Mauri.

School of Advanced
Business Studies,
Barcelona, 1954–1959,
García de Castro / Carvajal.

Opposite page:
Romeu house
(partial view and plan),
Cadaqués (Gerona), 1958–1963,
Correa / Milà.

beneath whose parabolic arches he built apartments in a way that capitalized on the curvilinear nature of the existing situation. The result— now lost as a result of an overzealous restoration of La Pedrera—was in a style very typical of the fifties, which he also applied in his Cadaqués apartments. It should be noted that this work was done with artisanal materials and methods in a realistic response to contemporary circumstances.

Not far from these experiments, but working within a more restrained formal repertoire, Barba Corsini built the Mitre building between 1959 and 1963. This is another double slab block, with courtyards and vertical communication links separating two lines of apartments that are symmetrical except for their balconies, which adapt to their orientation. The aim in this building—successfully achieved—was to offer a global type of housing-with-lifestyle, insofar as it designed in communal services such as day care and laundry facilities, cafeteria, pharmacy, and centralized services, in tune with the contemporary notion of the *unité d'habitation.*

The midpoint of the decade saw the start of a phenomenon which, although apparently small-scale and frivolous, was to prove extremely fruitful. The village of Cadaqués, on the coast of Gerona, became a sophisticated holiday destination for the most cultivated elements of Barcelona's middle class. Not just for them, in fact, as visits by the likes of Marcel Duchamp and the fact that Salvador Dalí lived nearby made the place internationally famous. The architecture built there up until the middle of the following decade used Cadaqués as a testing ground for solutions and approaches that would then be fine-tuned in larger-scale commissions.[22] Two houses designed by Correa and Milà—the 1956 Villavecchia house and the 1962 Romeu house—provided the parameters for these experiments.

In the first of these houses, the designers provided benchmarks for this type of project. Transforming a fisherman's house into a holiday home called for a major modification of the distribution while keeping the constructional and dimensional characteristics intact and contriving to keep the operation invisible from the outside. Achieving this low a profile required the finest of sensibilities and talents. In the Romeu house, the intention was quite different. As Terradas explained:

The form imposed a priori by the solution of three interlocking hexagons respects the real conditions of the geographical context. The hexagons have been placed in such a way that the house's physical space is constituted not only by what is under the roof, but also by the exterior spaces to which the geometrical forms give shape. Thus, the way the house's external walls echo the stone of the local landscape creates the idea of a continuous, uninterrupted skin which often makes the actual geometry disappear, opening up and giving shape to the exterior space.[23]

Other architects worked in Cadaqués—Barba Corsini, Terradas, Harnden and Bombelli—but it is Coderch's work that is most relevant to our purposes here. His 1957 Senillosa house could be seen as the response of a master to his disciples. Comparisons between it and the Villavecchia house provided controversy and object lessons then, and still do today.

The intensity and subtlety achieved in the houses just considered were objectives beyond the reach of more ordinary programs, and the series of works discussed next were conceived along lines consequent upon functionalist ideas.

From 1953 to 1961, López Íñigo, Subías i Fagés, and Giráldez Dávila built the Montbau housing estate and, from 1958 to 1966, the southwest unit of the El Besós estate, the latter in collaboration with Giralt i Ortet. Both schemes were carried out by Barcelona's Municipal Housing Authority, the aim (pursuing urban renewal ideas derived from CIAM) being to create whole neighborhoods with an identity of their own on the perimeter of the city to satisfy the enormous demand for housing on the part of shanty town dwellers. As their designers intended, neighborhoods such as El Besós did indeed acquire a distinctive personality, though it was not part of their intention that they should end up socially marginalized as they have. Slab blocks, orientation providing the only variation, became the motif of the periphery in the late fifties and early sixties.

The slab block, variously clad from a restricted selection of materials, had many exponents during this period, and its use was not limited to

School of Law,
Barcelona, 1957–1958,
Giráldez / López Íñigo /
Subías.

Meridiana dog track,
Barcelona, 1962–1963,
Bonet Castellana / Puig Torné.

Opposite page:
Architects' Chamber of
Catalonia,
Barcelona, 1958–1962,
Busquets.

La Caixa building,
Barcelona, 1968–1973,
Busquets.

housing. The School of Law, designed by López Íñigo, Subías, and Giráldez, is a good example.

The School of Advanced Business Studies was designed in 1954 by García de Castro and Javier Carvajal, with the collaboration of Bassó and Gili. This is one of the best Spanish buildings of its period: parallelepipeds stand on a rigorous ground plan of rectangles organized into function zones by circulation patterns and illumination. The facades reveal the grid of the structure, and their composition makes neoplastic use of masonry and carpentry.

Bassó and Gili's design for the Gustavo Gili publishing house also dates from 1954. This building is again composed of a series of volumes, each taking its shape from its functional purpose. The same architects also designed the Atenas cinema, now destroyed, which showed how analytical architecture, as described above, can be applied to a program offering more options for spatial organization.

Robert Terradas was another architect of influence, both through his design work and as a professor at the School of Architecture. His buildings are very revealing of architects' preoccupations during this period. The clear-cut, orderly facade of the 1956 Caja de Ahorros Provincial bank headquarters building on Calle Roselló; the combination of traditional materials like stonework with modern compositional solutions like the continuous window, in a 1957 building for ENMASA; and the combination of blocks in his 1959 School of Engineering, reveal that these were the dominant principles in Barcelona architecture in the latter half of the fifties.

A survey of the buildings constructed to establish the SEAT car factory during that same period points toward the same conclusions. Between 1954, when Ortiz-Echagüe, Echaide, Barbero, and de la Joya built the employees' canteen, and 1960, when the two first-named built the laboratories, this team of architects, working all together or in groups of two, created a collection of clean-cut buildings in which the dominance of the modern discipline typical of their period is very evident: glass boxes, their structures visible or veiled by brise-soleils . . . they used the entire repertoire judiciously and with skill.

At the end of the decade, Antoni Bonet Castellana, working with Josep Puig Torné, built the Canódromo Meridiana dog track in Barcelona. It takes its form from the structure whose compositional system is summed up with analytical precision in the following description:

> The two levels with ground plans in the shape of parabolic sectors are dissimilar in horizontal projection, demanding a solution where ground plans and elevations make play with the geometry of the different curvatures resulting from pushing the structural order to its ultimate consequences. Since all the solid-web girders that give it shape derive from one horizontal plane, the roof is warped, creating the impression, when it meets the plane of the brise-soleil, that the grandstand is also doubly parabolic in ground plan.[24]

This was architecture enriched by the involvement of formal and geometric components, and its optimistic structures defined the period.

The discipline having been mastered, certain architects were to indicate avenues for exploration. J. M. Fargas and E. Tous, who in the sixties explored an architecture of visible structure encased in a glass box, had been applying these notions as early as 1955 in their Mandri building, designed in conjunction with J. Amat. In 1959, with a competition-winning design for the headquarters of the Architects' Chamber of Catalonia and the Balearic Islands, Xabier Busquets began work on a building which—in contrast with the city he had inherited—demonstrated the principles of the modern. This was an influential building, and, in exemplifying the overall efforts being made by architects to find new formulas developed from the strictly contemporary, it explains the activity of the subsequent decade.

This consideration of Spanish architecture has so far treated the subject as if it were a tale of two cities, Madrid and Barcelona, with nothing happening elsewhere. This was, indeed, the case until the sixties as far as architecture of any reflective content and influence was concerned. In these two cities alone did the density of new building, contacts, and exchange engender shared concerns and an intensity of discourse that, disseminated through journals, congresses, and other links, generated enough impetus to exert influence and become known and published, albeit timidly, beyond Spain.

Even so, a great deal of architecture was designed and built in other parts of the country. The postwar reconstruction has already been mentioned, but the amount of building that went on in the north merits particular

Opposite page:
SEAT office building
and depot on Plaza Cerdà,
Barcelona, 1954,
Ortiz-Echagüe / Echaide.

Right:
Grandas de Salime
hydroelectric power station,
Oviedo, 1953–1954,
Vaquero Palacios.

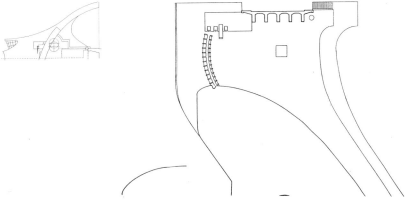

attention. In the Basque country, and particularly in Bilbao—a city that soon recovered its industrial stride—the building activity of the forties attempted to reconcile traces of regionalist tradition with the functionalist precepts that had been adopted before the war and meshed well with the idea of industrial modernity.[25] From Muguruza's houses in Fuenterrabía and Zuazo's Consulado cinema in Bilbao, to the neighborhoods designed by Imaz, Germán Aguirre, and Lorenzo Blanc, also in Bilbao, and Unánue's groups of low-cost housing in Guipúzcoa, the big names of Basque architecture were closely involved in housing.[26] In office and industrial buildings, Galíndez, Apraiz, Guinea, Aguinaga, Ispízua, Cárdenas, Fontán, and Smith made outstanding, soundly designed contributions. This situation continued into the fifties, with architecture characterized by disciplinary precision, as exemplified in the efficient ground plans and restrained facades of the Alaberga housing built by Martiarena in Rentería, and in the housing on Bilbao's Gran Vía avenue by Aguinaga, Aguirre, and Imaz: here, clues to Zuazo and Gutiérrez Soto's Bilbao origins are clearly discernible.

Outstanding educational buildings in Bilbao included Jesús Bastarrechea's School of Industrial Engineering; the Teacher Training College by Germán Aguirre, Álvaro Líbano, and Navarro Borrás; and the San Bonifacio school by Emiliano Amann. All these opted firmly for the compositional approach of using split and articulated volumes and facades analytically broken down into their elements, very much in the taste of the fifties. Also very typical of the style of this period is the beautiful, optimistic La Galea golf club in Getxo, where Eugenio María de Aguinaga made skillful use of triangular modules beneath a bold, overhanging roof. However, the epic Basque project of this period was the basilica of Aránzazu, mentioned earlier in the context of Madrid, where it was conceived by Laorga and Sáenz de Oiza. Other important works, which also originated in Madrid in the sense that they were competition responses, were the church of Nuestra Señora de los Angeles, by Carvajal and García de Paredes, and the church of La Coronación de Nuestra Señora, by Fisac, both in Vitoria; and the San Mamés Football Club Stadium grandstand, by José Domínguez Salazar, Carlos de Miguel, and Ricardo Magdalena. They are all very much of their period, particularly in their emphasis on deriving form from structure. Luis Peña Ganchegui also made an impact during the sixties. His 1958 Vista Alegre tower in Zarauz, built with Juan M. Encio, launched him as an important, creatively autonomous force.

In Navarre, Víctor Eusa, an important figure in the early years of the century, produced less work in the forties, although the basilica of El Puig, in Estella, is on a par with his earlier creative expressiveness. In 1954, he built the Aurora building, and in 1956 the Santa María la Real school: extraordinarily personal works which had little influence on the course of the architecture of this period.

In Andalusia, perhaps because regional architecture was so firmly rooted there, the classical exerted less pressure than in central Spain.[27] Building activity, which declined throughout Spain in the early fifties as a result of economic stagnation, was represented in Seville by a few notable housing developments: that of La Estrella, by the Medina Benjumea brothers, and the Virgen del Carmen and Los Diez Mandamientos estates, by Luis Recanséns, are some examples. All made a significant local impact in that, though not innovative, they introduced the modern block to a city whose own traditional form of collective housing—tenement-type buildings known as *corralas*—was outstandingly successful and efficient. There were other ways of reconciling local tradition with modernity, some involving a degree of almost surrealist humor. Examples of this could include Alejandro de la Sota's colony-village of Esquivel mentioned earlier, and José Rebollo's work in Córdoba, such as the bull ring in his home town, which is exquisitely ironic in its handling and use of traditional clichés such as arches, tiles, and grillwork. The impact made by Rafael de la Hoz was considerable. Working with García de Paredes, he built the Córdoba headquarters of the Chamber of Commerce in 1953, an early work which, in its decorative elements and furnishings, provides a precocious glimpse of so-called informalist architecture. In the course of this decade, de la Hoz built several houses in Córdoba, the most outstanding being the 1955 Canals house and the apartment building on Calle Cruz Conde. Both are mature, brilliant works, especially the latter, which is a beautiful piece of urban work; it was later added to, thus completing the block and showing subtly how continuations of projects can succeed.

Poorer, smaller, parts of the country than those already mentioned also qualify as distant provinces. In Asturias, architect and painter Joaquín Vaquero occasionally revealed his artistic abilities in buildings where his formal skills came to the fore. Examples are the 1954 Grandas de Salime hydroelectric power station and its 1964 equivalent in Proaza, whose juxtaposition of concrete and electricity seems to symbolize the modernity that was by then inevitable.

Chamber of Commerce,
Córdoba, 1951–1952,
García de Paredes / de la Hoz.

Vista Alegre tower,
Zarauz (Guipúzcoa), 1958,
Peña Ganchegui / Encio.

At times, history seems determined to make its presence felt, causing events to cluster around specific dates. Nineteen sixty-two was a case in point, a year of important political decisions that reflected the profound changes of recent times. These decisions were, in their turn, to accelerate new events. This was the year that saw the introduction of a Press Law that marked the start of liberalization, and the publication of books by the likes of Sartre, Neruda, Beckett, and Brecht that were to exert a formative influence over the minds of the sixties generation of university students. It was also the year of the launch of Spanish television, and of the start of large-scale production of SEAT cars, the first to be manufactured in Spain since the Civil War.

All of these events, consequences both of the international consolidation of the Franco regime and of Spain's industrial and productive normalization, were symptomatic of a liberalization that was rapidly seized upon, showing its first results in 1965 with student strikes bringing about a prolonged closure of the universities, priests holding demonstrations, and—for the first time since the war—a weekly magazine being published in the Catalan language.

In the face of the combined pressure exerted by the economic development policy of the early sixties and the social tensions and political demands emanating from the university, the regime reacted with a similarly dual strategy: police repression, which had the effect of strengthening emergent student associations such as the FUDE (Spanish Democratic University Federation) and the FLP (Popular Liberation Front), and the approval of a new education plan in 1965. This plan reduced the length of architecture studies from seven years to five, and filled lecture rooms by easing the academic requirements for acceptance into architecture programs. The extraordinary increase in student numbers during those years, which was to continue up to the mid-nineties, marked a significant change in the teaching methods and in the education that architects acquired. Architecture schools could no longer guarantee a desk per student, and students came to lectures bringing plans they had drawn at home, keen to talk about them with their peers—rather than with their teachers—and keener still to discuss what they had been reading.

One important effect of this overcrowding in universities was that it created a substantial market for publishers. The 1962 Press Law, the increase in the population's purchasing power which resulted from the money sent home by Spanish emigrants to northern Europe—significant during those formative years of the Common Market—and the entry of foreign currency generated by the huge influx of tourists, all fueled a renewal of the publishing industry.

Until that time, the few architecture books that students had been able to lay their hands on had been Latin American publications, produced mainly by Argentinian and Mexican publishing houses. From then onward, publishers such as Blume and Gustavo Gili set about translating and publishing everything of interest being written abroad, turning Spain into the country that was most adept at absorbing foreign books—during the following years, the first translations of key books, such as Aldo Rossi's *L'architettura della città* and Robert Venturi's *Complexity and Contradiction in Architecture* were undertaken in Spain. This publishing boom not only represented the sloughing off of years of isolation but also changed the academic profile of architects, who from then on were much more widely read and began to venture increasingly into the field of criticism.

Page 40:
Hydrographic Research Center and Hydraulics Laboratory, Madrid, 1959–1962, Fisac.

Commentary on the state of Spanish architecture was marked during this period by the appearance of two books that shared the same title: *Arquitectura española contemporánea*.[28] The first book of this name, written by Carlos Flores, appeared in 1959, and the second, by Lluis Domènech—explicitly intended as a continuation of the first—in 1968. As for specialist journals, in addition to *Arquitectura* and *Cuadernos de Arquitectura* mentioned earlier, which continued to be influential, *Hogar y Arquitectura*, edited by Carlos Flores and focused primarily on public housing, enjoyed a wide readership.

Carlos de Miguel, the indefatigable editor of *Arquitectura*, was the prime instigator of progress during this period. It was he who involved Oriol Bohigas in 1959 to foster a series of encounters between the architects of Barcelona and Madrid: between them they organized the small-scale conferences known as *pequeños congresos*.[29] Architects from the provinces, such as Peña Ganchegui, were also drawn to these events, and derived from them the support and the expansion of horizons that were to alleviate the isolation of their situation. Another crucial factor was the participation of foreign architects such as Nuno Portas in 1962, Sandy Wilson and Aldo Rossi in 1964, and Peter Eisenman in 1969, and their consequent involvement in the Spanish discourse with results whose importance is well recognized.[30] By the end of the decade, then, there was a relatively confident Spanish presence in international circles.

An important product of the new climate in publishing was the appearance in 1966 of *Nueva Forma*, the first architecture magazine not affiliated with an official institution. It was edited by Juan Daniel Fullaondo[31] with the financial backing of the Huarte Group, a consortium linked to the construction company and family of the same name, which had become established as the most important patrons of art and architecture of the period. Over the various phases of its existence, the magazine exerted a decisive influence on architectonic culture not only in Madrid, where it was published, but throughout Spain as a whole. Its effect in two areas merits particular mention: it provided critically oriented exposure for what we now call the modern tradition, keeping several generations of architects up to date and equipping them with matter for discussion in the process; and also, with more specific intent, it provided exposure for the architecture then being built in Spain, especially in Madrid. Fullaondo determinedly promoted an "informed" architecture, finding his material in the dialectic between the two poles of architectural progress in Spain: Catalonia—where it was consolidated around Barcelona's *Escola*—and

Madrid—for whose potential, nascent school he claimed the title of *Organicismo madrileño* (Madrid organicism).

From what has been said so far, it will be clear that prospects were promising for Spanish architects at the start of the sixties. Expansion in tourism and industry, made possible by Spain's new international status, meant that though the profession's informational and cultural structure was small, it was agile and efficient and there was plenty of work on the horizon. The frantic reconstruction of the postwar and renewal period was over, but economic expansion was just beginning. By triggering an explosion in the number of architects, expansion would eventually create a shortfall of work, but not until the nineties, after years of prosperity. The architecture of the sixties was shaped by two main cities, Madrid and Barcelona, particularly since in the distant provinces only a few isolated architects had anything original to say.

The Organic and the Modern in Madrid

In the previous chapter, it was seen how architecture in Madrid in the mid-fifties achieved the cultural objective it had been pursuing for half a century: that of becoming an integral part of its geographical environment. We shall now see how, without delay, architects embarked on an exploration of new avenues, parallel to the activities of their colleagues in the rest of Europe, and to which critics like Bruno Zevi gave the name "organic" architecture.

The influence of Zevi, essential reading for Spanish students in the late fifties, is discernible in the most significant pieces written at that time by Madrid's young architects: Inza, Fernández Alba, Fullaondo, and Moneo.

Carlos de Miguel, already encountered as promoter of the small-scale conferences, was the moving force behind Madrid architecture in the sixties, as indeed he had been for the twenty years before. He was instrumental in bringing many and notable visitors to the Spanish capital, among them the great Alvar Aalto,[32] about whose visit Rafael Aburto relates a telling anecdote:

> We took Aalto to the Escorial—we always took visitors there—to impress him with the monastery, which we held in great awe, and so we had a lunch table prepared at the Hotel Felipe II, from which splendid views of the building could be had. Once there, we went out onto the terrace, watching the Finn's face to gauge his first impressions: Aalto walked to the balustrade, saw the monastery, turned round and sat down with his back to it. He didn't give the building a second look, nor did he say a single word about it.

Like Aalto, during the sixties the architects from Madrid ostentatiously turned their backs on that sort of historical architecture, which was not to be allowed to interfere with the pressing need to find new approaches. As the title of Fullaondo's magazine implied, the architecture of Madrid required new forms. While the general conviction among intellectuals and students was that the whole of Spanish society needed "re-forming," by offering such forms the "organic" label architecture seemed to be fulfilling its role.

Perhaps all it takes to bring about great changes are the right circumstances and the will and talent of a small group of people. Around this time, a figure emerged at the opportune moment who was able, enthusiastic, and sensitive, and who attracted around him a handful of northerners like himself. Juan Huarte, from Navarre, was the son of the veteran builder and businessman who was to construct such significant works as Muguruza's monument to the dead of the Civil War, the Valle de los Caídos, and Zuazo's government buildings, the Nuevos Ministerios, and among whose stonemasons Oteiza designed and carved the pieces that won him the prize at the São Paulo Biennial. Juan Huarte emerged as a patron supportive of artists keen to produce work unconnected with the regime. Prominent among the many artists he took under his wing was the sculptor Jorge Oteiza, a passionate and rebellious spirit, whose experiments with the concept of space spurred architects on in a similar direction. During this period, he abandoned his depictions of exhausted, suffering figures in favor of experiments with metaphysical boxes whose walls opened up to create an effect of vast spatiality despite their smallness.

Huarte also financed the *Nueva Forma* journal, which, under Fullaondo's decisive and cultivated guidance, provided exposure for the work of Oteiza and of such painters as Canogar and Antonio López, systematic examination of the great masters of modernity, and a showcase for contemporary Spanish architecture. He interspersed his critical texts, which were flowery and allegorical, with only apparently random quotations from James Joyce, and out of an amalgam of all this—Zevi, the constructivists, Oteiza, Joyce, the spoils of his eclectic culture which he called his "pirate's cabin"—emerged the concept of organic architecture, an architecture rich in expressive impulse and sensual spaces, as opposed to what he mockingly called "that less-is-nothing" architecture.

Torres Blancas building, Madrid, 1960–1971, Sáenz de Oiza.

One of the tower blocks built in Madrid during this period took on legendary status: this was the Torres Blancas building, so named because it was to consist of two white concrete towers. It took eleven years to build, from 1960 to 1971, and over this period it provided an ongoing educational demonstration for Madrid's architects as they watched it grow, formwork succeeded by gray, rounded concrete components, in a thrilling, large-scale building lesson. The Torres Blancas building, fortuitously situated on the road leading into Madrid from the direction of Barcelona and the airport—the probable reason for de la Sota's half-ironic, half-jealous nickname for it: *los propíleos*[33]—became a symbol of the architecture of Madrid. Like an architectonic Minerva, it was the brainchild of Sáenz de Oiza, but as major buildings always do, it involved the work of many. Juan Huarte instigated the project, and it was he who selected the architect from Navarre. According to Huarte, Sáenz de Oiza told him with characteristic intellectual coyness: "Don't ask me, ask Molezún—he's the best," and proceeded immediately to make hundreds of drawings and a sequence of home-made models.

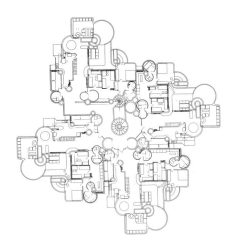

It was the young Moneo, a fellow Navarrese and a student at the time, who took organicism into Sáenz de Oiza's studio, triggering the change of direction from the *ville radieuse* to the Wrightian skyscraper, and it was Fullaondo (another northerner, from Bilbao) who, having replaced Moneo in the studio, drew formwork plans and publicized the project.

Another legendary building of the period was the Artistic Restoration Center designed by Fernando Higueras and Antonio Miró. This building, which was only completed a quarter of a century after it was designed, was commissioned by an enlightened administration keen to express its support for contemporary culture. Also brutalist in its use of concrete, it explored the organic qualities of circles and structural ribs, and was a thing of beauty during construction, being drawn and photographed by Antonio López, master of the reinstated figurative mode. The friendly relationship between the architect and the painter is important, for it shows how, from within his exploration of the organic, Higueras was already expressing his interest in the figurative as early as 1962.

In the Lucio Muñoz and Santonja houses, both built in 1962 and both for clients who were painters, and in the warm, serene Hortaleza housing estate, these architects deployed the constructive elements of architecture in their most direct role as disciplining factors: tiles, wood, and weathered granite exhibited their natural qualities without disguising their role in the building. Corners were corners, roofs and facades no longer aspired to the realm of abstraction that encouraged architects to call facades "faces" and windows "voids." This was a different kind of realism from what we saw in Catalonia, which consisted in accepting social and economic realities; here it was more a case of calling a spade a spade. It would be true to say that a new figurativeness flourished in architecture during this period in a way that it was not to do in painting and sculpture until a decade later. As the likes of López had been doing since the fifties, Higueras and Miró now alternated their experiments between these two areas, the realist and the organic, rooting their designs for large-scale, formal commissions and competitions, such as the hotel in Lanzarote, in the latter.

Fisac, who had become the architect most frequently in the public eye, the one whose opinion the newspapers always sought, was now embarking on an avenue of investigation that was to provide the central axis of his work for decades to come. Fascinated by the malleability of concrete —which undergoes what amounts to metamorphosis in the building process, turning from a semiliquid substance into an extraordinarily hard and resilient material—he explored the use of formwork, both for roof structures and for external walls, developing techniques that emphasized the construction process and thereby achieved expression and form. During the process, he invented and patented a series of hollow beams, using posttensioned concrete in a way whose potential has still not been fully explored, which he called "bones" because of their obvious similarity in section to organic forms. Fisac, who with a sarcasm typical of his native La Mancha had for years been describing his own work as *arquitectura del mondongo* ("gut architecture"), now became the most literally "organic" of his contemporaries. His most intense work of this period was the Hydraulic Laboratory in Madrid, built between 1960 and 1962.

Artistic Restoration Center
(currently, the Instituto de
Conservación y Restauración),
Madrid, 1961–1970,
Higueras / Miró
(Drawing by Antonio López).

Lucio Muñoz house,
Madrid, 1960–1963,
Higueras / Miró.

Convent of El Rollo,
Salamanca, 1958–1962,
Antonio Fernández Alba.

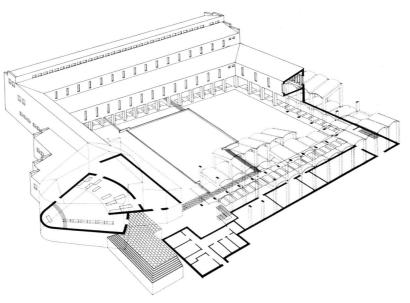

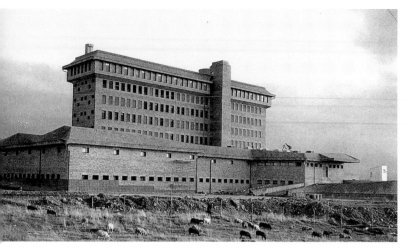

Antonio Fernández Alba, whose fascination with the theory of composition aligned him with musicians like de Pablo and plastic artists, was the author of intense, difficult texts and of a series of drawings that explored spaces and associations triggered by the notion of the circle, growth, and intersection. Together, these made him the most authoritative and influential architect of the Madrid school in the early sixties. Buildings designed by him late in that decade, such as the Convent of El Rollo in Salamanca and the School of Santa María in Madrid, showed in their elegant poverty the perfect assimilation of all the previous generation's preoccupations: harmony with vernacular architecture, as shown by the use of local materials, and familiarity with and involvement in contemporary movements, as revealed in his personal interpretation of Scandinavian architecture. His design for Gijón, built in conjunction with Javier Feduchi, demonstrates a command of the curve that explains his importance as professor at the Madrid School of Architecture, where he introduced the teaching methods used by Johannes Itten at the Bauhaus, making him a key figure in the modernization of teaching that occurred at that time.

Curro Inza, who qualified a year after Fernández Alba and who collaborated actively with Carlos de Miguel in the journal *Arquitectura*, was a person whose extraordinary humanity and love of life were reflected in his architecture. The sausage factory he built in Segovia between 1960 and 1963 exemplifies a way of working very much of its period. The project was defined after four sets of drawings and plans, more impressionistic than precise, and actually took shape during the building process itself. Using very cheap methods, he built a factory in which expression was achieved through a formula much loved then and for some time to come: the use of a single material, and that an almost vulgar one, brick tile. In a departure from its usual application, this material clothed the whole building, appearing to particular effect in roofs and eaves where its shape was more justified. In buildings such as the 1962 Café Gijón in Madrid and the 1968 Hotel Alfaro in Logroño, Inza demonstrated how his version of the organic derived more from his own exuberant humanity than from a culturally influenced decision.

Sausage factory,
Segovia, 1960–1963,
Inza.

Gómez Acebo house,
La Moraleja,
Madrid, 1966–1968,
Moneo.

Opposite page:
Parish church of Almendrales,
Madrid, 1961–1964,
García de Paredes.

Centro building,
Madrid, 1965–1967,
Alas / Casariego.

In the remodeling of the monastery of San Benito, planned by Miguel Oriol, Dionisio Hernández Gil directed an exhibition of constructive virtuosity: the new part, built in smooth shapes of exposed or plastered ceramic, was an extension of the old stone building and achieved beautiful spatial continuity true to the organic approach typical of its time.

The work of Rafael Moneo completes the catalogue of exponents of this tendency. Moneo had achieved prominence through his writings and his involvement in the organic architecture controversy. On his return from a long period abroad, principally in the Academy in Rome and in Scandinavia (where he worked with Jørn Utzon), he designed a small project: the Gómez Acebo house in the Madrid suburb of La Moraleja. Beneath its rectangular hipped roof, the layout of this house was a small-scale variation on Wrightian principles. An elaborate route leads through its spaces and elements: pillars, beams, cornices, and fireplaces, as realist as those described in the work of Higueras. Although these two architects moved apart in their later work, their earlier similarities are undeniable.

Some Madrid architects remained resistant to the kind of formal experimentation discussed so far. They continued to explore the principles that had inspired the previous decade—ideas such as the relationship between form and function—and what their work may have lacked in youthful enthusiasm, it gained in maturity and serenity. García de Paredes's work from this period displayed considerable continuity with his earlier concerns, and the supremely beautiful hypostyle hall of the parish church of Almendrales, built between 1961 and 1964, used the most modest materials even then. So industrial a material as cement-asbestos took on a religious mystique in the modulated light admitted by plastic skylights. In Málaga's Belén church and convent, also built between 1961 and 1964, the church filled the narrow site, with the monks' cells placed on top, under the roof, where the required secluded environment was easily achieved. In 1964, García de Paredes built the Zaidín secondary school in Granada. This strictly rational building, designed to be built rapidly, became a model for subsequent school buildings. Experiment had no place here, only efficiency.

Javier Carvajal, who moved to Madrid after working in his home town of Barcelona, also collaborated regularly with García de Paredes, for example in the School of Telecommunications Engineering in Madrid built in 1960. This restrained, functionalist building was very much dictated by the complexity of the brief. In the mid-sixties, however, Carvajal moved successfully into an architecture that was formally denser while retaining his earlier functionalism in precise layouts. In the two houses he built in Somosaguas, strongly handled concrete extends into overhangs, recesses, and gutters, creating environments that cried out to be used in the cinema, as Carlos Saura actually did in a film about psychological introspection. In 1964, in his Spanish Pavilion for the New York World's Fair, Carvajal used the idea of the Spanish patio with rough walls, ceramic floors, and long pools of water to public and critical acclaim.

Others who remained faithful to modern principles, albeit tempering the details, were the architects Genaro Alas and Pedro Casariego, who worked as a team. In the Centro building in Madrid, the folded metal cladding and arched portico they designed gave a certain approach-

ability to the volume. Nearby, in Calle Orense, they also built the Trieste building in 1972 adopting similar techniques.

Julio Cano Lasso belonged to the same generation as these architects and shared certain similarities with them, although his work from this period shows him to have been influenced by organicism. In the Satellite Communications Center, built in Buitrago de Lozoya in 1967 in collaboration with José Antonio Ridruejo, while the layout showed a concern for circulation and function, the use of cylindrical forms wherever use permitted gave the exterior a variegated shape.

Cano Lasso's expressed ideals of constructive simplicity and modesty were more clearly exemplified in the apartment building on Calle Basílica in Madrid. This half-block project, designed in 1966 with Alejandro Blond and Alfonso García Noreña, used brick set in broad mortar seams to create unbroken, almost monotonous facades on which the bay windows are the only salient features. Completed in 1974, this building

School of Telecommunications Engineering, Madrid, 1960, Carvajal.

Settlement of Caño Roto, Madrid, 1957–1961, Íñiguez de Onzoño / Vázquez de Castro.

was extremely influential. The architects must be given credit for having anticipated a whole series of concepts, concerned with emphasis on type, which emerged at that time. The Calle Basílica building and the Urumea building in San Sebastián were to be regarded many years later as models of this school. It is worth stressing this shift in dominant models for urban development among architects and town planners. The decade that had begun in the sway of the slabs and rows of two-floor houses typical of the modern tradition (the Caño Roto estate designed by José Luis Íñiguez de Onzoño and Antonio Vázquez de Castro, completed in 1961, is a splendid example) ended with a revisionist enthusiasm for the housing block, characteristic of inner suburb developments.

This section concludes with an account of certain figures who, although not involved in the organic movement—indeed they almost represented its converse—continued to be considered masters by many, including Fullaondo, who dedicated two issues of his magazine to them. Two such figures, who often worked together, were José Antonio Corrales and Ramón Vázquez Molezún, already mentioned in these pages. In 1965 they built one of the most beautiful houses in suburban Madrid for Jesús

Apartment building on Calle Basílica, Madrid, 1966–1974, Cano Lasso

Huarte house, Puerta de Hierro, Madrid, 1965–1966, Corrales / Vázquez Molezún.

Huarte. In the wealthy suburb of Puerta de Hierro, where most houses are characterized by conspicuous expense, Corrales and Vázquez Molezún built a house that occupied most of the large site and yet was barely visible from the outside. Protected by extensive sloping, flat-tiled roofs, alternating with others topped with soil and plants, it opens onto a sequence of inner courtyards. An analysis of the layout reveals how perfectly the house functions, with interior spaces enjoying a high degree of independence created within outer walls of clinkered brick of the same color as the roof tiles, which are all that can be seen from the outside amid the vegetation that covers large parts of the house.

Finally, we must take a look at two well-known figures who provided a counterpoint to the predominant organic movement. While Sáenz de Oiza's Torres Blancas building, Higueras's Artistic Restoration Center, and Fernández Alba's architecture and teaching set the parameters of that discourse, de la Sota and Cabrero represented the most purist continuation of the modern.

With the Maravillas School Gymnasium in 1962, Alejandro de la Sota reached the pinnacle of a career already described here. Capitalizing cleverly on a difficult, steeply sloping site with a marked change in grade between the access and the street levels, his gymnasium achieved a very imaginative internal structure. The interior space was quiet and athletic, its light entering from between large convex structural ribs. The measured punctuation to the facade provided by the lines of its structural elements and the texture of its materials made further formal expression superfluous.

Although he remained active, de la Sota's reputation waned over the following years as a result of his explicit rejection of the current trend of experimentalism. "Pornographic magazines!" his students remember him exclaiming about the architectural publications of the time. In 1963, he built an apartment building on Calle Prior in Salamanca and the CENIM National Center for Metallurgical Research buildings on Madrid's university campus. These buildings, constructed with pre-fabricated panels, possessed a hardness that highlighted their presence despite their small scale. Importantly, they also constituted a statement about renunciation, a concept of vital importance for de la Sota, who wrote:

> We must appreciate things at the point where they almost cease being
> what they are—at their very rudiments—where so much of
> their superficiality has been removed to expose their true essence,
> the notable quality that exists in every building.[34]

In 1966 he built the Sports Pavilion in Pontevedra and in 1967 the César Carlos residence hall on Madrid's university campus. The latter was an exercise in illusionism: the volumes of the complex were skillfully distributed, with rooms in two tall blocks and services in another, lower one, partially below ground level. Their outlines were blurred with a shiny greenish cladding so that they seemed to merge, the conjuring trick being given a final flourish by a glazed gymnasium that linked the tops of the two main blocks.

Cabrero likes to refer to the period of his work when iron featured prominently in his designs as his "constructivist" period: examples of it include the Arriba newspaper building constructed in 1961, and the Puerta de Hierro house and the Glass Pavilion in Madrid's Casa de Campo park, built with Jaime Ruiz in 1964. Iron appeared in beams, in columns, even in lintels. The lintel is a basic, intelligent structural device, a builder's way of spanning the void. Weight is lifted from the ground and kept up in the air to enable people to walk underneath. Prehistoric dolmens used rigid lintels, log cabins used flexible ones, and the Greeks combined the two, inventing the definitive convention once and for all. What a thrill it must have been for builders when iron arrived on the scene in the nineteenth century. The beautiful straight lines that could be obtained! The excitement of spanning such voids with such little mass! Cabrero had been forced to manage without iron in the early fifties, when he was building his apartment block on Avenida de América in Madrid. There he made a virtue of necessity and resolved his essential architecture with vaults and

Maravillas school gymnasium, Madrid, 1960–1962, de la Sota.

buttresses, the structural tension being absorbed by braces incorporated into the mortar. Iron was a precious, and hidden, material. When the furnaces of Altos Hornos began rolling and shaping steel, he at last had access to the hard, dry, straight line that he needed for his lintels. It was during this period, with structure reduced to angles and the building process to the iron lintel, that Cabrero built his most directly poetic work.

Arriba building,
Madrid, 1960–1963,
Cabrero.

Glass Pavilion,
Casa de Campo park,
Madrid, 1964–1965,
Cabrero / Labiano / Ruiz.

César Carlos
student hall of residence,
Madrid, 1967–1968,
de la Sota / López Candeira.

Having fulfilled its objective—the cultural reinstatement of Catalan architecture—and having achieved modernity, the R Group saw its older members, such as Coderch and Sostres, detach themselves from the group, unhappy with what they considered to be style choices. The reins were promptly seized by their heirs. Oriol Bohigas and Federico Correa complemented each other to great effect in the period that followed. They spearheaded the finest Catalan architecture, rebels acknowledged their leadership, little could be achieved outside the ambit they created, and between them and the youngest architects, often products of their studios, they succeeded in establishing a style in the true sense of the term—a school with its own intellectual aims and approaches—which became known as the Escola de Barcelona. The city was a style setter once again, as it had been during the *modernisme* period. Mainland Spain has not produced an equally identifiable style since.

Oriol Bohigas was a creative force during this period—indeed, he always was—providing the momentum for its most effective achievements. Not only did he unite the Barcelonans about him but, by means of the small-scale conferences, he also established links between Madrid and other Spanish cities, gradually becoming something of a champion of the periphery. Federico Correa's contribution was to broaden horizons—which he achieved with the apparently superficial and detached foppishness of the *flâneur*—to embrace the international dimension that every culture needs if it is to avoid descending into provincialism. A former collaborator of Coderch's, he provided a counterpoint to the latter's work in projects built jointly with Alfonso Milà during this period. They used small-scale, sophisticated, domestic commissions for the Catalan middle classes as a testing ground for defining the strong decorative traits that characterize Catalan architecture in the second half of the twentieth century. The significance of Cadaqués has already been discussed: these architects reflected idyllic summers in a collection of apartments and studios, the design elements of which—such as fireplaces, low seating, fluid environments and spaces, shaded terraces, and earthenware floors—served to show the rest of Spain, still sitting in high-backed chairs, how they should be living in a decade of major world changes.

This stylistic revision paralleled an equivalent one in teaching, also heavily involved in politics during this period. Correa, recently appointed professor at the School of Architecture, taught the most active students—Domènech in 1959, and the future members of the PER studio in the sixties. These years saw the start of student protests, which culminated in the serious uprising of 1965; repercussions were to be various in the years that followed. In 1967, disillusionment in the official school led to the creation of the EINA design school, with Rafols, Cirici i Pellicer, Alemany, and Correa as professors. The latter, along with many more, was expelled from the ETSAB, the Barcelona School of Architecture, in 1969, in one of a series of repressive measures that were powerless to halt the course of events.

In an article entitled "Una posible Escuela de Barcelona"[35] (Possibilities for a Barcelona School), Oriol Bohigas set out the characteristics of such a school, going on to name its constituent studios: Correa and Milà, PER, Bofill, Domènech, Puig and Sabater, Rodrigo and Cantallops, and MBM. These did, indeed, become the hub of architectural activity, though, as we shall see, there were other studios which, while varying the theme slightly, also belonged to the Escola in stylistic terms. As to its characteristics:

Residential home for the elderly, Lérida, 1966–1968, Domènech / Puig / Sanmartí / Sabater.

> [Given that] Catalan architecture commissions come from the Catalan middle classes, in contrast to Madrid commissions, which are of an official nature, [works should be characterized by]:
> A willing, conscious, and informed adaptation to the inconvenient realities of these commissions and to the technological situation of the country.
> An attempt to adhere firmly to the principles of the rationalist tradition (fine-tuning the understanding of the term rationalist, used in its logical rather than its historical sense).
> A realistic avant-gardism which requires both an open approach to building and a rupture with established codes. In essence, this is a question of communication.
> Pessimism. A taste for critical, radical, and ambiguous attitudes.

In fact, these characteristics were emblematic of the nature of Barcelona society, or at least of its most cultivated layer: a vitalist, sensuous attitude that reveled in small details. All this gave rise to an architecture that could be said to derive its inspiration from urban culture, as opposed to the rural, vernacular inspiration that Coderch had chosen. Bohigas criticized this earlier model to some effect, declaring it to be traditionalist escapism from the deeper concerns of the modern.

A paradigmatic example of all this was Correa and Milà's extension to the Trias y Godó factory in 1962. These same architects had recently completed the Montesa factory where, respecting the requirements of the modern, they had determinedly used a tough, technological material, called Durisol, which did not live up to the expectations aroused by its name. The results were disastrous, and the new commission for another factory provided them with an opportunity to reconsider some of the principles in which they had believed so fervently hitherto. Consequently, the material chosen for the Trias y Godó building was brick, and it was used to build shapes that echoed the existing factory building. Having demonstrated in the previous decade its definitive adoption of the formal principles and resources of the modern heritage—also known as the International Style—Spanish architecture was now in a position to carry out research at a more local level. After the recovery of the architectural discipline, Correa and Milà now focused on the matter of construction, placing emphasis on an almost timeless technology. Brick became virtually the only material deployed in the fabric of buildings, and in time this idea of achieving unity in building through the almost exclusive use of one material was to become a stylistic characteristic of the emerging Escola.

The Meridiana building designed by Bohigas and Martorell was equally representative of its time. The formal structure imposed by several stories

Madre Güell
student hall of residence
Barcelona, 1963–1967,
Cantallops / Rodrigo.

of tightly sited dwellings was given a fine, firmly rhythmical facade. Arcaded at ground level, this facade was dominated by highly figurative balconies, as opposed to abstract recesses, placed at intervals that were both functionally efficient and compositionally pleasing. This, and the acceptance of the location, on the edge of Barcelona's inner suburbs known as the *ensanche*, gave the building its industrial, rather proletarian tone and revealed its realist intent. This building, which completed a series on Calles Escorial, Pallarés, and Roger de Flor, encapsulated the core concerns of the MBM studio. Reinforced by other projects such as factories and single-family houses, and by the publishing activities of all its members, particularly Bohigas, this studio played an important role in shaping the stylistic definition of the Escola. Its influence spread throughout Catalonia initially and then throughout Spain's periphery, slipping progressively, as always happens in these cases, into gradual misuse which would eventually trigger reaction, not least from Bohigas himself.

A similar attitude is discernible in the Madre Güell residence hall, by Rodrigo and Cantallops, where the rigorous use of brick helped to endow the cloister with an atmosphere of tranquillity and seclusion.

In the early sixties, the studio made up of Domènech, Puig, Sabater, and Sanmartí was the most representative one of the Barcelona school, despite the fact that they came originally from Lérida. In Gimenelles in 1965, they built a small agricultural complex using simple forms whose geometric squares and diagonals seem ahead of their time. A year later, this same team pursued the geometric, combinatory route further in their residential home for the elderly in Lérida, a building very typical of the Escola. In addition to the use of brick as a unifying material and the elegant deployment of windows, window boxes, and eaves, the design was ruled by a determination to build a civilized environment, treating the home's corridors and passageways as if they were the streets of a small village.

Another member of this Barcelona group was Ricardo Bofill who, despite his youth, was a prominent figure of this period. Brilliant and controversial, he possessed no Spanish academic qualifications and was therefore excluded from the official chambers. In 1964, he won the FAD prize with an apartment building on Calle Nicaragua in Barcelona where, on the pretext of evading its northern orientation, he used abstract planes of brick. In this building, and in other urban projects such as that on Calle Compositor Bach, he operated within the concepts we have been describing, albeit tinged with a certain critical irony directed at the bourgeois city.

In issue 15 of the international architecture journal *Zodiac* (1965), dedicated to Spain, Ricardo Bofill wrote an article analyzing the state of Spanish architecture. His attitude of critical detachment scandalized official bodies, and he was thought to have gone too far even by the most left-wing students. Unlike the students' involvement with social issues, his stance was not intended to oppose the Franco regime, but rather to challenge bourgeois society as a whole. Over the years, Bofill would cast off the *gauche qui rie* attitude that characterized certain circles in Barcelona, in a triumphal ascent to the position of global architect who, with an international reputation and offices in various countries, and mysterious

or surprising financial and political connections, obtained commissions for projects involving vast amounts of money. Earlier in his career, however, he designed and built the Xanadú building in Alicante, where he used the opportunities offered by this tourist commission to invent forms and interior spaces that were entertaining and unorthodox. Designed in 1967, the Xanadú was ahead of its time in its criticism of modernity, such as authors like Robert Venturi were then expressing in print. In the mid-sixties, Bofill was one of the Escola's imaginative young architects, the other wild ones being Lluis Clotet, Oscar Tusquets, Pep Bonet, and Cristian Cirici, the constituent members of the PER studio.

The PER, as they were known in those days, usually worked in twos: Bonet with Cirici, and Clotet with Tusquets. Their buildings were steeped in irony, as were their public appearances at which, with their Barcelona football shirts, pop-star haircuts, and love of the saxophone, they exuded a relaxed, almost anarchistic attitude to life that in no way interfered with their grasp on reality and on the value of things. Consider the example of the Penina and Fullà houses designed by Clotet and Tusquets in 1967. Although they presented these buildings as pessimistic and absurdist, they were actually rooted in an optimistic attitude as revealed in their logical and independent approach to the limiting factors, like the shape of the site, which defined their brief. The Penina house is revelatory of the sometimes contradictory issues that concerned this team, and of how they obtained their architectonic solutions from that very dichotomy, criticizing the ideology of the bourgeois society while according importance to comfort. Approaching architecture from the comfort angle, the user's angle, was something that Clotet and Tusquets had learned during their collaboration with Correa—they recall that he was the first to use carpet in the Reno restaurant—and that could be reconciled with protests against conservative habits. Lluis Clotet recalls that in those "progressive" times they lived without furniture, and designed things such as lamps and hearths intended to stand directly on the floor. The Penina house, through the absurdist magnificence of its shape, criticizes the absurdity of dividing town plans up into lots, yet the interior is comfortable.

In 1965, Sostres built the Noticiero Universal newspaper building. The man who ten years earlier had shown his mastery of the modern language in the Ciudad Diagonal, where he expressed his own interpretation of modernity, went on in the Noticiero building to provide a foretaste of the disciplinary interpretation of the city and of architecture that would later be propounded by the members of the Tendenza. In the Noticiero building, a flat facade without cornice, true to modern principles, was composed of repetitions of a single balconied recess of vertical proportions—figurative features against an abstract expanse.

Also around 1965, Coderch marked the start of his evolution toward a more sensuous abstraction with his Hotel de Mar in Palma de Mallorca, where he created a skin for the building and interpreted the supporting structure as something at the service of the organism within that skin, concerned with orientation—an external factor—and circulation and use patterns—an internal factor. In the Girasol ("Sunflower") building in Madrid he extended this interpretation. The skin was again made of ceramic panels and wood, and in this case it contained apartments oriented toward the sun, as the name suggested, breaking with the rectangular geometry typical of the inner suburbs where this building was located. Perpetuating the functionalist-organic ideal, the structure of the Girasol apartments attempted to replicate the layout of freestanding housing and, in particular, that of the Uriach house.

During this period, almost certainly influenced by the urban nature of his commissions, Coderch's oeuvre entered a new phase, superseding the previous one that had been heavily rural in inspiration. Starting with the buildings already described, through the Banco Urquijo apartment blocks in Barcelona (built on a site formerly occupied by bus garages, and therefore nicknamed *las cocheras*), up to his most ambitious urban designs for the competitions for the ACTUR Lakua in Vitoria and the Kursaal hall in San Sebastián, working sometimes with Valls and other times alone or with his sons, Coderch continued to expound the importance of the outer wrapping. In buildings designed for other uses, such as the Trade offices in Barcelona, the skin was still the dominant feature—in this case it took the form of a glass curtain wall, a skillful revival of a half-forgotten Miesian solution. Here, though, the glass was applied like scales, the aim being to produce an epithelial rather than a technological effect—an effectively ironic touch unmatched by his contemporaries.

In Barcelona, the architecture of the sixties was dominated by the members of the R Group who were to define the Escola. But they were not alone; other architects—more than can be mentioned here—also made their contribution. Some must be singled out, if only briefly: a loyal disciple of Coderch, Lluis Nadal's interpretation of architecture could be said to have emerged from his mentor's famous declaration: "Geniuses are not what we need." His work aspired to nothing more than realism and suitability, and demonstrated that this apparently modest approach was the way to make restrained, efficient buildings. The Marqués de Alella winery and the Matadepera school, built in 1969, are examples of an attitude which, recalling Louis Kahn, makes them seem very contemporary.

Enric Tous and Josep María Fargas, in important commissions such as the Banca Catalana building in 1969, explored a technological approach involving the use of glass in roofs and of stark exposed structures, not far removed from some of Coderch's ideas, achieving successful buildings in the process. The inclusion of vegetation from the planning stage made the constructional techniques more digestible. Xabier Busquets falls into a similar category: his office block for the Caja de Ahorros y Monte de Piedad savings bank in Barcelona is another brilliant building.

Elaborating on a 1964 project, Manuel de Solà-Morales and his son, Manuel, built the Porvenir-Muntaner building in Barcelona in 1967. Characteristics identified as typical of the Escola—the use of brick and the direction of recesses—were deployed in much the same way in this building, which, fitting readily into the nineteenth-century city, contained a strange and charming solution of courtyards and corridors: skillfully updated variations on the bourgeois house.

The term *periferia* was a popular sixties coinage that emerged from the culture of Barcelona to describe the rest of Spain, as opposed to its core—Madrid—thereby establishing a certain identity for these neglected areas. This evocative term reflected the reality of a situation in which decision-making powers were very much concentrated in the capital of a then very centralist state. This situation affected architecture in various ways. It caused commissions to be allocated in large numbers to Madrid-based architects, and this in its turn caused many to move to the city over many years, creating large work forces in its established studios. However, it also generated rebellion against the status quo (the very term *periferia* was a token of this rebellion), reflecting increasingly insistent rumors about political autonomy and establishing Barcelona as capital of this periphery and a source of considerable influence in years to come.

Although the periphery only produced architects of importance and established an identity for the very diverse parts of the country of which it was composed in the seventies, from the early sixties it saw progress in this regard in the form of Luis Peña Ganchegui. His work from the early sixties onward, while clearly rooted in the material and cultural conditions of the Basque country, did not represent regionalism in the same way as the Basque architecture of the recent past. It soon proved that architecture could be created from the provinces without recourse to regionalism or reference to Barcelona or Madrid. Peña's work thus served as an exemplar for all architects working outside those two cities. His work stood out in two areas: in the construction of small housing complexes in the villages of Guipúzcoa province, and in the treatment of urban spaces. An example of the latter is the Plaza de la Trinidad in San Sebastián, built in 1963, a splendid demonstration of how to design a public space by interpreting the lifestyle of its inhabitants. Here the architect incorporated a *pelota* court and tiered seating into the plaza, and adapted it to the party walls and the slope of the hillside in order to create an overall effect that is both functional and natural.

Peña worked hard in the village of Motrico and to particular effect in buildings such as the housing on Calle Ibaibarriaga, built in 1963 near the church of Silvestre Pérez, and the Aietzu complex, built in 1964. Despite the modest scale of the commission, there is a fluency and live-liness to this architecture that is simultaneously sound and restrained. Its "naturalness," a product of lack of pretension, was firmly grounded in layouts perfectly suited to the requirements of consumers whose way of life he knew well. Peña Ganchegui became a yardstick for younger generations, and was later made head of the San Sebastián School of Architecture when it was founded. (The fact that at first this was admin-istratively dependent on Barcelona's demonstrates the latter's status as capital of the periphery.)

Although it was not completed until the seventies and could not make its influence felt until then, a building designed in 1968 by Moneo, Marquet,

Unzurrunzaga, and Zulaica belongs to the period under consideration. The Urumea building in San Sebastián, mentioned earlier, is a complex one, for although the curved balconies of the exterior place it firmly within the period, the layout is so strongly disciplinary in its acceptance of the urban block patio and of the "through-light" model of apartment that it qualifies as a premonition of the predominant tendency in the Spanish architecture of the seventies.

Building in Bilbao continued much as described in the previous chapter: solidity and size characterize the neighborhood of San Ignacio, designed by Basáñez, Argárate, and Larrea; expressionism the buildings developed by Fullaondo, Líbano, and Olabarría; and a gentler version the buildings constructed by Íñiguez de Onzoño. In Vitoria, far from the industrial traffic of the coast, José Erbina created elegant buildings such as the Ofesa factory, with its smooth skin and rhythmically distributed openings.

While Peña Ganchegui enjoyed critical success from the start, the same cannot be said of José Bar Boo in Galicia—then considered the back of beyond—who used local materials, particularly traditional granite ashlar, to build housing in an international expressionist style.

Urumea building, San Sebastián, 1969–1973, Moneo / Marquet / Unzurrunzaga / Zulaica.

Vázquez house, San Miguel de Oia, Vigo (Pontevedra), 1963, Bar Boo.

The list of this period's architects representative of the part of Spain in which they worked must include Erwin Broner.[36] Born in Munich, he settled in Ibiza in 1959 and became the principal exponent of what later consolidated into the Ibiza style, whose origins date back to the architectonic discovery of the island by himself and the GATEPAC architects many years before. A painter, he was the founder of the Ibiza 59 group and a moving force in the island's cultural life. He built many houses up to 1971—the Broner and Kaufmann houses in 1960, the Sinz house in 1964, the Paniker house in 1966, and the Weber house in 1971, to mention but a few. Using conventional building techniques, whitewashing walls, providing shade with pergolas, canopies, and blinds, he created spatial combinations—interior and exterior—looking out at sea- and mountainscapes or in at secluded patios, which unquestionably justify his choice of lifestyle. Broner, who often worked with Ramón Torres (they built the Sandie apartments together in 1963), launched an architectural approach that was hugely successful and, as we shall see, continues to be so.

Josep Lluis Sert, who discovered Ibiza architecture at the same time as Broner, also returned to Ibiza. There he built the Calle Muralla house and designed the Can Pep Simó development, several of whose houses he built. Germán Rodríguez Arias, the first member of the GATCPAC group to settle in Ibiza, also worked on the same development, building in the same vein as his colleagues.[37]

In Andalusia during the sixties, things carried on much as before. The same architects already mentioned continued working, with some younger talent emerging, but their work achieved little exposure. Some examples are Pablo Fábrega, who built a cultural center in Villamartín, Cádiz; Carlos Pfeiffer de Fórmica, who worked in Granada; Francisco de la Corte with his vocational training workshops in Huelva; Luis María de Gana's bull ring in Marbella; and Jaime López de Asiaín, Ángel Díaz, and Pablo Fábrega's School of Industrial Engineering in Seville. The only Andalusian architect whose work achieved wider recognition during this period was José María García de Paredes, whom we have already seen established in Madrid.

Murcia was an atypical case: while architect Valentín Rodríguez[38] fulfilled the local role

Can Pep Simó development, Santa Eulalia del Río, Ibiza, 1965, Sert.

Architects' Chamber of the Canary Islands, Santa Cruz de Tenerife, 1968–1971, Díaz-Llanos / Saavedra.

typical of the periphery, a truly exceptional figure emerged in the form of Emilio Pérez Piñero. He qualified in 1969 and died in a car accident in 1976. On the basis of his experiments with molecular, spherical, and foldable structures, he built the geodesic dome for the Dalí Museum in Figueras. His premature death deprived Spain of an experimental architect who was breaking promising new ground in the same fascinating territory that interested the likes of Buckminster Fuller and Frei Otto.

If any part of Spain was peripheral during this period for geographical reasons, it was the Canary Islands. Lacking a School of Architecture (eventually one was founded in 1968); cocooned by an idyllic climate which, paradoxically, proved more of a handicap than an advantage in architectural terms; dependent on an economy inextricably bound up with the vagaries of the tourism sector, Canary Islands architecture, which

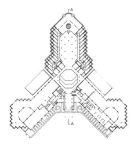

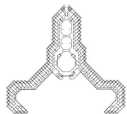

before the war had produced such pioneering figures as Miguel Martín from Gran Canaria and Marrero Regalado from Tenerife,[39] was virtually an unknown quantity on the mainland at this time.

From the early sixties on, however, there was a major upsurge, and by the end of the same decade solid results were already discernible. Two significant projects by Javier Díaz-Llanos and Vicente Saavedra illustrate this. For twenty years, from 1963 on, these two architects worked on the Ten-Bel tourist complex in southern Tenerife—a hitherto uninhabited area, covered only by native vegetation—to create a complex of apartments organized around interior gardens using a constructive repertory of volcanic rocks and prefabricated cement elements and a formal repertory of prismatic volumes and strong white concrete planes whose direct impact matched well the lush subtropical vegetation. Unfortunately, this eminently successful solution did not provide the model for many later tourist developments. Between 1966 and 1971, the same team built the headquarters of the Architects' Chamber in Santa Cruz in a style suggestive of British and Italian brutalism, a relative of metabolism, which sat easily amid the craggy mountains and volcanic rocks of the Tenerife landscape. This building's dense concrete and solid volumes are expressive of a response to the local geography, and the same approach is recognizable in the best Canary Islands architecture produced since that time. Thirty years on, the building is still valid as what its architects intended: a demonstration, between waterfront and mountain, of an urban architecture that works.

Late in the decade, in 1969, Rubens Henríquez, working with collaborators Félix Sáenz, Fernando Isidro, and Felipe Amaral, built a series of multitiered housing blocks staggered on the hillsides of Ifara that offered a convincing alternative solution to the problem of urban growth in difficult topographies such as those of the Canary Islands. Time has shown it to be a successful one, but again, unfortunately, its example has not been followed. The same is sadly true of other tourism-generated projects such as Higueras and Miró's hotels in Lanzarote, and the hotel built in Maspalomas by Corrales and Molezún—all exceptionally fine buildings.

Lanzarote is the island that has survived the tourist onslaught best, largely owing to the efforts of César Manrique. A sculptor and landscape artist whose smaller-scale work was formally very exuberant, Manrique's projects for the island demonstrated remarkably fine judgment and constructive skill. Inspired by him, roads similar in color to the volcanic rocks and painted to merge with the landscape lead to projects of various kinds designed by Manrique, such as the Mirador del Río vantage point and the Jameos del Agua volcanic grotto, all typified by their sympathy with the landscape. Manrique continued working for several decades more until his death in 1992.

Nineteen seventy-five was a pivotal point, the year when Franco died, bringing about the end of one political regime—the dictatorship—and the start of another—parliamentary monarchy.

The period during which the change was consolidated is known as *la Transición*—the Transition. Historians will probably never agree about the exact timing of such far-reaching changes, since the Transition can be said to have started earlier or later depending on whether it is viewed from a social, political, or other perspective. From the viewpoint that concerns us here, changes affecting client and commission (those essential elements of architecture) occurred gradually, speeding up or slowing down in pace with the devolution of political power to the various regions into which the state was organized. As regards the figure of the architect and his style and ideology, the process is impossible to identify since the same architects were practicing before and after the change of regime. In other words, it was the source of commissions that changed: Madrid became weaker and the various autonomous governments became stronger, but the personnel and ideas of architecture remained the same. It is important to realize how society had evolved in the years leading up to the death of Franco. With the exception of a few reactionary regime faithfuls, the populace was fully aware of the need for the political change to a democratic society while simultaneously accepting, despite the urgings of more radical opinion, that it was not worth resorting to violence to achieve this in the lifetime of the dictator. It would come about of its own momentum when he died. After being concealed beneath the uniform of a regime that no longer represented it, during the Transition society started wearing its own clothes. Architecture played a part in this process, for it had been waiting for this change and was prepared for it. The drama of earlier years gave way to optimism, as we shall see.

As described in the previous chapter, the works of the organicists and of the Escola had already come of age in the period since 1965. Spanish architects moved forward in the direction of theory and criticism. Several highly influential magazines came into being, and access to seminal books had a marked effect on students' training. The magazines established in the previous decade continued to be published, but ceded ground to new ones of a more ideological slant. *Nueva Forma*, for example, continued to be published until 1977, but, with its initial organicist fervor burned out, it was given over to publishing monographs on Spain's leading architects, taking part in more controversial current affairs only from the sidelines.

Plaza del Tenis,
San Sebastián, 1975–1976,
Peña Ganchegui,
sculpture by Chillida.

In Barcelona, *Arquitecturas bis* made its first appearance in 1971 and lasted until 1983. As the name was intended to suggest, its aim was not to propound one specific artistic ideology but rather to provide a panoramic ideological showcase.[40] The magazine was launched by Oriol Bohigas and Rosa Regàs, with a very eclectic and influential board of directors.[41]

Bohigas, the architect who had been so active in R Group in the fifties and had defined the Barcelona *Escola* in the sixties, continued to be a key figure in his city's cultural life in the seventies.

Also in Barcelona, *2C Construcción de la Ciudad* appeared from 1972 onward. This magazine's moving spirit was Salvador Tarragó, active cultural agitator,[42] early translator of Rossi, and without doubt the most active Spanish member of the Tendenza. *2C*, in some measure a counterbalance to *Arquitecturas bis*, published certain highly (as it were) "tendentious" monographs on Aldo Rossi and Giorgio Grassi, and on Catalan figures such as Cerdà and Torres Clavé, which proved to be very opportune reassessments.

Completing the range of Barcelona-based magazines was *El Carrer de la Ciutat*.[43] Edited with critical zeal by Beatriz Colomina, its modest small format and cheap paper smacked of a persisting underground style.

Books such as Juan Benet's *La inspiración y el estilo*, Joseph Rykwert's *On Adam's House in Paradise* (translated into Spanish in 1974 as *La casa de Adán en el paraíso*), the works of Manfredo Tafuri, Giorgio Grassi's *La costruzione logica dell'architettura*, and above all Venturi's *Complexity and Contradiction* and Rossi's *Architettura della città*, both written in 1966 and translated into Spanish at the start of the next decade, were hugely influential and helped build faithful followings for Venturi, Rossi, and Tafuri. With an eye to the growing number of students and young architects, publishing houses were quick to publish relevant book series.[44] The result was a genuine transformation of the cultural profile of architects, who were becoming increasingly well-read and whose professional interests and work habits were influenced in consequence. One result of this in the seventies was that young architects became interested in joining schools as teachers. These new educators, trained during the turbulent years surrounding 1968, made up a generation that polarized teaching and stretched the limits of the profession to such an extent that, when *Arquitecturas bis* brought out an issue in 1978 on architecture in Madrid, it entitled it "28 arquitectos no numerarios" (28 Architects without Tenure; see below).

With the benefit of hindsight, it could now be said that the Transition was experienced in architecture as a reawakening of an old controversy: that of turning to history for lessons in the discipline's formal repertory versus turning to the new and the vernacular. In other words, continuing to speak in classical language as opposed to the neologisms of a changing world, which seeks expression through new voices. In short, a rather refined controversy, in contrast with the more visceral, intuitive explosion that occurred in the sixties. The seventies were, then, a period of reading, reflection, and maturity.

It is vital to realize, however, that despite the amount of reading and interchange of opinions and influences, the objective being pursued remained unchanged. As will be seen, reassessing the meaning and uses of history equipped Spain with a more informed approach to interpreting the modern.

Madrid's Movida

The early seventies in Madrid was an intense period of reading and reflection. It was also a time of self-identification.

By dint of dogged opposition to the regime from the university, leftist ideas had gained a dominant position by the end of the sixties. This meant that the moral tone that had come from the Catholics in the forties and fifties now came from the left, bunkered in the university and in the labor organization Comisiones Obreras. Lecturers openly defended this political liberalization, and social conscience and the social role of the architect were prime subjects for discussion in the early seventies. While urbanism had been the choice area of study in the previous decade, the seventies would look to the relationship between architecture and city for its solutions.

Since the late sixties, painters in Madrid had been showing a growing interest in the figurative, reclaiming it from abstraction. Now they established links with the architects who, in parallel, had become increasingly interested in architecture's relationship to the city. Antonio López, Paco and Julio López Hernández, and, later and with a different slant, Luis Gordillo, Guillermo Pérez Villalta, and Juan Navarro Baldeweg—to name but a few painters connected to architecture by area of interest or training—were influential in architectural projects of this period.

The intensity of experience generated by reading, embracing libertarian ideals, and the dizzying rate of political change in the buildup to the big change, produced an acceleration of ideas that found its most public expression in a phenomenon that became known as *la movida*. This word, borrowed from local slang and meaning "an event that comes about when a small group of like-minded people get together to achieve something," became a media buzz word at the end of the decade, but if it meant anything at all it was the surge of activity and interchange that, in the libertarian glow of the approaching change, helped equip people working in Madrid with a cultural identity.

That said, however, architecture in Madrid was the sum of parts contributed by architects very different amongst themselves, though they can be categorized to some degree. Two lines of inspiration or predominant ideas divided loyalties from the start. On the one hand were the architects who consulted the technical evidence for formal resolution of the architectonic object, interpreting the modern in a very orthodox way. On the other were those who accepted the new stress on urban analysis as an enrichment of the modern—this was almost their identifying feature—and as part and parcel of the architectural project.

These ideas, only roughly outlined here, were not, of course, mutually incompatible, but Madrid's architects could be divided into those who inclined primarily in one or the other direction. The technically inclined ones had sound, convincing models to refer to. In the city itself, Alejandro de la Sota became a *maestro* figure for many who attended his unforgettable classes at the School of Architecture, and through the example of his own work. Models outside Spain included the highly influential Gowan-Stirling partnership, which had been the best-known foreign practice from the late sixties onward.

From early on, adherents of urban analysis, avid readers of the Italian authors mentioned above, included a highly authoritative exponent in the person of Rafael Moneo. His training had been meticulously orchestrated: he had worked in Sáenz de Oiza's studio while still a student, and after qualifying had joined Utzon's studio in Denmark. He won an Academy of Rome scholarship and subsequently returned to the Madrid School of Architecture as a lecturer. There his clear-sighted judgment and eclectic knowledge, present in the essence of all his projects, won him his first disciples, before he eventually occupied a chair in Barcelona. How this came about is an interesting story.

An academic event occurred in Madrid 1971 that, though specifically focused, was to be far-reaching in its national effects. Competitions were announced for three academic chairs, in Madrid, Barcelona, and Seville. Five candidates came forward: Alejandro de la Sota, Federico Correa, Antonio Fernández Alba, Rafael Moneo, and Alberto Donaire, listed here in order of age. Apart from this last, who was the Seville School of Architecture's official candidate, the candidates presented very different profiles, though all brilliant. De la Sota had been Madrid's most influential architect, and would be again, though critical interest in him had waned for the moment; Correa, the only Barcelonan, was an outstanding figure in Catalonia; Fernández Alba was the Madrid School of Architecture's most prestigious teacher, perceived as a political figure and as an overt exponent of the recent organicist movement. The up-and-coming Moneo's presentation was the most brilliant and relevant. There were simply not enough posts for teachers of such caliber, and the dilemma was dealt with in a very revelatory way. Perverse objections on the part of the panel—such as the fact that Correa was not a professor—produced an equally perverse result, though on the silver lining principle some good came of it: Fernández Alba won first place and was made professor at Madrid; Donaire was given second place so that he could take Seville, and Moneo was given Barcelona. This was hugely beneficial both to the Barcelona school and to Moneo himself, who cleverly capitalized on the cultural platform that the city offered in the seventies. Moneo surrounded himself with a group of young lecturers—Mora, Piñón, Bach, Viaplana, Llinás, and Torres among others—who in time would

Lecture room building, School of Science, Seville, 1971–1973, de la Sota.

become some of Barcelona's most prestigious architects. His influence as academic and teacher was profound, not only in Barcelona and Madrid but throughout Spain. Moneo's presence as a teacher in Barcelona while maintaining his professional practice and influence in Madrid established a change in the relationship between the two cities: the nation's critical hub revolved around Rosa Regàs's desk at *Arquitecturas bis.*

In 1978, *Arquitecturas bis* devoted a double issue to the architecture of Madrid. It featured a series of buildings and two leading articles by Rafael Moneo and Antón Capitel, respectively, along with reflections on recent work by architects of the city in question. Titled "28 arquitectos no numerarios" (28 Architects without Tenure), it presented the work of several teams of young architects who had in common the fact of being teachers without tenure at the School of Architecture; people with little work, but busily employed at teaching. After making the point that he was not referring to a "school" as such, Moneo declared that the young architects

> do not disdain culture, and try to use theoretical problems as one of the yardsticks against which to measure the practice of this new understanding of the profession. The recently qualified architects whose works are featured here are well-informed architects, *au fait* with what magazines publicize and present as good, who discuss and involve themselves in an architectural debate that extends beyond strictly national boundaries. I believe that this change is worthy of comment, especially given that one of the accusations that used to be made against the Madrid school was its lack of culture, though it was credited with intuition. The attention that Madrid's young architects pay to the outside world is reflected in their work, and could be said to be one of its most obvious characteristics. But it must also be admitted that alongside this attention is a prudence that suggests a belief in the ancient Delphic dictum "nothing to excess." This balance of forces makes it difficult to place the group within any one of the tendencies currently unsettling the waters of architecture.[45]

Among the works featured, the Bankunión and Bankinter buildings were presented as current trendsetters. The Bankunión was designed and built by Corrales and Molezún between 1972 and 1977. When this almost abstract, scalariform building was completed, it became a monumental presence on Madrid's Paseo de la Castellana, and to the man in the street it stood for architecture at its most modern.

Bankunión building,
Madrid, 1972–1977,
Corrales / Vázquez Molezún.

It is metallic (a beautiful red anodized aluminum), exhibits pipework of varying sizes on the exterior, and is roofed with a version of the barrel vault whose effect is mechanical rather than classical. This is what earned the building its nickname of *la cafetera* ("the coffee machine").

A building of Alejandro de la Sota's, attributable to the technical tendency, was not featured in the magazine, no doubt because it was built in Seville. This was the lecture hall built for the university in 1972—a stern building, with severe walls and thin slit windows for light control, with a strict metallic structure outlining the large, cold spaces of the interior.

The Madrid issue of *Arquitecturas bis* closed with another building, again attributable to the technical tendency, that became a landmark. The Banco de Bilbao was Sáenz de Oiza's contribution to that period's new buildings in Madrid. It has the proportions of a small skyscraper in glass and metal and, along with Torres Blancas, is still one of the best tower blocks in Madrid. In formal terms, it is a highly intelligent compromise between the cubist *pile d'assiettes*, splendid for visual impact but inconvenient in use, and the functional glass parallelepiped. Structurally it is made up of a sequence of concrete trays projecting from a sturdy nucleus on large cantilevers on which the intermediate floors sit in groups of four. The rhythmic variety created by the different floors is capitalized on for the location of cleaning galleries and glass sun canopies that differentiate the floors according to their orientation, achieving beautiful vibrations of level, light, and shade and giving it a mechanical look.

Other architects from Sáenz de Oiza's studio worked on this project with him, among them Francisco Alonso de Santos, Alfonso Valdés, Javier Vellés, and José Carlos Velasco, all of whom would subsequently build works of their own. Like Ferrán and Mangada and others already mentioned, these architects can be considered disciples of Sáenz de Oiza, who, together with de la Sota, was Madrid's grand master in the seventies.

José Carlos Velasco built a professional training center in Teruel in 1972. This is a very direct building in which all the constructive elements both declare their function and perform a precise role in the overall composition. Examples include the drainpipes and the heating system chimney, which stands out from the body of the building and is placed to one side of the wall that it crosses vertically. The same wall is punctuated horizontally by continuous balconies with long windows and balustrades. The architectonic device that provides light for the long, schematic staircase on the rear facade is topped at roof level by a raised superstructure with large windows. The unequal overhang created by this device achieves an imposing crowning feature for the roof and the blind wall gable end. The restrained modesty of the materials used and the serviceable tone of the construction create a building that, though forceful, is charming rather than tough and uncompromising.

Also in 1972, Javier Vellés built a series of professional training colleges, notably in Santander and Seville. He worked in collaboration with José Manuel López-Peláez on the latter of these, creating a very straightforward building. Roofing, circulation, illumination, and ventilation were the key conceptual elements of its design. It is composed of a deep-perspective barrel vault made of glass, iron, and cement blocks, the materials deployed in their most naked and unembellished state. The lecture rooms are distributed on either side of the vault. This dispassionate, efficient, self-referential design could be placed on the outskirts of any town just as a car could be parked at any curb.

Javier Vellés and María Luisa López Sardá designed a shade-garden leisure center for Cercedilla, in the mountainous countryside outside Madrid. As in the previous buildings, this is another example in which all the elements and forms derive from some aspect of the construction process, whether an interface, structural support, or characteristic of a material. Stone-banked platforms staggered against the hillside are shaded by a series of flat surfaces composed of squares of wood and wire that filter the light, replicating the effect of the branches and leaves in the surrounding woodland. In this building, wood and shadows are deployed to soften the structure's shape.

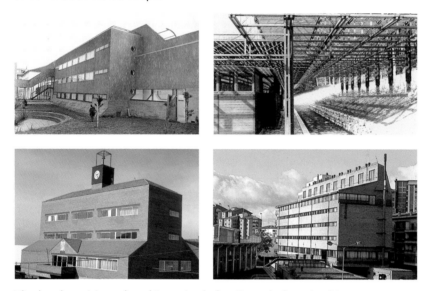

From left to right and from top to bottom:
Boarding school, Talavera de la Reina (Toledo), 1975–1977, Manuel de las Casas / Ignacio de las Casas.

Shade-garden leisure center, Cercedilla (Madrid), 1976–1979, Vellés / López Sardá.

Alcorcón Town Hall, Alcorcón (Madrid), 1973, Cabrero.

Vocational Training Center, Teruel, 1972, Velasco.

The brothers Manuel and Ignacio de las Casas belong in this same tendency. Their boarding school in Talavera de la Reina, Toledo, reveals an awareness of English architecture and a command of Castilian building tradition. Traditional local materials, brick and daub, are used in combination with glass and a circulation-oriented formal structure. The restrained scale and the dynamic of the successive spaces are notable in this building.

The much-cited Bankinter building was designed and built between 1973 and 1976 by Ramón Bescós and Rafael Moneo. Even before completion it had become Madrid's first example of the programmatic interpretation of architecture so typical of that time. Moneo had already declared this as an interest in his Urumea building, discussed earlier. The importance of the Bankinter building was enhanced by its success beyond the city itself. For the first time, Madrid's architects saw foreigners converge on the Paseo de la Castellana to see the most modern building in both the Old

Bankinter building,
Madrid, 1973–1977,
Moneo / Bescós.

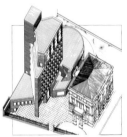

Top and center left:
Manuel de Falla Concert Hall
(general view and detail
of the interior),
Granada, 1975–1978,
García de Paredes.

Bottom left:
Casa de la Lluvia,
Liérganes
(Santander), 1978–1982,
Navarro Baldeweg.

Bottom right:
Architects' Chamber
of Western Andalusia,
Seville, 1977–1983,
Perea / Ruiz Cabrero.

and New Worlds. And indeed, it would be true to describe the Bankinter as the first building designed on the basis of a totally clear, rigorous, and competent interpretation of the theories that perceived the architectural project as a direct product of urban analysis. Critical opinion was tired of the functional metaphor and of mechanical, linguistic, and organic analogies, and now demanded a return to the intrinsic discipline of architecture. Type, character, and urban shape were once more the concepts that dictated the architectural project, whose role was not only to improve the city but also to explain it. Moneo's illustrative and pedagogic leanings are consistent throughout his oeuvre. But the theories of the Tendenza, of which this building could be considered the most brilliant example, are not the sole influence here: other interpretations of the city, as expressed in the contemporary writings of Venturi and others, are also in evidence. Consequently, we should now interpret it as a dissertation on the application and meaning of the compositional theories that succeeded the modern. This didactic building demonstrated Moneo's maturity, and in conjunction with some of his written work, such as "On Topology," published in *Oppositions*, earned him the academic authority that he has enjoyed ever since.

Another building of this period that proved influential among the disciplinary tendency, though far less in the public eye, was the Alcorcón Town Hall, in Madrid, completed by Francisco Cabrero in 1973. Critics such as Antón Capitel recognized in this building an affinity with disciplinary ideas and with those of Venturi. The Town Hall is a volumetrically emphatic building, made of the most ordinary materials used in a conventional way—brick, aluminum detailing, iron lintels, and exposed concrete beams—but deployed so as to emphasize certain immediately symbolic elements: clock, weather-vane-topped tower, escutcheon, balcony. These features have an almost kitsch feel in the context of the building's overall sobriety; the principles evinced here, Capitel declared, place Cabrero in a position where

> he will in a way, and unwittingly, preside over the group of architects who are seeking a new urban approach; and it is on the basis of aspects such as this that his work will be appreciated, and the old Trade Union building, hitherto condemned as negatively ambiguous architecture, will take on an emblematic value.[46]

In a quiet but very confident way, José María García de Paredes was also an influential figure, becoming Spain's leading expert in the design of concert halls. Andalusian in origin, though he practiced from Madrid, he was an important teacher at Seville's School of Architecture and the author of the Manuel de Falla Concert Hall in Granada in 1976. This enormous building takes its place to stunningly beautiful effect on a site as sensitive as the side of the hill on which the Alhambra stands. To achieve this, the bulk of the concert hall, designed with the precision of a violin maker, is broken up and fragmented externally, creating a series of ceramic volumes charged with expression despite silent expanses of wall.

In 1975, after a prolonged dearth of opportunities of this official kind, the Architects' Chamber of Western Andalusia announced a competition for the design and construction of its new headquarters in Seville. The position of the site, right in the city center, raised the vexed issue of placing modern architecture in a historically consolidated environment. The winning project by Enrique Perea and Gabriel Ruiz Cabrero was rooted in issues in which these architects were primarily interested at the time. They analyzed the clash between the nineteenth-century three-story buildings on the square and the city's six-story 1950s buildings, and extracted the formal theme for the corner site from that very contra-diction. After selecting the most suitable complex form for the conditions imposed by the brief, they organized the project around an interpretation of the patio as a semipublic space, appropriate to the building's function. An understated box of superb local brick, whose excellent quality per-forms well as the building's interface with the city, provided ample leeway for the composition of the interior. The finishes incorporated elements, both superficial and more integral, derived from the formal repertoire of Seville architecture: sun canopies, *azulejo* tiles, large apertures in high walls, all of which imbued the building with a slightly kitsch feel which in later years would be read as regionalism. The fact that this project won the commission gave credibility to opting for a disciplinary approach while still engaging with the modern, at least among its architects' contemporaries in Madrid.

This predominant tendency coexisted well with the other, technical tendency mentioned above, and Madrid's architecture continued to develop vigorously in these two directions during this period, which is probably why later stances such as postmodernism and deconstructivism were not to find much favor among the city's architects.

The Casa de la Lluvia ("Rain house"), built in Santander in 1979, announced the arrival on the architectural scene of Juan Navarro Baldeweg, already an established and influential figure in his role as lecturer on the elements of composition at the Madrid School of Architecture, and in the plastic arts as a painter. It marked the start of an architectural career that would soon take him into the international arena. Standing halfway up a gentle, green-meadowed hillside, the house is an exercise in lightness, where the constructional elements—windows, roofs, pergolas, and drainpipes—become elements of the composition as the sum of parts. These elements—the drainpipes are a good example— are interpreted as parts of a machine, working mechanical parts, and are drawn with clever irony by someone who, perhaps because of his love of one-of-a-kind machines, cannot help seeing all machines with affection and skepticism in equal measure, an attitude that allows him a free hand when giving things shape.

Is there such a thing as Catalan architecture? In 1976, *Arquitecturas bis* devoted its thirteenth issue to a retrospective of works built in Catalonia during that decade, similar in content to the magazine's double issue on Madrid of 1978. An introduction by Oriol Bohigas started by posing the above question. In a brilliant rhetorical exercise, Bohigas argued that the existence of various tendencies in architecture was, if anything, proof of cohesion among the architects of Barcelona: "It is not that they lack identity, but rather that they are adapting to new approaches, alert to and actively aware of the experimentation that generates new objectives, while remaining within the authentic framework of their own culture."[47] The buildings featured in the magazine, representative of various tendencies, were also interpreted in a piece by Helio Piñón, whose observations are interesting in a different way, coming from someone who, because of his age, had not been part of Barcelona's Escola:

> Whatever the case, one trait that the different attitudes represented have in common is their obvious acceptance of theories both authorized and clearly identifiable in the international debate about architecture. This fact should not surprise us, considering the increasingly universal dimension that architectural theories have been taking on, and the capacity for assimilation that characterizes Barcelona's recent architectonic culture. . . . While I do not feel that my arguments need to be backed up with specific examples to prove my point, it seems relevant to consider the emergence and continuity of *Arquitecturas bis* from this perspective.
> The date when it was launched coincides with a breaking of the *impasse* in which the theory and practice of architecture had become trapped by the end of the cycle defined by the protagonism of the Barcelona school. The frustration generated by the crisis over the principles on which the school had based its relative opportunism—not so much about the role assigned to architecture by capitalist society (remember that Oriol Bohigas mentioned pessimism as one of the group's characteristic traits in 1968), as the validity of the analysis and proposals it produced—gave way early in 1974 to a new situation in which attempts to reformulate old issues came from various quarters.[48]

Piñón's diagnosis, accurate in all its details—the only questionable point being his focus on 1974 as the starting date of the new situation, of which more later—shows that the Escola had had its day. This was a consequence both of the formalist mannerism into which it had declined through the sort of misapplication and banal imitation that follow on all successful aesthetic movements, and of the cultural rescue operation effected by the reading of texts mentioned earlier. A connection could, perhaps, be made between this particular occurrence in Catalan architecture and the more general situation in Spanish society as a whole. In the sixties, the success of the Escola's philosophy represented Catalan culture in retreat: with the region's language prohibited by the regime, along with any expression of Catalan culture, the populace and especially the bourgeoisie withdrew into a world of comfortable, carpeted interiors that were bastions against the regime—which, in the larger context, was slowly dying. When the regime changed, the nationalistic feelings that had taken refuge in the domestic—so homogeneous, and so typically Barcelonan—could be expressed publicly, and architecture, which until then had served as platform and mouthpiece for social aspirations, could apply itself with greater conviction to issues more specifically within the scope of its discipline. In short, to paraphrase the monarchical declaration: "Barcelona's Escola is dead, long live Catalan architecture!" It is important to realize that this architectonic transition occurred before the death of the dictator, social changes anticipating the political change that must inevitably follow.

This shift from the domestic to the descriptive occurred gradually, not at a stroke. The apartments in Sant Feliú de Guixols designed by Lluis Domènech, Lauri Sabater, and Roser Amadó date from 1970. The building stands beside a preexisting tower, though it does not refer to it compositionally. Quite the contrary, for the new building is a straightforward volume, its understated facades punctuated by uniform apertures. Although the interior contains traits typical of the Escola in which these architects were active participants—the living room's built-in elements are an example—features of the exterior, such as the top-floor arcading and the small square windows and the way in which they are grouped, are clearly indicative of a degree of formal identification with the Tendenza.

In 1972, Lluis Clotet and Oscar Tusquets completed a little house that they named the Georgina Belvedere. As in the previous example, the ground plan shows that sense of the domestic at which the Escola was so accomplished, but the irony evident in the Belvedere indicates that there are other allegiances at work here. Astutely aware of how ridiculous little holiday homes with delusions of mansionesque grandeur can be, the architects exploited this summer house's disguise to solve a problem they considered superficial only in the literal sense. Far from being a negligible question of appearances, this was not so much an exercise in disguise as an attempt to resolve two issues: appearance and comfort. The treatment of the pergola, pilasters, and balustrades, solid or painted on, carries the grasp of the vernacular and the kitsch to the finest detail, turning this little building into perhaps the best and earliest representative in Europe of the area of interest so brilliantly examined in the writings of Robert Venturi.

On the Italian island of Pantelleria in 1972, Clotet and Tusquets were confronted with a dry, windy natural environment whose inhabitants eke out a subsistence agriculture on terraced slopes. The architects tackled

Left and center:
Georgina Belvedere
(general view and plans),
Llofriu, Gerona, 1971–1972,
Tusquets / Clotet.

Right and opposite page:
Vittoria house,
Pantelleria, Italy, 1975,
Clotet / Tusquets.

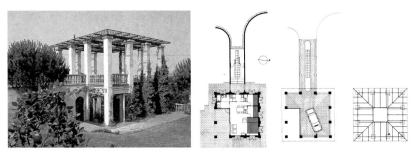

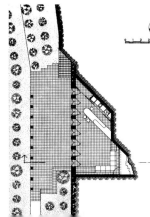

the paradox arising from situating a comfortable holiday house in such an austere setting by dressing a very Barcelonan configuration of domestic rooms, efficiently distributed with geometric angularity, with an arrangement of concrete pilasters, which like the shiny flooring condense the quintessence of a classic Mediterranean ceramic stylobate. Its architects describe it thus:

> The new building, unavoidably visible because of its size, makes no attempt to resemble either the popular architecture of the past or the commonplace pseudo-Mediterranean architecture that uses white rounded surfaces and little arches. The spirit of the dark, austere *danusos* (local farm buildings) is preserved in this strange, newly built ruin, whose concrete pillars form a timeless, classical, orderly screen behind which the varied pattern of every day life goes on.

In short, integration with the landscape is achieved through identification with the classical and the vernacular. The other half of the PER studio, Pep Bonet and Cristian Cirici, designed the Bonet house, which its archi-tects declared to have been inspired by local farm buildings. It anticipated the new influences in its typological appreciation of elements of marginal architecture.

Equally advanced are the towers and ventilation shafts designed by Jordi Garcés and Enric Sòria, built in Sabadell in 1971, which in the context of the surrounding landscape take on a dignified quality somewhere between the archaeological and the metaphysical, between ruin and remains.

Two very significant works—the Calle Galileo building and the Frégoli building—were built in Barcelona during this Transition period by architects of a new generation who erupted onto the scene with ambition and daring. The Calle Galileo building, designed by Gabriel Mora, Helio Piñón, and Albert Viaplana, was built between 1974 and 1976. This was a minor commission for small apartments on a site in a narrow-streeted built-up area, but the architects rose above the limitations of the brief, opting for a fan-shaped ground plan reminiscent of Aalto and using elongated stairways to define a dramatically long space. They cleverly contained these ambitious features within a discreet facade with large apertures, which allowed the interior to breathe.

Esteve Bonell's Frégoli building, built between 1972 and 1975, is another example that transcends the narrow constraints that some briefs impose. Bohigas observes of this building:

Despite starting off within the tortured forms derived from the mannerism of the Barcelona school, during the building process it gradually changed direction toward a new neorationalism, triggered by a desire to erase progressively the overexpressive imprint of the little functional anecdote. . . . By the end of its own evolutionary process, the building had almost become a simple prism, in which the structure and the beautiful graphic quality of the facade are undifferentiated. It must be said, however, that as a consequence of the doubts tackled during the process, the building presents certain errors of syntax and elemental formalization, such as the open staircase which stands out as an odd element, creating a double contradiction.[49]

In their directness and ambitiousness of form, these two buildings demonstrate their architects' urge to push beyond both the obsolete tradition of the Escola and the influence of their reading. How they achieved their objectives in the second half of the decade will be seen, but the stance adopted by their former *maestros* in the meantime merits some attention.

The MBM studio (Martorell and Bohigas having been joined some time previously by David Mackay) continued to be a fundamental point of reference. Without question, their most significant building from this period is the splendid Thau school, completed in 1974. Disregarding the influences that were inclining younger architects toward territory of the kind described above, this building shows more affinity with the programmatic work of figures of their generation such as Stirling and Van Eyck, its construction governed by analysis of use and circulation, particularly appropriate considerations when designing a school. The central space serves as a hub around which use patterns are configured, and the inspirational idea behind the project and its formal execution follow on from these, achieving a coherence not often found in Spanish architecture. This stubborn adherence to modern attitudes on the part of MBM, parallel to Coderch's despite the considerable differences between them, was to have its repercussions in years to come.

Coderch built the French Institute in Barcelona between 1972 and 1974. Bru and Mateo comment:

The proposition of the autonomous, inward-looking building, contrary to a positive appreciation of urban continuity, is an attitude characteristic of modernity, and one to which Coderch's work is particularly susceptible. Hence his isolationist urban work—think of his urban housing, of which the Girasol building in Madrid is a paradigmatic example. It reflects this stance perfectly, the building's autonomous character being accentuated by the way it willfully renounces contact with the preexisting environment, and is formalized from within its own system of logic, without reference to any engagement with its surroundings.[50]

This refusal to establish contact with the existing environment, which probably stemmed from a trait of the architect's character (or a fad

From top to bottom and from left to right:
Thau school, Barcelona, 1972–1975, Bohigas / Martorell / Mackay.

Frégoli I building, Barcelona, 1972–1974, Bonell.

Llinás house, Begur (Gerona), 1978–1980, Llinás.

Apartment building, Cerdanyola (Barcelona), 1976–1979, Clotet / Tusquets.

sustained for so long that it amounted to the same thing), needs to be evaluated from two angles. It not only provided evidence of Coderch's independent stance, but also served a more collective function of keeping alive the practice of a particular interpretation of architecture—uninfluenced by contemporary discourse—bearing in mind that at that time, the interpretation of the city and appreciation of the preexisting environment were current issues.

The isolationist quality of the French Institute building is reinforced by Coderch's use of a compositional theme discernible in his work from the Barceloneta house onward: the notion of a skin that wraps the house and delineates the most disciplinary interpretation required by the notion of the facade. Here, windows flush with ceramic cladding dispense with any trace of molding. This building is reminiscent of Sostres's Noticiero Universal building mentioned earlier. Though Sostres was no longer active as an architect at this time, his influence was disseminated by an issue of 2C devoted to him. With the new appreciation of these architects in the mid-seventies came a recurrence of interest in matters modern.

Work by Clotet and Tusquets dating from this period is representative of this interest; their apartments built in Cerdanyola between 1976 and 1979 are a case in point. An interest in the modern is evident not only in the maisonette layout of the apartments but also in the materials used, such as the metalwork displayed in the galleries and access stairs, whose only decorative content derives from their own constructive logic.

The same could be said of the Science Museum in Barcelona, where, between 1979 and 1980, Garcés and Sòria restored and expanded an existing industrial building, resolving the composition by means of extensive brick and glass walls which are abstract in conception.

Similarly, in the Cerler ski station apartments in Huesca, built between 1976 and 1979, Jaume Bach and Gabriel Mora manipulate modern and traditional elements simultaneously. Among the former are the choice of apartment type, very much in the central European tradition, and certain details such as porches and pillars; among the latter are the vertical apertures, the masonry, and the balustrades.

Josep Llinás announced his presence in the architectural panorama with a beautiful building at the close of that decade. This house, built for his parents in 1978, makes a clear statement in favor of modern architecture. The simplicity of this habitable parallelepiped, the lightness of the roof and supporting columns, the confident use of glass, the placement of the building in its setting, and the comblike configuration of gallery and rooms are all stylistic devices honed in the fifties.

The interest shown by Catalan architects since the start of the seventies in issues raised by the likes of Rossi and Venturi could be said to have given way toward the end of the decade to a renewed interest in the modern. Reassessed, and in stylistically appropriated form, this was to be the dominant theme of the exultant, optimistic eighties.

The seventies were also a period of important change as regards centers of architectural activity. In Spain's silent periphery, an increasing awareness of place created new focuses of activity, and from the middle of the decade onward Madrid and Barcelona no longer held exclusive sway. Peña Ganchegui has been mentioned as a singular figure in the previous decade, designing from the specific perspective of the Basque country. The disciples he attracted consolidated as a group around San Sebastián, so that it became a new focus.

Capitalizing on the cultural stance of the intellectual Julio Caro Baroja who, working from his home village of Vera de Bidasoa, was writing about the Basque country's anthropological and urban situation, Miguel Garay and José Ignacio Linazasoro set up a study center. They succeeded in obtaining the backing of the Cultural Commission of the Architects' Chamber, and organized, among other events, the San Sebastián Architecture Weeks to which they invited the most active theorists of the time, so that Rossi, Krier, Scolari, and Grassi came face to face with Bohigas, Solà-Morales, Sáenz de Oiza, Fullaondo, Sambricio, and Moneo. The direct relation-ships struck up between the former group and these younger architects and others, including Unzurrunzaga, Galarraga, Íñiguez, and Ustarroz, who attended the events from Pamplona, reinforced a specifically Basque architectural movement characteristic of this period.

In 1974, Garay and Linazasoro completed their Ikastola, a Basque school in Fuenterrabía, Guipúzcoa province. It demonstrates an advanced, balanced, and sustained understanding of texts exploring the relation between architecture, city, and territory, themselves simultaneously rooted in the thinking of contemporary Basque authors such as Caro Baroja. This is a building charged with the youthful verve of the *opera prima*: uncompromising, white, its volumes clearly drawn, it stands alone in a rainy natural environment just like the country houses of that part of northern Spain. This solid quadrilateral is evocative of the laconic Basque culture which looks to the ancient for authenticity. It was a much publicized building, for, as we have observed, it clearly encapsulated the concerns of contemporary European culture, and was rapidly classified as Tendenza-related, though equally heavily influenced by Silvestre Pérez.

In 1976, Navarrese architect Patxi Biurrun built a house that was again very much of its time. The conceptual tension that informs all his work is present in his location of a sculpturesque white shape with a flat roof within a settlement of unadorned tile-roofed stone buildings, the difference making it stand out in an unreal way from the rest of the village.

Manuel Íñiguez and Alberto Ustarroz's restaurant in Cordobilla-Erreleku, in Navarre, is volumetrically imposing. Using some preexisting buildings and adding several new ones, they grouped a complex composed of long-roofed wings around a tower. The component parts—heating duct, gable end, the arrangement of windows let into a wall—are handled in a way that reveals an ongoing interest in historically consistent elements of the

discipline. The whole creates a classic—in the sense of ahistoric—effect. In appearance, it could be an ancient villa or a rural mill.

In 1975, Luis Peña Ganchegui built the Plaza del Tenis in San Sebastián, in collaboration with sculptor Eduardo Chillida. The difficulties posed by the powerful elemental qualities of this site on the Cantabrian coast were masterfully handled with the creation of splendid stepped surfaces, geometrically precise and impressive in scale, where Chillida's iron sculptures comb the wind (his group sculpture is entitled *Peine de viento*) and water gushes through clefts in the granite with the force of the tides.

At the close of the decade, between 1978 and 1980, Garay and Linazasoro produced another fine building: the Mendigorría house, a large apartment building, somewhere between rural and urban, of a kind often found in northern Spain. Despite its severity, this building achieves a charming quality, created perhaps by the soothing use of symmetry, the compositional arrangement of windows, drainpipes, and imposts, and the precise, "architectural" tone of the patio, stylobate, and galleries. The interior distribution makes optimal use of the concept of distributive discipline, the rooms grouped around a corridor in a comfortable, unforced way.

Galicia, another part of the country with a rich and ancient culture of its own, also raised its own architectonic voice in the mid-seventies. In common with all Spanish architecture of the period, two enduring basic tendencies became identifiable among Galician architects at this time. On the one hand were those who took Alejandro de la Sota, a native of the Galician province of Pontevedra, as their *maestro*, following his example to develop an architecture that was light, technical, subtle, and very Atlantic. On the other were the "disciplinary" architects who expressed another facet of the Atlantic through their use of granite and unadorned volumes. This period saw an intensification of the influence of Alvaro Siza Vieira, another Atlantic architect, who from his Oporto studio practiced a personally revelatory approach that was modern in essence and attuned to local place and culture.

César Portela and Pascuala Campos built a settlement for gypsies in Campaño-Poio. The work of these architects is usually inspired by the images and types of local architecture, and for this project they looked to gypsy caravans for their obvious relevance to its future occupants. The

Ikastola school, Fuenterrabía, (Guipúzcoa), 1974–1978, Garay / Linazasoro.

Opposite page: Gallego house, O Carballo, Oleiros (La Coruña), 1977–1979, Gallego Jorreto.

Rolando house-studio, Mairena del Aljarafe (Seville), 1980–1983, Vázquez Consuegra.

housing complex derives strength of presence from its location and from its curved roof shapes, but more important is the overall effect, whose highly evocative imagery is ambiguous in its simultaneous references to a collection of caravans and a group of *hórreos*, the raised, granite-built granaries that dot the local landscape. In short, it presents a group pattern both archaic and symbolically charged which is, as such, both enduring and contemporary in its relevance.

Manuel Gallego Jorreto's 1979 house, built of small stones and with a flat, cement-fiber roof covering a long bay, is set deep in a pinewood landscape and seems to be trying to debunk the notion of appearance. The inexpensive materials, the immediate, orderly distribution of rooms, the absence of artifice and pretension, all contribute to the air of serenity and dignity that emanates from this house. A new Galician architecture was starting to make its presence felt, though it was not to declare itself definitively until 1993, celebrated as a holy year in honor of St. James, eponymous patron saint of Galicia's pilgrimage site of Santiago de Compostela.

Meanwhile, a similar process was occurring in Seville. In 1977, the Madrid magazine *Arquitectura* devoted two issues to that city's architects. While declaring that it would be premature to speak of a Seville school, the introduction identified a series of traits common to the work of all the young architects featured: a common awareness of cultural distance and marginalization—national magazines never featured their work—and an obsessive determination that their work should incorporate modern principles.

The Sevillians were equally committed to analyzing the invariable features of the Andalusian house and city, gratifyingly viewed through the prism of the writings of Venturi and Rossi, and to the architecture of Terragni and the Bauhaus, models of an approach to life that Seville's architects had adopted. The factor that united them all was the city itself. Seville is a city charged with character, this being rooted in large measure in its own physical being and the nature of its buildings. The legendary reputation of cities often relates to their geographical position by a river, sea, or mountain; Seville's derives from the special relationship that exists between its inhabitants and its urban structure: streets, parishes, patios, and *fiestas* are the interface between climate and occupants that give it its character. Seville's architects do not approach the city merely as a scientifically analyzable entity with important implications for architectural projects: they engage it personally. Characterful streets constitute an experience; they are like people, while their people are monumental. Artistic feeling emanates from an awareness of bodily posture: the accomplished execution of oft-repeated gestures. It is acquitting oneself well during the Holy Week processions repeated year after year, or placing one's feet correctly in the choreography of bullfighting. Seville's architects take to the streets with their buildings.

Antonio Cruz and Antonio Ortiz were the earliest exponents, and their career has proceeded unfalteringly ever since. Their Calle Medina apartments date from 1973, the Doña María Coronel apartments from 1974–1976, the Calle Lumbreras apartments from 1978, and the Villanueva del Ariscal apartments from 1977–1978. A sense of the street and the patio informs them all. The best known and most brilliant of these is the Doña María Coronel building. Here a kidney-shaped patio provides a brilliant solution to the problem of achieving dignity in a domestic interior space. The irregular kidney shape allows the nonconstructed space to be distributed where it is most useful—something that could never be achieved with a regular circular or rectangular shape—and the interior corner of the party wall to be incorporated into the final configuration, creating a clear, specific shape. The way the apartments are distributed around the patio is as finely tuned, responsible, and sensitive as is the distribution of the apertures and the shape. This exemplary building reveals the precocity of these architects, providing salutary evidence of maturity achieved before the age of thirty.

Precocity and confidence are also in evidence in the houses built in 1976 by Antonio Barrionuevo and Francisco Torres. In the El Portil house and the Conil house, both single-family homes, the two main principles that inform the buildings are decisively and outspokenly stated: a determination to deal in strictly modern language and forms, and a confident acceptance that—at least in this area on the Cádiz coast—a house must be organized distributionally and compositionally around a patio. The various versions of these patios and their attributes—canopied terraces, porches, open-air staircases—take on a mixed character between roofless room and public place, an intriguing house/street ambiguity.

At this time, Guillermo Vázquez Consuegra, who over the years would become one of Seville's best-known architects, was engaged in the same concerns and aims as his colleagues. In his Rolando house, the various rooms are arranged autonomously around a central space, endowed with the status of independent units, almost buildings in themselves. In this case, the central space is also a patio, though more rural in character than in the examples considered so far, so that the overall effect of the house is something like a *cortijo*, an Andalusian farmhouse. The architect uses a similar device in the garden of the Olivares house, where the elements of patio, columns, window-perforated walls, and stairs all seem borrowed from the repertoire of public parks. This fondness for the rural and appreciation of craftsmanship, revealed in a direct, straightforward way of using ironwork, carpentry, and masonry, coexists with modern convictions and tempers them, achieving a local, personal tone and

Doña María Coronel building (courtyard and ground plan), Seville, 1974–1976, Cruz / Ortiz.

thereby creating a version of the modern free of any hint of the avant-garde.

Between 1973 and 1974, Gonzalo Díaz Recaséns and Fernando Villanueva built the School of Economics in Seville. In formal terms, this is an outspokenly simple building—a clear example of the interest in Aldo Rossi prevalent in Seville at that period—whose component wings are ranged around a long, vault-roofed space. This is another example where the outdoor public space is structured in accordance with the domestic brief of the *corrala*, Seville's characteristic tenement building.

All the architects mentioned so far trained at the Seville School of Architecture, though some, like the first four, completed their training elsewhere. This shows how firmly established the School was, and exemplifies the importance of this type of institution in consolidating identifiable local approaches and styles. There were few significant teachers at the School at that time, the most influential being Luis Marín de Terán, who emerged as a mature spokesman for certain contemporary theories—Venturi's, for example—which he disseminated in his lectures and writings. Working in association with Aurelio del Pozo and Enrique Haro, he designed buildings such as the housing on Calle Pío XII in Seville, putting the theories he taught into practice.

José Ramón Sierra was already a singular figure on the Seville scene. His work as a painter and member of the generation responsible for consolidating the abstract school in Seville, and his intense and unconventional allegiances with painter and poet colleagues in initiatives such as the influential magazine *Separata*,[51] give his work a distinct, plastic interest. In architecture, he has worked in association with his brother Ricardo, and together they have designed buildings of great plastic density, whose facades and interiors seem to create not so much architectonic forms as environments for ways of living and behaving.

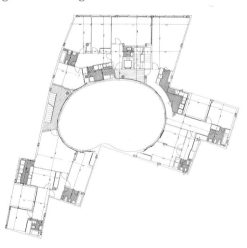

LEGITIMACY AND RESTORATION

It was in the eighties that Spanish architecture received acknowledgment for what had been a collective effort: consolidating the modern ideal. Though some Spanish buildings (the Bankinter, for example) had already attracted international critical interest by the mid-seventies, it was in the mid-eighties that Italian magazines, always the most alert to matters Spanish, began to feature works by Navarro Baldeweg, Piñón and Viaplana, and Cruz and Ortiz. The concealing wall around Spanish culture collapsed under the force of the interest sparked by the new democracy. The closed forum that had characterized Spanish architecture at the point where this book started was now being opened up, and it was patently becoming part of the international critical scene. In the mid-seventies, the legitimacy bestowed by the restoration of parliamentary monarchy produced a political background sound enough to provide the final impulse toward modernity. The failure of the attempted coup in February 1981 confirmed the fact that the road ahead was now open. The eighties were years when work and optimism abounded, and everything seemed easier.

Architectural magazines continued to be influential. At the start of the decade, two long-established publications reemerged. *Arquitectura* in Madrid and *Quaderns* in Barcelona, published by the respective Architects' Chambers of those two cities, targeted different areas. *Arquitectura* became an up-to-the-minute, eclectic, wide-ranging publication, with monographic issues devoted to specific architects and cities, while *Quaderns* opted for an editorial approach concerned with modernity in a more orthodox sense. Having started off as modest publications, both magazines now expanded in a way typical of this period, including the adoption of computerized color reproduction and typesetting techniques.

Halfway through the decade, *El Croquis* was launched as the personal venture of Fernando Márquez and Richard Levene, under whose skillful guidance it became the most widely read magazine. Giving detailed information not only about buildings but also about their background projects—something that not many publications manage to do successfully—they acquired a large and loyal readership, especially among students of architecture, and provided a showcase for Spanish architecture to foreign markets. Later on, *A & V Monografías* and *Arquitectura Viva* appeared on the scene, both headed by Professor Luis Fernández-Galiano, featuring in a systematically efficient and critically committed way architecture being built in Spain and abroad. It would be impossible to understand the development of contemporary architecture from our perspective today without reference to these publications. *Basa, Periferia,* and other magazines linked to professional chambers complete a publishing scenario that progressed from meager to overabundant during this period.

Museum of Roman Art,
Mérida (Cáceres), 1980–1985,
Moneo.

Spanish architecture produced in the eighties was characterized by two main traits: a collective embracing of the fundamental principles established by European rationalism at the start of the century, and an insistence on realism, emanating from a conscience comfortable with its own time, culture, and technique.

The first of these traits relates to something whose importance earns it frequent mention in this study, namely the obsession on the part of Spanish architects with recovering, or rather establishing, the modern. Despite so many years of discussing and analyzing the architecture of the modern movement while feeling that Spain had not been in at the start, and did not quite belong because of not having been actively enough involved in the thirties and forties, the old objective lived on. After the formal experiments of the Escola and organicism, which effectively defined these architects' own experience and local tradition, and after assimilating the impact of criticism in the seventies, in the eighties they took up the old ideal once more. Whereas outside of Spain the discourse about the architecture of the modern movement approached it in fundamentally stylistic terms—the American controversy between the Whites and the Grays and the emergence of postmodernism come to mind—Spain's several regions were as one in their faithful, unrestrained acceptance of modernity as an optimistic principle, a point of departure, a still viable and uncontaminated source of ideas. The stubbornness of the likes of de la Sota and Sostres was winning the day: in short, a nonstylistic appreciation of the modern was starting to hold sway. The recuperation of pre–modern movement architecture that engaged critical attention at this time did not produce as many postmodern exemplars in Spain as in other countries, but it did contribute to a way of understanding architecture whose benefits showed in an area of activity that became important later, namely the restoration of buildings.

The second trait was an insistence on realism. This term should be understood not in the ideological sense as in, for example, Italian cinematography, but in the sense of a dispassionate acknowledgment of the everyday.

In a finely tuned, precisely focused text written in 1985, Ignasi de Solà-Morales declared:

> Spanish architects have been wary of creating utopian illusions and have remained in touch with immediate reality, and this has kept them at an easy distance from the whimsical imaginings of unrealistic speculation. This may be attributable to the fact that, until the seventies, Spanish architects were able to practice their profession in comfort; or perhaps to a certain realism which makes every little problem into an opportunity for both experimentation and construction. Or, finally, it might have something to do with the fact that architectural training was closely combined with a strict technological apprenticeship.

The above is linked to a clear awareness of the state of the nation's technology, for as Solà-Morales put it:

> Added to this constant attention to physical reality was another equally important common characteristic: the loss of any faith in the avant-garde. There are a few exceptions, such as the almost messianic

quality that Ricardo Bofill injects into his work, even when it is used merely rhetorically. Another exception is the conceptual architecture of Juan Navarro and the Viaplana-Piñón group, whose work tends to be permeated by semiotic speculation. But most of the best Spanish architecture has lost all aspiration to avant-gardism in the programmatic sense of transforming reality.[52]

Bofill's messianic work could even be interpreted as a consciously over-stated response to a demand for tradition, and the conceptualism of Piñón and Viaplana's Plaza de la Estación de Sants as, strictly speaking, the metallic garden response to the slab of concrete.

The technical state of construction having been accepted in general terms, the options were skillfully capitalized upon, and buildings appeared in which the use of brick came to the fore, unthinkable in other countries. This example is a useful one in explaining the sort of traits that gave Spanish architecture its identity during this period.

Among the many contributing circumstances that led to the approach under consideration here, one merits particular mention: the new role of architectural restoration, a subject already touched upon. In 1977, Dionisio Hernández Gil was appointed Director General for the Fine Arts, and gathered about him, among others, architects such as Manuel de las Casas and Antón Capitel, with whom he developed a commis-sioning policy radically different from that applied previously. The administration was energetic in carrying out restoration work during this period, employing architects not for their level of specialization in this subgenre of architecture but rather for recognized professional effective-ness in earlier work, even if that had been in the most humdrum areas of architectural practice. In these years when reinstated civil society accorded importance to the recovery and use of the national heritage, the administration distributed many commissions among young archi-tects, giving them the opportunity to come to grips with constructional solutions and problems both deep and large-scale, and allowing them to acquire experience and a fine-tuning of their ambitions to design and create. This approach on the part of the (then Socialist) administration was not restricted exclusively to restoration. In fact it extended to almost all state services and was maintained subsequently, as an unchallenge-able philosophy, in the autonomous regional governments as their areas of responsibility gradually increased. This favorable situation was further enhanced by the fund of experience contributed by architects who, having been implicated in political activity before the Transition, were trusted by the new politicians in power: Bohigas, Solans, and Acebillo in Barcelona, Pérez Escolano in Seville, and Mangada in Madrid, to name but a few, opened up the city streets and plazas to fellow countrymen and architects alike.

This situation began at the start of the eighties with the consolidation of legitimacy and continued to intensify beyond the end of the decade, reaching its peak in 1992. Let us see how it all happened.

Plaza dels Països Catalans,
also known as
Estación de Sants Plaza,
Barcelona, 1981–1983,
Viaplana / Pinón.

If any region was ready to develop an autonomous constitution, it was Catalonia. The built environment of Barcelona, now a capital city again, was divided into areas of proven urban efficacy, such as its *ensanche* (inner suburbs), and others on the disorganized outskirts composed of massive housing blocks, built in the more recent past and intended to absorb immigration into the city. On the advice of professionals familiar with the city, successive elected city councils opted not for an ambitious general plan which would have been subject to rapid revision—as occurred in Madrid—but for the approach of tending all the city's wounds, whether large or small, such as urban voids, dysfunctional areas, and inadequate public spaces and services. As early as 1979, *Arquitecturas bis* examined the city with an issue titled "Arquitectura para Barcelona: la escuela, la vivienda y el resto verde" (An Architecture for Barcelona: Schools, Housing, and the Remaining Green Areas), whose very title analyzed the situation at the time. This was to change over the course of the decade as the remaining green areas came under development. In Moneo's contribution to that issue he wrote:

> After years of sad and distressing enforced inactivity, which Barcelona's architects often combated by concentrating on teaching, an unexpected event early in 1978 presented these professionals with the promise of a change of scenario. This was when Juan Antonio Solans, services representative of the Barcelona city government, started placing municipal commissions with prominent architects, thereby breaking with established practice and, most importantly, breaking the ice of the ever-tense relationship between the administration and architecture.[53]

The strategy adopted by Barcelona—later looked to as a model by cities both in Spain and beyond—was precisely, prudently, and decisively targeted, and had the virtue of being based on an acknowledgment of the specific nature of the city, so that in application it reinforced its character rather than altering it. Barcelonans' identification with their city, their self-satisfaction even, is both the source and the sustenance of the status it has achieved as capital city while retaining the homogeneity of the efficient, comfortable bourgeois city that it has characteristically always been.

This reclamation of their own culture took place across the board. In 1989, under the editorship of Bru, *Quaderns* devoted an issue to Jujol that covered the previous year's exhibition organized by Josep Llinás. The contributions revealed an interest on the part of Bru, Llinás, and others, such as Elías Torres, in this follower of Gaudí. Such recuperation explains how these Barcelona architects, responding to the way attention had been focused on discipline and history for some years, decoded Jujol in modern terms, thus investing their own objectives with authority.

Grasping this new, normalized political and economic situation, architects propounded the realist architecture mentioned above. They did so with particular finesse and, on occasion, by taking drastic decisions. Such was the case of PER architects Clotet and Tusquets, who split up their studios and made major changes to their architecture. Comparisons among the few (though sophisticated) writings by Lluis Clotet make this very explicit:

> An architecture that considers its prime objective to be the expression of a critical attitude in relation to its environment. By physical environment we understand not only the physical environment that surrounds the building, but also all the sectors by which, directly or indirectly, it was determined.[54]

Such was the PER studio's stance in 1969, one of political reaction that was active though pessimistic. In a paper delivered in Almería in 1989, Clotet declared his two "specific concerns, which are what I am most interested in developing in my current architectonic output. On the one hand, a concern for the economics of the building, which is to say economics in capital letters, and on the other, a concern for its relationship with its physical environment." He goes on to point out that lack of resources demands economy, which implies durability, and concludes that durability requires two qualities: good construction and versatility. His first thoughts, Marxist and structuralist in affiliation and critically directed at a very small, specific environment, namely the Barcelona of 1969, gave way twenty years later to opinions that were more open and generalized in the philosophical area (durability) and more direct in the programmatic area (construction and use).

These opinions are illustrated in the way the architecture of Clotet, using the construction process as a learning tool, explored the question "Is there no poetry in weight?"—challenging the lightness so thoroughly exploited by others in a way that was typical of his response to a uniform world.

In this second phase of his oeuvre, Clotet worked in association with Ignacio Paricio. The Banco de España building in Gerona, designed by them in 1982 and completed in 1990, is notable for the close relationship it reveals between architectonic form and construction. The architects use directness, and material and constructional evidence, to convey an image of the institution. This led critical opinion outside Spain to consider this building prototypical of the Spanish architecture of the period.

Extension to the Picasso Museum, Barcelona, 1981–1986, Garcés / Sòria.

Rehabilitation and extension to the Palau de la Música, Barcelona, 1981–1989, Tusquets / Díaz.

Oscar Tusquets, working in association with Carles Díaz, reacted even more drastically, rejecting all his earlier work. His ever-intelligent buildings sometimes seem to be trying to dress in a way readily comprehensible by the most banal observer. He now incorporated traditional elments into his architecture without the ironic tone with which he had used them in early works such as the Georgina Belvedere. This change should not simply be attributed to attempts to satisfy clients' and promoters' tastes, for in other fields such as oil painting, which he practices successfully, he reveals an interest in such things as moldings and shadows, and traditional materials such as ceramic and stone. The evidence is there to be seen in his fine paintings in the Palau de la Música.

Tusquets must have found working with old buildings very enlightening. They certainly taught him something that he had not learned from his history teacher, Sostres, who considered modernity to be ahistoric—that is, that the problems and concerns of architecture remain substantially consistent throughout time.

Jordi Garcés and Enric Sòria stayed truer to themselves, their work losing its abstraction and gaining plastic density. This can be observed by comparing their 1982 Social Center in Seo de Urgell, where the materials—brick, iron pillars, and copper canopies—seem to have their physical properties of color and light subsumed by the simple geometry of the lines, and their Picasso Museum in Barcelona, where an interplay of colored stones lines floors and walls.

Lluis Domènech, whom we have already met actively engaged through his architecture and writing in the discourse of Barcelona in the seventies, undertook a major project in the eighties. Working in partnership with Roser Amadó to plans drawn up in association with R. M. Puig and Joan Busquets, he tackled the urban organization of Lérida's historical center, essentially linking the base of the cathedral with the lower part of the city by means of the great wall and tower of the El Canyeret project. The wall retains the hillside and backs a long office building, its wavelike shape cleverly echoing the enduring character and variety of the landscape. The tower, which is triangular in section and usefully spans a considerable change of levels, stands tall, its civic image striking up a dialogue with the cathedral's ecclesiastical one.

Urban redevelopment of the El Canyeret district, Lérida, 1981–1990, Amadó / Domènech / Puig.

Banco de España, Gerona, 1982–1989, Clotet / Paricio.

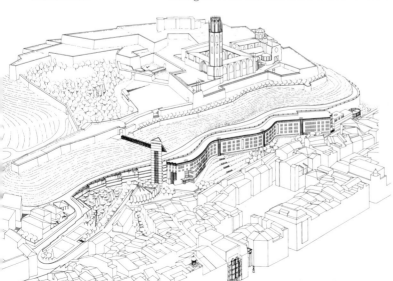

Jaume Bach and Gabriel Mora moved into increasingly fertile, plastic territory. The Bellaterra railway station in Barcelona combines elements of the modern tradition, such as powerful projecting features, counter-balanced by cantilever-supported facades constructed as composition-defining abstract planes, with traditional elements such as the great segmental access arch and the crowning cornice. The whole building is suffused in warm colors. Their Jujol School is even more plastic, as if in homage to the great architect, designer of the building that previously occupied this site, for whom it is named. Soft ochre- and blue-toned planes seem to float in the light that enters through precisely placed and angled apertures. Efficiency and versatility are Bach and Mora's weapons, even their proud boast. They have worked with rural elements in the Cavas de Sant Sadurní d'Anoia winery, while in the Olympic Village telephone exchange, perhaps obeying a brief that required the building to be divided into two, they resolved the composition with a daring contrast of volumes and materials, creating an enduring testimony to the Barcelona Olympics.

Piñón and Viaplana, a team that had already demonstrated their conceptual rigor as planners, teachers, and critics, seized the opportunity offered by one of the new situation's first significant commissions, Estación de Sants Plaza in Barcelona, to create the most significant urban-scale work of that time. Taking their cue from the slabs roofing the railway lines that run beneath this square, the architects took the radical decision to embrace hard paving and an absence of greenery. Their design presents an artificial version of nature using iron structures and metal canopies that cast shadows on granite surfaces at once forbidding and delicate.

Torres-Guasch
hardware store,
Ibiza, 1985,
Martínez Lapeña / Torres Tur.

Rehabilitation of the Ronda
and Baluarte promenades,
Palma de Mallorca,
1983–1992,
Martínez Lapeña / Torres Tur.

Horta cycling stadium,
Barcelona, 1983–1984,
Bonell / Ríus.

Subtly varying floor levels, undulating canopies, and columns unadorned at the base define spaces where children play. This square, nicknamed *la plaza dura* (the "hard square") despite—or perhaps because of—its delicate lightness, was much admired and won many followers. It still retains all its intelligent freshness.

Also during this period and in a similarly dense conceptual vein, but this time working with a much weightier piece, Piñón and Viaplana built their Sant Hipolit de Voltregà Health Center. Severe concrete beams and pilasters support a regular geometric form mounted on a gently stepped base. Whereas the granite of Sants square, and the lightness suggested by the railway and rain, had led to a certain sublimation of the modern, Sant Hipolit is endowed with a templelike classicism by the evocative properties of its base, column shapes, and architrave.

The plans and construction, between 1979 and 1984, of a building by Lluis Cantallops and José Antonio Martínez Lapeña were in the purest modern tradition. Their university department building in Gerona is drawn up in terms that are thematically very Barcelonan: white brick-built parallelepipeds slide horizontally and vertically to create an overall volume at once free and compact. Spaces are interconnected and grouped to meet the demands of use. Long horizontal windows, shaded from above by slatted shutters whose play of light and shade tempers the facades, admit plentiful light into the interior.

To declare Esteve Bonell and Francesc Ríus's cycling stadium in Barcelona the best-rounded building in Spain from that period is more than just a

pun. The building incorporates the sporting optimism and image of balance, speed, and lightness that modern bicycles suggest. Circles and ellipses, banked planes of dizzying outline, are contained within slim concrete slabs and slender pillars. Strict metalwork in uprights and handrails underlines invigorating images of the open air and modernity.

The work of Josep Llinás, who had announced his architectural presence with the house he built for his parents, demonstrated his continuing maturity with buildings such as a 1982 health center in Barcelona. Consistent characteristics show in the natural simplicity of its volumes, the linear strictness of its canopies, and the general distribution of the building in a manner once known as "functional" and which, the glamour of the label having faded, is here justifiably and correctly deployed.

It is unsurprising that Josep Llinás should have been commissioned to restore Alejandro de la Sota's local government headquarters in Tarragona—an extension of the concept of restoration to embrace contemporary buildings. The fact that it was necessary in this case provided an object lesson in the need for buildings to be systematically maintained so as to make restoration operations unnecessary, modern architecture

being no exception. It also served to highlight the fact that de la Sota's building had already taken on historical significance.

Another significant operation that triggered consideration of the deeper subtleties of architecture was the reconstruction—if that is the most apt term—of the German Pavilion designed and built by Mies van der Rohe for the 1929 International Exposition in Barcelona. The architects involved were Ignasi de Solà-Morales, Cristian Cirici, and Francisco Ramos. This exemplary piece of modern architecture, a lightweight monument, had been destroyed as was always the intention, yet all architects knew it by heart: it was an architectural legend whose image had been sublimated by the fact of its disappearance. The reconstruction destroyed a dream in exchange for a real building that, with age, will eventually match what the original would have become. A perfect mental image, the stuff of all nostalgia, was sacrificed to recover a piece of Barcelona's history and a testimony to its prestigious past.

It was at this time of recuperation of the modern that José Antonio Coderch designed a building that he never saw completed—the extension to Barcelona's School of Architecture. Reusing forms whose production was already an antiquated process, he created within a cladding skin so typical of his buildings an organism of white curves and overhead lighting evocative of the Mediterranean, which by today is showing the effects of wear and tear inflicted by an excessively large student population. Though not the most brilliant of his career, this building demonstrates Coderch's enduring *savoir-faire*.

The work produced by the studio of Elías Torres Tur and José Antonio Martínez Lapeña lies halfway between the Barcelona and Ibiza tendencies, or rather forms part of both. Ibiza's landscape of savine junipers and the rest of its particular flora, and a building tradition whose courtyards, mud walls, and terracing date back to the Egyptians, provide the setting for their Boenders house, built in 1983. Using opaque, earthy concrete blocks, they built an engaging sequence of generous, luminous spaces, creating an environment conducive to an aesthetically pleasing lifestyle. In 1984, they restored the church of L'Hospitalet in Ibiza, converting it into a meeting and exhibition hall. The restored building, which might still function as a church, consists of a collection of vividly colored mobile rooms mechanically adaptable to form very different environments. Scenes created with lighting and other devices, such as a moon that glides across the firmament when required, make this a stimulating place, with the sobriety of its arch and vault in ironic conjunction with its movable lightweight planes. In the Torres-Guasch hardware store, dating from 1985, mobile planes are once again used to brilliant effect, here opening and closing on a scene vivid with reflections of the harbor in the glass and metal surfaces of the shop's merchandise. Among this studio's prolific output are several important restoration projects, including the stairway for Ibiza's citadel and Bellver Castle in Palma de Mallorca. Here they continue to play with folding planes, albeit in stone—the citadel stairway capitalizes on the mute geometry of this defensive building, folding in upon itself and taking us on a little *promenade architecturale*.

Younger than these architects, Eduard Bru and Josep Lluis Mateo, who erupted onto Barcelona's architectural scene with their superb issues of *Quaderns*, built the Bastida school during this period. The longitudinal nature of the ground plan, adapted to its site along a watercourse, provided the architects with an opportunity to reinterpret modern functionality, albeit tempered here by urban and typological considerations.

One of the first buildings by Carme Pinós and Enric Miralles also dates from 1984. After a spell in the Piñón-Viaplana studio, they embarked on a professional career, first in partnership and later separately, that will be mentioned again in these pages. In their Fábrica de La Llauna, a factory converted for school use in Badalona, they created a new interior on the basis of the old. The autonomy of its rooms, the way ornamentation is derived from the varied assemblage of structural shapes, the incorporation of refurbished preexisting elements to work in tandem with the new, are a foretaste of their later works, modern orthodoxy being superseded by syntactical variations on the way elements are deployed.

Health center,
Sant Hipolit de Voltregà
(Barcelona), 1984–1986,
Viaplana / Piñón.

Bellaterra railway station,
Barcelona, 1984,
Bach / Mora.

With the devolution of power to the regions, or autonomous communities as they are known, and the consolidation of this new pattern of government, Madrid gradually lost architectural projects and commissions. It also shed a certain guilt about having been the headquarters of the centralist state, and this freed its inhabitants to look for a new identity. The city's cultural life became vibrant in the areas of film, music, painting, indeed in general, consolidating what had been fermenting since the time of the dictatorship. Architects made their contribution to all this activity: exhibitions and involvement in frequent competitions were opportunities for collective and public reflection. This was a period of recession that was tackled by the economic policy of the Plan General. The plan curbed physical expansion of the city, instead providing incentives to infill extensive inner-city areas as yet undeveloped. Efforts were made to consolidate the outskirts without expanding them, reinforcing public services in the poorly served outer suburbs, particularly in south Madrid.

The consolidation of the outskirts and the quest for a new identity directed Madrid's architects toward "poor" architecture, in the sense of using modest materials and pragmatic solutions to reinforce the realist tendency already noted. This was what occupied Madrid's architects at this period, along with work outside the city itself, very often in the form of restoration or rehabilitation projects for reasons already discussed.

Between 1980 and 1984, Rafael Moneo designed and built the new Museum of Roman Art in Mérida. This fine building owes the universal acclaim with which it was greeted to the close relationship between content and form that the project established. The construction—in cleverly selected, clean-lined long bricks, using walls and Roman-style arches and a ground plan suggestive of both basilica and dockyard— explains the building's use and meaning: it expresses the common conception of the Roman. This "Romanness" is present simultaneously in the construction, in the look of its decorative elements, and in the layout of some parts of the building, the overall organization of the rest being modern for the most part and divided up according to work areas. This museum was one of the first important buildings commissioned by the Directorate General for the Fine Arts, and it was influential for its relevance to reclaiming historical architecture, then an issue very much in international critical focus. In Mérida, Moneo makes definite pronouncements not only about how new buildings should be articulated within a historic city environment—in this case over an excavated archaeological site—but also about how to use perceptions of history as a storehouse of materials and ideas available for appropriation when the occasion demands.

The last years of work on the museum coincided with the construction of the Previsión Española insurance company building in Seville and the project for an extension to the Banco de España, both cases in which Moneo continued to explore the applications of history. In Seville, this is concentrated in a classical interpretation of the palatial facade, with

Pedro Salinas Public Library and Puerta de Toledo Social Services Center, Madrid, 1982–1989, Navarro Baldeweg.

Housing block in Palomeras, Madrid, 1981–1983, Frechilla / López-Peláez / Sánchez.

Four housing blocks in southeast Palomeras, Madrid, 1979–1982, Junquera / Pérez Pita.

orders of columns superimposed in a tripartite vertical composition and quoins, plinths, and eaves. The architect's use of history seems instrumental rather than respectful, and this is expressed even more baldly in the design that won the competition for the Banco de España extension, where he proposed an identical prolongation of the existing facade to front a conventionally modern ground plan—a stance perhaps more kitsch than classicist, for a design that was never built.

Madrid in the early eighties saw the consolidation of the reputation of Juan Navarro Baldeweg, whose exploratory architecture had long since been a source of interest to his colleagues. His first public building to create an impact was a rehabilitation and conversion for use as a museum of the Segura River mill buildings in the city of Murcia. Its key themes were the minimalist interpretation of elements, volumes, and wall, floor, and roof planes; the surface tension of the materials used (stone, concrete, and wood); and the abstraction achieved through historical motifs such as the cupola. Toward the end of the decade, he was already working on several projects, and in 1988 he completed the Puerta de Toledo Social Services Center in Madrid. This building is divided into various units, each of which tackles hitherto unresolved urban issues. The unit with the curved roof, for example, uses a simple yet powerful gesture to establish continuity with the excessive mass of the neighboring building, while an elegantly fenestrated parallelepiped similar in volume to the houses on Calle Toledo negotiates its interface with the plaza of the same name. These and other smaller units stand on a great podium of curved perimeter and gently profiled access steps. Navarro's strategy for recomposing the banal, fragmented city environment consists of adding new fragments that, from within the modest confines of the domestic scale and an apparent lack of formality, elevate banality into nuance.

Another architect of Navarro's vintage is Francisco Alonso de Santos, who, despite having few buildings to his credit, no doubt because of the conceptual toughness he presents, became a charismatic figure for his students in Madrid from this period onward, and an architect whose demanding designs fascinate many of his colleagues. In his house in the chic Madrid suburb of Puerta de Hierro, weighty slabs of granite two meters by one meter by 12 centimeters thick clad a dour facade in whose taut surface the apertures are governed in size and position by the demands of the interior. This house, where the hardness of granite is juxtaposed with the hardness of glass, provides a good explanation of his architecture as an assemblage of materials presented in such a way as to exhibit the conceptual intensity behind their selection.

Younger than the above, though allied to them in their understanding of the profession, Víctor López Cotelo and Carlos Puente completed two splendid buildings in 1985: the School of Pharmacy building on the Alcalá de Henares campus and the extension of Valdelaguna Town Hall. Even their early works reveal a maturity and mastery acquired during their years of collaboration with de la Sota. With the School of Pharmacy building, they showed their unwavering confidence in the contemporary potential of an orthodox approach to the modern. The decorative power of exposed viroterm, overtly strong beams, minimalist handrails, and run-

School of Pharmacy, University of Alcalá, Alcalá de Henares (Madrid), 1981–1985, López Cotelo / Puente.

Single-family house in Puerta de Hierro, Madrid, 1986, Alonso de Santos.

of-the-mill light fittings demonstrates the value they place upon such concepts as industry, economy, and tectonics. In the Valdelaguna building, they called on a gentler repertoire concerned with plastic values, as shown by the interiors painted in soft colors, which glow in the light filtered through wooden structures, and the whitewashed exterior surfaces. In their fidelity to the modern, these works by Puente and López Cotelo, along with others that will be examined later, strike echoes of different places and periods: Holland, Denmark, and the 1920s are represented regardless of time and space, enabling us to experience a continuity of time and geography in which memory and imagined reality coexist.

It was during this period, too, that Alberto Campo Baeza began building his direct, simple volumes enclosing white interiors. A disciple of both de la Sota and Cano Lasso, he has remained faithful to the modern, endowing his work with a highly personal tonal continuity using simple principles and straightforward formal solutions, all bathed in a purist, white light. His buildings became well known and critically acclaimed abroad early in his career.

With buildings such as the Agricultural Studies Department in Palencia, Ángel Fernández Alba likewise lent weight to the Madrid architects' use of the modern. Viewed from the outside, this college building has an industrial look about it, produced by the large windows, suggestive of ample light, let into the direct volumes of which the complex is composed. The use of metallic walkways and glass in the interior underlines the building's strictly industrial character.

This insistence of Madrid's architects on the modern and the realist was fairly unanimous and extended to, or rather showed its intent in, the building of low-cost housing, as we shall see later. However, there were some architects who stood apart from these concerns with other formal approaches of their own. A case in point is Javier Bellosillo. In his civic and religious center in Almazán, concrete elements that, though relatively small, are immensely powerful in their evocation of the totemic and primitive are grouped together to form a religious citadel. The bare concrete of the interiors, illuminated by slits through which the light enters like knife blades, determines spaces of an almost awe-inspiring religiosity.

Luis Burillo and Jaime Lorenzo explored a more expressionist direction. In their conversion of the Episcopal Palace in Tarazona for use as a museum, the relationship between the new building and the existing fabric is established through contrast. The materials of the new part, apparent by their modern nature, barely touch the sturdily built stone and brick walls and ceilings, while paving is laid like carpets. The result achieves sophisticated tactile effects reminiscent of the magisterial hand of Scarpa. The same strategy is in evidence in their reconstruction of Maqueda Castle as a police barracks—a commission that, like the previous one, exemplifies the restoration policy mentioned above. In this case, though, the building's larger scale allows for a series of skillfully achieved rooms within the precinct, turning the castle into a sort of citadel for its new purpose.

Previous architectural tendencies had stressed the importance of building mass housing. The need to rehouse a populace living, in some cases, in substandard conditions was tackled by building dense housing complexes on the city outskirts. Earlier town planning efforts, poorly organized and ill defined, had resulted in the building of sink districts such as Palomeras and Orcasur. Architects were now able to reorganize these, making effective use of a whole range of modern techniques for the grouping of housing, such as slabs, towers, and rows. The catalogue of solutions achieved includes notable examples, which share the repeated characteristics of realism, restraint, and modernist leanings. Manuel and Ignacio de las Casas worked in Palomeras, building five high-rise slabs that were required by planning stipulations to be over 20 meters wide. The team of Ferrán, Romany, and Navazo responded to the same requirement with perimeter blocks. Both teams solved the difficulties these posed by placing two rows of apartments with L-shaped ground plans on each floor, on either side of a longitudinal access passage. The L-shaped ground plan provides a very useful interior space, developed here with terrace balconies.

The first architects to suggest this adaptation of the old-style *corrala* tenement buildings, once so common in Madrid, were Estanislao Pérez Pita and Jerónimo Junquera, who made clever use of the model in their 1980 Yeserías building. In Palomeras they built four blocks, on plots over 35 meters wide, dividing each building into two rows, one of maisonettes plus a ground floor and another of thirteen single-story apartments. This second row is subdivided into three towers with four homes per floor, the towers connected to one another at their sides to make up the block. One appreciates the architects' concern to break up such a gigantic volume in an attempt to mitigate the overwhelming effect inevitably created by such high-density housing.

The problems posed by deep, long, high blocks were tackled by Javier Frechilla, José Manuel López-Peláez, and Eduardo Sánchez. They responded to vastness of scale by accepting its enormity, and designed a structure of broad galleries parallel to the longitudinal axis within brick facades perforated by large, identical stretches of wall that correspond to different rooms. The building's backbone is again the high, narrow *corrala*-type corridor. The most formally outspoken complex in Palomeras was that built by the team of Juan Montes, Pablo Carvajal, and Mario Muelas: the dimension of the blocks, which they interpret as brick-built volumes, is translated into potency by treating the planned-in curve as if it were a flat facade.

Another major rehousing operation took place in the Orcasitas district, where there were already notable examples from an earlier period. A large team that was actually an amalgamation of two—Alfonso Valdés and Javier Vellés being one, and Luis Mapelli with José Luis Romany, a veteran of public housing, the other—built an imposing complex of towers and perimeter blocks arranged, to use Valdés's description, like pieces on a chessboard. The continuity provided by brick and the strongly stated apertures give unity to the whole and resolve the blocks' interior courtyards in such a way that, despite the domestic nature of their clothes-hanging areas, they have something of the *plaza mayor* about them.

Left, from top to bottom:
Segura River Mills Museum
and Cultural Center,
Murcia, 1984–1988,
Navarro Baldeweg.

Valdelaguna Town Hall
and plaza,
Madrid, 1983–1986,
López Cotelo / Puente.

República de Brasil
state school,
San Fermín district,
Madrid, 1985,
Campo Baeza.

Right, from top to bottom:
Reconstruction of
Maqueda Castle,
Toledo, 1984–1987,
Burillo / Lorenzo.

Religious and civic
center, Almazán
(Soria), 1983–1987,
Bellosillo.

Agricultural Studies
Department,
Palencia, 1983,
Ángel Fernández Alba.

Social housing
in Orcasitas,
Madrid, 1977–1984,
Vellés / Valdés.

Social housing blocks
in Palomeras,
Madrid, 1984–1987,
Manuel de las Casas /
Ignacio de las Casas.

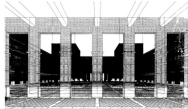

Social housing block
on Avenida Ramón y Cajal,
Seville, 1984–1987,
Vázquez Consuegra.

With the School of Architecture consolidated and Seville declared the center of government of the Autonomous Community of Andalusia, and as a consequence of the growing number of commissions that this generated, the city became established as Spain's third most important center of architectural activity. Because it represented such a large population—that of the whole of Andalusia—and because of its cultural and geographical characteristics, Seville was equipped to engender architectural approaches all its own. This recalled earlier periods, when the city had possessed artistic schools identifiable by their stylistic homogeneity.

As a professional and cultural group, Seville's architects contributed certain objectives to this situation. Explorations of architecture's historical values and their enduring relevance, an issue of critical interest during this period, were determining factors in the architecture they produced. Thus, the modern and the city, as fundamental categories in architecture, conditioned collective design and construction.

The first significant opportunity to be taken up by Seville's architects was the urban organization of the Pino Montano district. Antonio Cruz and Antonio Ortiz drew up the overall plan, which proposed a grid-pattern expansion of alternating square and rectangular perimeter blocks. This shows the influence on the plan of the new confidence in the perimeter block as opposed to the modern tower block as a solution for expanding cities. Even so, building depth was already orienting future projects toward a more recent housing type rooted in distributional solutions that had been explored with slab block projects in central Europe in the twenties. In other words, the modern was influencing the size and type of urban block to be used in extending the city. Courtyards within perimeter blocks, which precluded the possibility of building below ground level, would allow the idea of the patio to persist as a current motif, generating solutions specific to the social realities of life in Seville.

Of the perimeter blocks built under the auspices of the plan, those by Francisco Torres and Victoria Durán merit particular mention. Their use of maisonettes, and interiors and exteriors reminiscent of Viennese *Höfe*, seem to indicate historically recuperative intent. Antonio Barrionuevo's perimeter blocks placed the accent on the idea of the patio, not only in the way the blocks' courtyards were distributed and furnished, but—particularly—in the effort devoted to providing each residential unit with an outdoor space. This goal, again inherited from the modern housing block, was achieved by making terrace balconies as large as possible so that, even though not actually touching the ground or opening to the sky in proper patio fashion, by means of plants and canopies they took on the spirit of the Andalusian patio, here coexisting happily with the apartments' modern layout.

José Ramón and Ricardo Sierra's square perimeter blocks provided them with an opportunity to pursue their own particular interests. A cylindrical patio contrasts with the parallelepipedal volume, creating a double-

facaded interior space that absorbs the apartments' clotheslines and service areas. This allows repeated windows and balconies to feature in the exterior composition with restrained and uninterrupted continuity. The strongly jutting cement-fiber roof, the dramatic triple-height portals, and the shape of the shop recesses at street level, reminiscent of those of Renaissance cities, give each block the look of a palace, whose classicism is accentuated by the use of brick finished with flush lime mortar pointing.

In their housing block on Calle Hombre de Piedra, Cruz and Ortiz continued the exploration of the Seville dwelling seen in their Doña María Coronel building. Varied distributional and compositional solutions are lent homogeneity by the realist tone and lack of stylistic prejudice that characterize this building. The architects' range and lack of inhibition are discernible both in the modern layout of the apartments, some of them maisonettes and others traditional corridor models, and in the decorative elements, such as pilotis used together with moldings as well as balconies, handrails, window grilles, and canvas canopies. Patios and the access galleries giving onto them capitalize successfully on Seville-dwellers' capacity to understand the use of, and differentiate between, public and private spaces. Stylistic antecedents for this building would have to be sought in a particular local tradition, not at all avant-garde, in which modernist, art deco, and traditional elements were brought together in a provincial interpretation of the confusion and uncertainty of many decades earlier.

Guillermo Vázquez Consuegra built his Avenida Ramón y Cajal apartment building in Seville as an elongated block in which modern architectural issues are in evidence. They can be seen in the apartment layout, the curvilinear frieze, the access walkways with their banisters and canopies, and the long horizontal windows. All these features are combined with balconies and patios that acknowledge the validity of certain traditional concepts. What Vázquez Consuegra built here was his (typically effective) interpretation of the issue under consideration, establishing a personal model for his subsequent public housing projects.

Also belonging in this discussion are the La Corza apartments built in Seville by Aurelio del Pozo and Luis Marín de Terán and the Puerto de Santa María apartments by Antonio González Cordón, for both projects again reveal a concern, at the heart of Andalusian culture, to determine the relationship between modernity and tradition.

Beyond the field of housing, this period also saw the start of public commissions, a foretaste of the coming decade. In the Canal Sur Television Center building, the Díaz Recaséns studio developed the theme of an

Canal Sur Television Center, San Juan de Aznalfarache (Seville), 1985–1988, Díaz Recaséns.

Social estate made up of eleven units and one villa, El Puerto de Santa María (Cádiz), 1982–1985, González Cordón.

Opposite page: Housing estate in Pino Montano, Seville, 1982–1983, Antonio Barrionuevo.

oblong fortress contained within a facade-cum-defensive wall. The building is composed and distributed internally around a succession of patios, each with its specific function—as in an Andalusian farm, or *cortijo*—communication within the whole complex being provided by various types of passage, walkway, and corridor, like parapets of a fortress. The *cortijo's* airy dovecotes and solid towers are here transformed into an aerial tower and skylights. Turning to a rural theme, such as the *cortijo*, for inspiration has been frequent and automatic and has worked well when applied to buildings located in parts of the urban periphery in the process of consolidation.

Galicia began to emerge as a new center of architecture in much the same way as Seville, albeit more slowly, keeping pace with what was going on in the La Coruña School of Architecture (founded in 1975), the principles favored by whose architect-teachers gradually gained a hold, as seen in our observations on the seventies. César Portela and Manuel Gallego Jorreto were still the most representative architects, but new names were emerging, of whom more later.

Capitalizing on the stonemason's craft, still very much alive in Galicia, César Portela designed a series of country houses that called on a very pared-down vocabulary: granite perpend walls, tiled roofs, brightly painted metal detailing, and concrete structures. Although the concrete piles and the distribution of bathrooms and kitchens are clearly modern, the clear-cut volumes perforated by square windows and fronted by large glazed mirador balconies also show traditionalist leanings.

Manuel Gallego's career, meanwhile, showed the influence of the new tendencies, which he incorporated in his later buildings. Between the Gallego house, mentioned earlier, and the Veigue house, his work acquired a milder tone revealed in an awareness of the slope and the plane, and in the nuances of semienclosed spaces, contained yet continuous. Richness of nuance and spatial continuity are also brilliantly evident in the Chantada cultural center, notable for the variety and appropriateness of its skillfully combined materials, giving the traditional and the modern equal contemporary relevance.

October 1990 saw the inauguration in Bilbao of an exhibition of neoclassical architecture in the Basque country.[55] Not only did this recall a period of particular brilliance but, more importantly, it explained what had led the Basque architects of the decade just past in a different direction of their own. For indeed, while architectural thinking in the rest of Spain was, as we have observed, informed by modernity and realism, the Navarrese and Basque engagement with apparently opposed issues—such as the persisting validity of architecture's profound truths beyond time and place in approaches to the local, the native culture—gave a particular cast to their work, expressed formally in projects that could be termed neoclassical, using the word in its widest sense. The exhibition's organizers, Javier Cenicacelaya and Íñigo Saloña, designed projects that tackled these issues in depth, despite smallness of scale. Their multipurpose hall in La Rijada, Vizcaya, added to the church and *pelota* court, completes a tiny acropolis. The building uses the model of the hall or palace salon, with a single volume surrounded by a peristyle of Tuscan columns without entablature. Though typologically ambiguous, the absence of religious symbols makes the building's civic function clear.

In 1985, Miguel Garay built a cultural center in Pasajes, Guipúzcoa, a building in which symmetry, emphatic entrance arch, moldings, divided central window, and decorative motifs derived from nature constitute an ornamental whole emblematic of the building's function and of an interpretation of Basque culture.

The housing block in the center of Vergara, Guipúzcoa, also dates from 1985. In reference to the solid compactness of the town's typical houses and mansions, José Ignacio Linazasoro used traditional elements such as cornices, the compositional pattern of plinth, central body, and frieze, and differentiation by means of materials between main and lateral facades to achieve a new building absorbable by the existing urban environment. His acceptance of traditional values is also demonstrated in the structure and distribution of rooms in the interior.

Navarre's architects probed further in the same direction. In buildings such as the health center in Lesaka, completed in 1987, Manuel Íñiguez and Alberto Ustarroz explored a classical essentialism, discernible in the precision and sobriety of their moldings and the directness of their volumes, that allies them—within the vast family of classicists—with those neo-Greeks who pursued immutable principles so rigorously.

Navarre's austere climate and landscape can also be interpreted in a conceptual way, as exemplified by Patxi Biurrun's Tajonar housing block, which exhibits the sturdy materials of which it is built.

Valencia possesses an exemplary building in its modern art museum, the IVAM (Instituto Valenciano del Arte Moderno). This cleverly and elegantly designed building represents a precisely focused response to the city's real cultural situation. With this museum, and others being installed in rehabilitated old buildings, Valencia is acquiring a concentration and homogeneity of museum resources, the fruit of a well-grounded campaign, that contrast with dispersed activity in other areas of artistic production. Such culturally dispersed preoccupations can only be matched by an artistically hybrid response, as is the case, in painting, of the Equipo Crónica group, whose work combines the brilliant local sense of the baroque with pop art and modernist composition. The IVAM building not only strives to show the people of Valencia the most important contemporary art from Spain and abroad, but also functions as a dynamic center of local culture. Hence the interest of an exhibition entitled "Arquitectura valenciana: la década de los años ochenta" (Valencian Architecture: The Decade of the Eighties), inaugurated in March 1991. More than forty buildings demonstrated the scope and some of the characteristics of the architecture of Valencia: appropriateness to and inspiration in climate; an underlying culture hybrid in its nature; and a more nuanced predominance of official commissions than in the rest of Spain. Of these three characteristics, the last two perhaps provide the most useful clues to a difficult question: given that Valencia is one of

Spain's most dynamic and creative regions economically, why is this not reflected in its architecture? Another point highlighted by the exhibition was the significant number of buildings completed around 1990.

Valencia has some of the most outspoken examples of the disciplinary architecture practiced in Europe in the sixties. Two architects, Carlos Salvadores and Manuel Portaceli, working alone and in various partnerships, were key figures of this tendency. Both worked on converting a palace to accommodate the Valencian parliament, and the building shows certain characteristics typical of their work: adaptation of the old in combination with new building, with a taste for simple, direct forms, straightforward distribution, apertures that are sober in their composition and detailing, and materials that are few in number and noble in character. Giménez Condón and Salvadores built the regional government's General Archive and Library Coordination Center, and Giménez Julián and Salvadores built the IVAM. While both these buildings share the characteristics just described for the Valencian parliament building, their programs have less to do with formal public occasions and they interpret the architectural discipline in a different way. The functional aspects of circulation and illumination provide the motif for the archive building, giving a linear model dominated by repeated flights of stairs. In the case of the IVAM building, the motif is provided by the modern references of the diagonals and the canopy-topped glass plane.

Arturo Estévez house, San Martiño de Salcedo (Pontevedra), 1980–1983, Portela.

Cultural center, Chantada (Lugo), 1987–1990, Gallego.

The disciplinary tendency made its presence felt at the IVAM exhibition organized in 1991 with the directness of its designs, reclaiming order in a scenario overly fertile in formal areas and rooted in late flirtations with organicism or opportunistic postmodernism. Also notable were expressions of confidence in the modern, seen in two tendencies that were to fare better in the coming decade: the technical tendency and essentialism.

Representative of the first of these are three buildings completed in 1989: the Dinesa building in Paterna, whose architects José María Lozano and Ignacio Pascual we shall observe producing increasingly accomplished buildings; Miguel Martín Velsaco's Rector Center at Paterna Technology Park, a building whose contained volume is fronted by a glass and stilt facade; and Francisco Candel and Luis Carratalá's health center in Picasent, which confidently applies compositional and distributional principles typical of functional architecture.

Toward the end of the decade, a small but established group in Alicante began to put forward an architecture both restrained and essentialist. The small, single-family house designed by Javier García-Solera and built in Alicante's Lomahermosa housing complex in 1987 is modern in distribution, daytime and nighttime zones being divided between two soberly built volumes joined by a glazed box. Equally sober and modern is the health center in Mutxamel by Carmen Rivera, completed in 1990: a white box, whose only exterior punctuation is provided by long windows and understated continuous shutters, contains a central space lit from overhead. Completing this series of small, white, modern buildings is Dolores Alonso's Such Serra printing works in Alicante, completed in 1989. In this case, all choices are informed by coherence and simplicity, from the distribution of work spaces to the signage, all illuminated by consistently clean light derived from lamps, slatted windows, and skylights.

Santiago Calatrava deserves a separate mention. This architect qualified at the Valencia School of Architecture in 1973 and took further qualifications at the Zurich Polytechnic in 1979. Having gone on to international success as what is known as a global architect, he built Valencia's first large-scale project between 1986 and 1989: the 9 de Octubre Bridge.

After a period of negligible activity, Murcia returned to the critical spotlight in an unexpected way in the sixties, on the sole basis of Robert Venturi's mention of its cathedral facade in his book *Complexity and Contradiction in Architecture*. The art of the late baroque period, of which that facade is an example, seems to parallel the fertility of Murcia's abundant fruit- and vegetable-growing area, the *huerta*, yet the architecture built in this region in recent years is outstandingly simple. As early as 1982, Enrique Carbonell and José María Torres Nadal won the commission for the headquarters of the Caja de Ahorros Provincial Savings Bank. Their design is a simple volume incised with long windows, containing an interior in the modern tradition where the richness of the materials, communicating the corporate image, is the sole salient feature. Torres Nadal also designed two works in the middle of the decade that demonstrate his mastery of these architectural formulas. In his three houses among lemon trees in Murcia, 1985, and the children's vacation camp in Calarraona, 1988, his architecture is one of pared-down, brick-built volumes in which the accent is provided by the elements freely disposed in its smooth-surfaced walls: mobile windows and stepped platforms establish a language whose syntax is determined by measured distances.

A complex of 66 low-cost housing units built in Albacete in 1983 is by José María Hervás and Fernando Retes. The complex, which is organized in strips and calls on the modern formal repertoire, relates readily with its arid environment through the use of very bright colors.[56]

Making architecture in the Canary Islands has its difficulties. Though at first sight the benign climate might seem to work in the architect's favor by freeing him from many practical demands and thus leaving scope for invention, he in fact has to struggle with limitations imposed by isolation and distance on the materials at his disposal, both physical and mental.

Single-family house
in Lomahermosa,
Alicante, 1986,
García-Solera Vera.

Valencian parliament,
Valencia, 1988–1995,
Salvadores / Portaceli.

Texaco gas station,
Santa Cruz de Tenerife,
Canary Islands, 1981,
Artengo / Martín Menis /
Rodríguez Pastrana.

This perhaps explains particular characteristics of Canary Islands architecture of the eighties: a sensitivity to materials, expressed by capitalizing on the tectonic qualities of volcanic stones and making almost impossible efforts to achieve sensuality with cement products, and a determination to build up a cultural structure for the islands to compensate for their distance from focuses of intellectual activity. Canary Islands architects have achieved this last through the brilliant operations of the Architects' Chamber, the moving force behind fundamental initiatives such as *Basa* magazine (joined by *Periferia* from its twelfth issue on) and the Manuel de Oráa Prize.

Since *Basa's* first issue, published in December 1983 and devoted entirely to announcing the competition for the first Oráa Prize, both initiatives have proceeded hand in hand, and they are now firmly established. Consequently, studying the output of both institutions is essential to an understanding of the islands' architecture. The first Oráa Prize, in 1985, was awarded to the gas station built for Texaco by Felipe Artengo, Fernando Martín Menis, and José María Rodríguez Pastrana, and brought these new architects to critical attention.

The long-established architects Francisco Artengo, José Ángel Domínguez Anadón, and Carlos Schwarz may be represented by their School of Law and Economics buildings at La Laguna, Tenerife, built between 1979 and 1983. Standing on a solid plinth of volcanic stone, this complex is like a grid-structured fortress in which concrete blocks, rhythmically etched by high windows, alternate with courtyards shaded by vegetation.

Also in La Laguna, Agustín Cabrera and Nieves Febles completed a rehousing project in 1987. The architects solved with considerable skill the difficulties implied in relocating occupants in new houses, which must also allow room for future growth, using the site to accommodate a complex at once compact and porous, whose layouts make the most of modest conditions with a strategy cleverly adapted to the brief and location.

Regions even farther than the Canary Islands from centers of diffusion would take a while longer to produce anything noteworthy. The halcyon years of the nineties were to provide the opportunity.

Castilla y León conference
center and exhibition hall,
Salamanca, 1985–1992,
Navarro Baldeweg.

The years leading up to 1992, the much-celebrated quincentenary of Columbus's first expedition to the New World, flew by in a whirlwind of frantic activity. Construction prices rocketed; skilled labor—concentrated as it was on the work being undertaken for the major events that were in the offing—became scarce, and new, opportunistic companies were set up to soak up a seemingly endless flow of money. With the Socialists firmly entrenched as the party in power at the time, the state focused its political and economic program on three extremely ambitious events. Two of these, the Universal Exposition in Seville and the Barcelona Olympic games, were huge accomplishments; but the third, the celebration of Madrid as Cultural Capital of Europe, met with only lukewarm success. Although the Expo and the Olympics devoured the lion's share of the investment, the sheer momentum of these events, added to the political necessity of improving the hitherto inadequate public services, pulled the country onward and upward in an unprecedented building frenzy.

In successive years, however, the impetus degenerated into excess and the investment into debt. Thus, hard on the heels of the pre-'92 frenzy came the post-'92 crisis. Controversy about the architect and his work was sparked off, and the press, associations in favor of free competition, and even the courts got involved in cases such as that of the Sagunto theater, the sports center in Huesca, and the M-30 ring road housing estate, of which more later. It might be thought that the very success achieved by '92 architecture attracted the attention of some sectors, but the truth is that in those years of crisis, the prevailing trend of the new economic and social relations that were taking hold was toward greater control over architects and greater limits on their decision-making capacity and responsibility. For some, the increasing complexity of architectural construction demanded the involvement of other technical experts, with the consequent sharing of responsibility in the planning and running of any construction project. For others, the Architects' Chambers, the professional associations of architects in Spain that set minimum fees and other financial terms on building work, were in breach of the constitutional principles of equality before the law. At the same time, in an attempt to reduce university subsidies, the state cut the length of university programs, and public opinion wondered whether architects had too much authority to carry out their formal research and express their taste. Unlike the preceding decade, the nineties drew to a close under a gray cloud of pessimism.

This seemingly meaningful watershed of 1992 was not as clear-cut as it appeared. In actual fact, the architecture made in Spain in the years that followed forms part of the same "period" as that of the years before. The following pages will take us down the home stretch of a history that is still drawing to a close. After a look at how the post-'92 crisis fitted into this history, we will be in a position to appraise this last half century, when Spanish architecture achieved modernity—the latest modernity—although it admittedly did so tardily.

An Olympic City

Rehabilitation and extension
to the airport terminal,
El Prat de Llobregat
(Barcelona), 1989–1992,
Bofill.

Orrganization of the
Vall d'Hebrón area,
Barcelona, 1989–1992,
Bru.

Municipal sports center,
Badalona
(Barcelona), 1987–1991,
Bonell / Ríus.

Few cities have ever made so much out of an opportunity presented by history. Barcelona was able to do so because the occasion came along at just the right time. In the eighties Barcelona was reaching maturity: it had in place the social, professional, and political structures that gave it the ability to grasp the opportunity without a moment's hesitation or the fear of taking a single false step. In the years leading up to 1992, Barcelona was the most dynamic city in Spain, in the Mediterranean, and, in my view, in the whole of Europe, and perhaps even beyond. What is even more satisfying is that the pace has not let up since. Although the city has undergone a dramatic transformation, it has essentially remained true to itself and has kept its intimate, discreet atmosphere, its efficient services and quality of life, the assets of mercantile and bourgeois cities that posses their own culture and territory. Despite being a magnet for culture, tourism, and finance at an international level, Barcelona still conserves the appeal of a city with a provincial personality at heart. In what other city in the world today can one find a stock broker, an art dealer, a *patissier*, a vendor of electrical appliances, and a heart specialist all within easy reach?

For Barcelona, the great benefit of the Olympic operation was the substantial improvement it made to its infrastructure, although the most striking visible advantage was its new architecture. The ring road that linked the city with the surrounding area, the opening up of the city to the sea, and the gaining of a port in the Olympic Village are all important in historical terms, but the image that was flashed around the world— before the games themselves were so brilliantly set in motion—was that of its new buildings. The intense relationship that existed between the architecture built in the city and a small, compact group of architects numbering no more than two dozen must be quickly stressed here. Apart from a select handful of leading international names like Siza, Foster, Calatrava, Isozaki, and Moneo, the architects resident in Barcelona— some from their position as clients (Bohigas, Acebillo . . .) and others from their drawing boards—baked and devoured the whole architectural cake with an efficiency that defies criticism and defines the city.

The Barcelona of the nineties was the outcome of a long-running process of internal reflection that the locals ironically termed *la cultureta* (mini-culture). Architects who lived in Barcelona were both satisfied and demanding with their city. Despite the fact that their view of architecture was quite homogeneous as regards its characteristics and its origins, two subtly different manners or approaches could be detected in the nineties. The first of these stemmed from the Barcelona tradition, from the philosophy developed by the architects of the city since the sixties: that of the most direct heirs and even members of the R Group, who received head-on the impact of Rossi and Venturi as mentioned in earlier pages. The second approach corresponded to those architects, for the most part younger than the ones just mentioned, for whom we could borrow the labels of neomodern or simply modern. They were the ones who, as in the rest of Spain and the world beyond, laid claim to the authenticity of the modern movement's manner of doing things. The difference between Barcelona architects and architects from anywhere else, their own peculiarity so to speak, is the continuous reference—present in many different guises—to a situation of their own that they insist on interpreting, in the light of the changing insinuation of the culture. Given that the barriers between these two groups are not always well defined, the work produced by them will be described here without acknowledging the switch from one group to the other, leaving it up to the readers to establish the barrier, or rather the transition—if they think it appropriate.

After the deaths of Coderch and Sostres, it was Federico Correa and Oriol Bohigas who became the fundamental points of reference for the profession. Correa won the competition to redesign the area of Montjuïc for the Olympics, a task that he carried out both prudently and successfully. With Bohigas ensconced in a position that was closer to that of a client than an architect, MBM produced works that pooled strength and professional ability. The layout of the Olympic Village reveals their predilection for varied forms and geometric patterns.

This list of names must be lengthened by the addition of others who have consolidated their influence in recent years. From the School of Architecture, Manuel de Solà-Morales has turned urbanism into a subject that goes beyond the old concept of town planning and illustrates his stance on the design of large urban swaths. As an architect, he confidently deals with major decisions on the issue without balking. The example that comes to mind here is the Moll de la Fusta promenade, built in 1987, where the architect's confidence in developing a huge area without fear of monotony, supported only by a section that is repeatedly used throughout the design, demonstrates his effective use of parts—bridges, stalls, and benches—as the area gradually becomes lived. Further confirmation of the correctness of a major town planning decision can be found in the Illa Diagonal building, designed in collaboration with Rafael Moneo, where the massive dimension of the urban block is controlled by combining the laws of stereotomy with the laws of repetition. The clever design and magnificent size of the windows that break up the endless plane richly carved in stone guarantee its success. It is easy to detect the American roots of this strategy: one could almost be talking about the gigantic apartment block, without forcing the image of a skyscraper on its side.

Ricardo Bofill, who by this time had given up his position as Barcelona's promising local architect to become an international architect-cum-entrepreneur, kept some major clients in Spain (the Madrid City Council was one). His design for the new terminal of El Prat airport in Barcelona, despite the intended international nature of its glass box, is one of the most Catalan of his recent works. By combining the modernity of glass and some very Ove Arup–like structural solutions with concrete Doric columns and palm trees, Bofill was able to present his building to the user as the international validation of all things Mediterranean.

Carles Díaz and Oscar Tusquets, the latter of whom takes pride in his being the only architect to defend Bofill—"He is a genius, I don't know what kind of genius, but a genius nonetheless"—adopted working

Illa Diagonal building, Barcelona, 1986–1994, Moneo / Manuel de Solà-Morales Rubió.

Alfredo Kraus auditorium, Las Palmas de Gran Canaria, 1985–1997, Tusquets / Díaz.

formulas that modern architects scorned: architects for a speculative housing developer (José Luis Núñez, chairman of the Barcelona Football Club), propagandist-illustrators for the press (*El País* Sunday supplement), or urban set designers for a royal wedding. But they never lost their profound sense of what architecture is all about, and with the Las Palmas auditorium, built in the late nineties, they created a decisive volume that stakes out its place on the Canary Islands shoreline, defining the territory— a stone mass erected in the style of the ancient castles along the coast.

Lluis Clotet and Ignacio Paricio worked, commission after commission, with a well-tested strategy that gives their output enormous continuity. They display their mastery over the logical process of architecture—the distribution of parts—by starting with the main volumes and gradually moving down to the details, which are given great importance and autonomy within each work. Thus, in their 1988 proposal for Granada's sports center, they first worked out a clear formula to distribute the uses of the building by placing huge courtyards or corridors between buildings designed with strong forms. The same clarity was maintained within the sports area itself through a categorical geometric distribution of tiered seating, access ways, and ceilings. In essence, the outcome is a very classical tetrastyle structure that develops a hierarchy in which the playing rectangle is the dominant area, both formally and symbolically, onto which open all the less important spaces of the spectator seating. These concerns, and others of Andalusian inspiration, extend to the window and cornice details and to the tiled portico that helps give the ensemble the attractive and surprising look of a bull ring. Like the 1996 Badalona swimming pool complex, this work exudes the playful air that characterizes these architects' oeuvre. In Clotet's own words: "If, as Kahn said, architecture is a higher order that contains other orders, then the question is to discover when the playing field allows you to make any kind of move."

The Vall d'Hebrón *pelota* center and the Hotel Plaza in Barcelona confirmed Garcés and Sòria's professionalism, which is very much in the Barcelona tradition. In the *pelota* center, the relationship between the playing areas, with strong overhead lighting, and the access ways, with much softer illumination, is the best idea of an ensemble devoid of expression on the outside. In the Hotel Plaza, built with Jordi Ruiz and Rafael Coll, the architects were determined to endow the external volume with a powerful presence in view of the dimension and strength of the neighboring buildings and empty spaces. This aim was also reinforced by the arrangement of apertures of elementary shapes and sizes in a Mondrian-like surface grid and the inclusion of other details such as the clock.

The ensemble of buildings constructed in Mollet del Vallés by the brothers Roberto and Esteban Terradas revealed their ability to bring order to a complicated area made up of very diverse constructions. Using as a basis the successful functional solution found for the Olympic shooting range (where the architects solved the problem of sight lines for the first time) and the Police Academy, they resolved the ensemble by accepting the original layout of the plot and capitalizing on its huge dimensions. The different buildings stand quite naturally in a line along a lengthy communication axis, in a way that seeks to be effective without being pretentious.

In 1987, the Tàpies Foundation commission proved to be the ideal opportunity for Roser Amadó and Lluis Domènech to show their skill in turning a renowned building—one that pioneered Catalonian *modernisme*—to a new use and reinterpreting its details along suitably abstract lines to house Tàpies's art. The following year, the same architects had more freedom to display their love of form in the Barcelona Archives of the Crown of Aragon. In this case, the untidy urban scene, together with the compulsory viewing point of the building—seen from a car traveling at speed—enabled Domènech and Amadó to set out a contrast of daring volumes and geometries in which the triangular forms that are responsible for the building's presence cut rooms and passages at angles.

It is also possible to detect a movement that is linked to a diagonal, or rather to a diagonal arrangement of the axis of an ellipse, in another geometrical exercise, albeit not such a strict one. This is the Badalona sports center designed in 1987 by Bonell and Rius and derived from their cycling stadium seen in the previous chapter. On this occasion, the interior of the building—with its magnificent spatial solution derived from the centrality and environmental continuity that the ellipse allows to the rectangular playing floor, and its constructive quality determined by the neat structural and lighting solution—is far more convincing than the exterior, where the mouth of the main gangway might be deemed somewhat excessive and difficult to understand in its urban location.

Toward the end of the eighties, Jaume Bach and Gabriel Mora gradually simplified their language. This simplification, which was already hinted at in the Olympic Village telephone exchange seen in the previous chapter, became even more drastic in the Tarragona incinerator plant, where the industrial nature of the commission prompted the use of stark volumes.

New building for the Archives
of the Crown of Aragon,
Barcelona, 1988–1993,
Amadó / Domènech.

Housing in
the Olympic Village,
Barcelona, 1990–1992,
Martínez Lapeña / Torres Tur.

In the Tarrasa hockey stadium, Bach and Mora developed an architecture
with limpid planes, on the ground or suspended in the air, that had much
more modern and Nordic roots. This has been their most powerful work
yet, made up of skylights ordered like sphinxes, light and airy projecting
canopies, and taut lighting towers.

Although it is a cliché to say that Heliodoro Piñón and Albert Viaplana are
minimalists, it is the unavoidable truth. Not merely relying on minimal
expression, their approach seeks to create an impression by using less
than what is formally essential. Evidence of how they have been judged,
not only by members of their own profession but by the market itself, is
the 1990 Hilton Hotel commission in Barcelona, where they took their
urge to eliminate elements to the extreme of avoiding the street itself, which
has to be sought inside the building. In the housing estate designed that
same year for the Barcelona Olympic Village, they had to adapt to the
"pattern set out by the designers of the plan. . . . The Village was divided
up into small sections to achieve this end: it was—we were told—one of
its virtues." This complaint, voiced by the architects, helps to explain the
occasional unfortunate detail in this work, such as the alignments of the
main facade, the impossible corner, or the invasion of what should have
been free interior space by intrusive elements. Despite all of the unnecessary elements forced upon the design, the architects made good use of a
fine, conventional ground plan and a repertoire of materials that was
perfectly adequate for the exterior—wooden overhangs, vitrified tiles, and
glass—to configure lines and volumes that are both forceful and gentle.

On the opposite side of Avenida Icaria, Franc Fernández and Moisés
Gallego built a training pavilion, adapting its rectangular, direct geometry
to the given corner with great difficulty. Later they worked with Pere Riera,
José María Gutiérrez, Montse Batllé, and Josep Sotorres on the Montgat
school and sports center, also in Barcelona, where they wielded the same
geometric arguments, but with a greater freedom that bore fruit. In this
case, the clean orthogonal lines and serene scale of all the parts create a
successful hall—a beautiful wooden box whose structural elements are
disguised behind the taut wooden skin of the box instead of standing out
as they usually do in programs of this type. The light that pours in cross-
wise can be controlled through huge parasols that, like the structure itself,
really only stand out on the outside.

Between 1990 and 1992, Elías Torres and José Antonio Martínez Lapeña
also built an apartment building in the Olympic Village. Taking advantage
of its position at the end of a city block, they skillfully turned the site into
a crescent that surreptitiously accepts the odd diagonal and ends in a
tower of nautical section that looks out onto the Mediterranean, making
clear reference to Coderch's masterful building in La Barceloneta and
skillfully and smoothly solving the ground plans of the blocks and houses.

Before leaving behind the Olympic Village, one last thought is in order. It
must be pointed out that Barcelona architects are extremely critical of the
village's layout, which they claim is both random and fickle. It is true that
it made a multiplicity of diverse and often ridiculous forms necessary—
aside from some very successful constructions like Clotet's little towers

and Bonet's "chalets," which, nevertheless, have a rather startled air about them. Whatever the case, its rather quaint look will be better judged with the passage of time, and one day this village will be regarded as the expression of Barcelona '92, with its own particular sense of design or its own interpretation of the Mediterranean and its way of life. It may even end up taking on a similar role to the one played by the Pueblo Español, the "Spanish Village," vis-à-vis the 1929 exposition.

Torres and Lapeña's Mora d'Ebre hospital in Tarragona, dating from 1988, is a piece of sober, disciplined, and effective architecture, in contrast with some of their other works that are full of sly references and tricks, revealing a double personality full of cheeky self-confidence that means we can expect surprises from them anywhere and at any time.

Surprise is not the word that best suits the architecture fashioned by Josep Llinás. The strictest, noblest sobriety in classical modernity would be a more apt description, in which Coderch's influence shares a place with de la Sota's. In the 1989 library of the School of Civil Engineering, nothing is placed at whim and nothing is devoid of meaning. The simple parallelepiped is unassumingly cut into sections to serve functional areas that only stand out when they really need to: in the library, where the image of modern efficiency is conducive to silent study. Llinás also built a secondary school in Torredembarra, in the southern part of Catalonia, in 1996. His starting point was the square ground plan around a courtyard that is so functional in these programs. The white volumes—to bring light to education—join together with the naturalness of geological formations.

Modern tradition was interpreted quite differently by Josep Lluis Mateo with Jordi Moliner and Jaume Avellaneda in their 1990 Badalona Law Courts building. The gray, concise volumetric design of the exterior gives an early indication of their taste for other modern values: invention and tension. Granite turned into plates, mounted on a technological framework, clads an interior designed on crossed geometrical lines, where the leading role is given over to the staircases and their metallic interplay of banisters, handrails, braces, and trusses, which also crisscross in precise

Hospital, Mora d'Ebre (Tarragona), 1982–1988, Martínez Lapeña / Torres Tur.

Casa de la Caritat center of contemporary culture, Barcelona, 1990–1993, Viaplana / Piñón.

Law Courts, Badalona (Barcelona), 1986–1990, Mateo / Moliner.

Opposite page:
Library,
School of Civil Engineering, Barcelona, 1987–1989, Llinás.

Housing block on Calle Carme, Barcelona, 1992–1995, Llinás.

Secondary school, Torredembarra (Tarrragona), 1993–1996, Llinás.

Juvenile correction center, Palau de Plegamans (Barcelona), 1984–1986, Bru.

profiles. Pierced, this gray, tense skin gives way to a modern, fast-moving, efficient replica of an ideal system of justice.

In 1984, in the juvenile correction center in Palau de Plegamans, Eduard Bru made the volumes of the building hug the line of the mountain, whose shape he corrected artificially through cut and fill. Long, sloping tile roofs, lattices, and whitewashed walls endow the work with a rural air, as if only Mother Nature could look after the disruptive youngsters who live in the center. Bru is also the architect behind another of Barcelona's major successes: the open space of the Vall d'Hebrón Olympic area finished in 1992. This work takes a low-key, natural approach to a subject that was much in vogue in Barcelona at the time, namely the relationship of nature and building in large urban areas. Other well-known examples of this emphasis are the Santa Cecilia gardens by Torres and Martínez Lapeña, or Piñón and Viaplana's Plaza de Sants. The unusual urban position of the Vall d'Hebrón commission, next to a ring road, was a source of inspiration that went beyond the winding layout of roads and paths and embraced the use of typical motorway elements, such as overhead walkways or low steel guard rails. These features, together with "artificial" ones such as the synthetic lawn, are interwoven in proper pop art fashion with grass and reed elements that play the role of a decidedly unconventional, inspired nature. The most important aspect of the project was that the park, brimming with unexpected contrasts, could only be built once the new, complex road structure was solved, in a site dotted with convents and other properties, through terracing and paths.

Vall d'Hebrón was also the site of one of Carme Pinós and Enric Miralles's most renowned designs: the archery pavilion built in 1991. The architects like to explain it as a work of land retention in a site characterized by the unevenness of its ground, proof of their satisfaction at the way they turned nature's strength of weight and movement into the design itself in the form of beams, cantilevers, and conveniently dropped walls. In the Igualada cemetery of the same year, Miralles and Pinós created an extraordinary atmosphere out of negative concepts such as death, neglect, and ruin. The site, which could have been a forgotten quarry or rubbish dump, was

fashioned from powerful concrete that holds back the added earth with elegant curves. The materials seem to have been reused and recycled. There are planks stuck into the ground at random, stone gabions imprisoned by barbed wire, and rods that crisscross to form fragile, unstable bars.

Once they went their separate ways, the former Pinós-Miralles partnership was closely scrutinized by the critical eyes that turned each of them into a leading light of the international avant-garde group of architects—a group that has an increasing number of Spanish representatives among its members. Pinós was in charge of the work designed by both partners for a school in Morella, a complex that was perfectly integrated into the striking geography of its site. It was slotted neatly into the landscape—under the castle that crowns the neighboring village—through the wise choice of colors, the concrete work, and strategic interruption. It is a great comfort to see such proof that it is possible to experiment architecturally under the very eyes of nature and history. Before his untimely death at the age of forty-five, Miralles made a heroic stand when the Huesca sports center (1988–1994) fell to the ground due to a flaw in its execution. As the scandal hit the front pages, Miralles simply took note of what had gone wrong and reerected the structure like a phoenix rising out the ashes.

To continue the metaphor of flight, the Hotel Rey Juan Carlos I designed by Carlos Ferrater (and built together with José María Cartaña in 1992) invites the user to embark on a journey into the future. Like a spaceship traveling through an atmosphere that offers no resistance, the building displays its geometry on the outside and develops its internal organization around a luminous empty space or vacuum that sucks the traveler in. There are some symmetries in the ground plan, but these simply explain how the freer-than-free form obeys the laws of that unknown atmosphere. In 1996, Ferrater added a fitness center to the hotel's facilities by picking

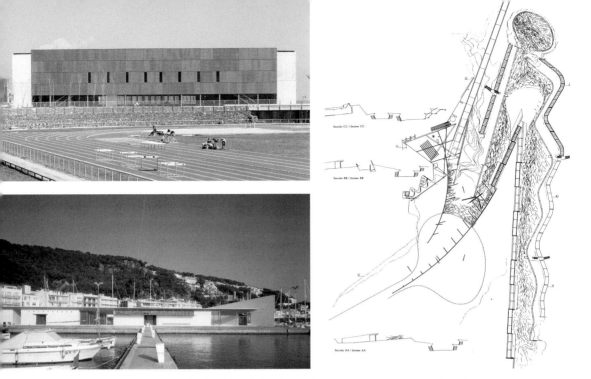

up the building's broken-plane geometry and burying the volume under the sand on a star-shaped pattern that leaves the central space open to the sky. The L'Estartit sailing club, which Ferrater built with Gerardo Rodríguez and Juan Díaz between 1990 and 1992, is a much calmer building, where the only traveling is done by the boats moored there. Nevertheless, the forms used for the building are somewhat reminiscent of sails, as if they sought some sort of complicity with the vessels anchored nearby.

So great is Barcelona and its identification with Catalonia that it overshadows the rest of the region. However, there are a few architects whose work has been capable of overcoming this dominance. Arcadi Pla is one such, whose oeuvre in Gerona is both wide-ranging and well constructed. One of the best examples is the school in L'Estartit, where he reacted to the disorderly periphery by constructing a work that looks in on itself, picking up on school typologies as universal and consolidated in their tradition as the Turkish *medersas*. In the case of the El Molí sports center, he designed an extraordinarily powerful building, taking advantage of its great length, which is skillfully emphasized through the whiteness of the block, the glass walls, and the white metal detailing that enclose an effective, luminous space within.

Before leaving behind the architecture being produced in Catalonia, let us take a look at the work of the youngest architects who, like those in the rest of Spain, are putting their efforts into so-called neomodern approaches. Two houses built by Tonet Sunyer and Jordi Badía—one in San Gervasi and the other for Alberto Herrero—follow a plain, serene ground plan broken by a small number of nonorthogonal details. The secret of this architecture lies in the placing of a door, a bath, or a window. They are small white or brick buildings that only stand out against their background through their subtle firmness when seen and touched.

In the mid-nineties, Manuel Ruisánchez and Xavier Vendrell displayed a notable maturity in works such as the Barcelona sailing school. The geometry of this building is dictated by the huge rectangular sports area placed—together with the auxiliary spaces—inside a powerful parallelepiped put together with carefully prepared concrete walls and enclosing planes painted the color of good-quality wood. In 1996, they gave further proof of this gentle understanding of architecture in the Riumar school in Tarragona.

Miguel Roldán and Mercé Berengué also designed and built a school, the El Pi, in Sant Pere de Ribes in 1996. Although forced to reuse existing buildings, they managed to make the old and the new sit comfortably together without jarring by choosing a traditional arrangement of classrooms around courtyards in a grid shape. The concrete and ceramic materials enclose spaces containing ramps, stairs, and some out-of-place volumes that add an element of surprise to the prevailing order.

The strictly utilitarian and technical nature of a municipal vehicle pool and waste collection depot, like the one built in 1996 by Esteve Aymerich and Ton Salvadó in Gerona, can sometimes be the perfect occasion to try out less conventional materials and forms. That is exactly what the architects did here, lining elementary volumes—inspired by the containers themselves—with ribbed sheets, sustained by a structure where the bars are the unassuming stars of the show. The highly dignified way this seemingly modest service is dealt with is really the best way to build a city.

In Banyoles, Gerona, Josep Miàs built a shop as if it were a stage on which the clients could play themselves. He turned a plot between party walls within the medieval layout of the town into a peripatetic work based on ramps and stairs between lights, mirrors, and clothes.

With, almost literally, four walls, in 1995 Xavi Claramunt, Pep Valls, and Se Duch built in Barcelona's Galería del Passatge a space with the capacity to transform itself into something else, thereby meeting the needs that an avant-garde—if that word still has any meaning—art gallery requires. The multipurpose nature of the space is heightened by the public passage that invades the premises and is used in exchange for the space itself.

If housing—and minimal housing above all—was the field that most favored architectural research and experimentation in the early years of the twentieth century, in the nineties other programs—the ones we are looking at now—seem to be the most suited to the task. In a bar, the sensorial relationship that the customer builds up with the space through sight, taste, hearing, and balance can on occasions go beyond the bounds of normal experience. What would be the most conventional actions in any other place can lead to unusual experiences there. Movement up and down a staircase or within a large crowd of customers and the unsuspected relationships that can be forged between them, the way someone sits at the bar or acts in the toilets, are all areas that allow certain architectural concepts to be explored with greater freedom in these commissions. The Tubobar, built by Josep Salló, Josep Miàs, and Francesc Pla, confirms this theory.

Seville's constructive history is a contrast of light and shade, a history where periods of dazzling activity have been followed by long periods of romantic neglect. Seville hummed with constructive frenzy when it was the seat of the Almohad kingdom, or the capital of trade with America, or the venue for the 1929 Exposition. During the intervals between those times, however, its structures languished and decayed. This cycle, repeated over and over in Seville down the ages, has meant that the city's moments of building activity are tantamount to times of reconstruction when the city has had to rebuild and restore its fabric to former glory. Nineteen ninety-two, the year of the Expo, was the latest in the long line of such moments of constructive euphoria. Seville's architecture always makes use of traditional materials: not just because the buildings are seemingly rebuilt with the stones and timbers of their own decline following the lines drawn of old, but also because the best examples of this architecture today are, as always, those that seek answers in tradition instead of form; their why and how instead of their design.

Colombina Library, Seville, 1989–1991, J. Ramón Sierra / Ricardo Sierra.

Calle Torneo, Paseo de Juan Carlos I, La Cartuja walkway (1990–1991), by Leonhardt / Viñuela, engs., and aerial view of the Expo 92 grounds on the Isla de La Cartuja (1986–1992), the river, and the historical quarter of Seville.

José Ramón and Ricardo Sierra must have felt at home working among books and paintings in the Colombina Library. All things old are an omnipresent feature here. The Sevilles that have successively existed in the past have left their trace in this building. There are Almohad arches, incomplete niches, broken walls, and gentle paintings on fine baroque doors that have been cleaned but not restored. All things new—the things that have been added—keep a low profile in this atmosphere where extras seem unnecessary. There is an underlying feeling that finishes are the result of pure need: the marble floors, which could not have been otherwise, and the use of white, which is much more than just a chosen color. It is the tool used to create an atmosphere that can be breathed in, on which portraits of learned canons and other upstanding Sevillians hang. There is a dense air about this architecture that prevails over the sought-after simplicity. An air that seems inevitable, the consequence of the passage of time or of the hours upon hours spent poring over books.

The Catalana Occidente building presented the Sierra brothers with the challenge of constructing an office block on a wide avenue in the process of consolidation. The long, narrow, seven-story-high block determinedly

took on two obligations: to come up with a dignified response to the urban requirements, and to find an effective solution for a rather banal office building ground plan. It was not just a question of resolving the facade itself; it was also necessary to analyze the position and attitude of new buildings in a section of town where the widths of the streets and their general dimensions do not match those in the traditional city. The task entailed defining a new street and specifying its new use.

The La Maestranza auditorium was located in a more central area of town and had to meet stricter image requirements than the examples seen above. By building the "city's ear," Luis Marín de Terán and Aurelio del Pozo completed the series of buildings—including the Torre del Oro, the

Previsión Española building, and the Real Maestranza bull ring and theater—that stand opposite the river and Calle Bétis. In a daring gesture, the auditorium was given the perfect shape of a cylinder, was enveloped in powerful high, pierced walls—which act as both structure and drop curtain—and was finished off with a theatrical flourish, stuck behind the masklike ancient facade of the Real Maestranza bull ring.

Following a different approach, in 1991 Antonio González Cordón turned a set of obsolete industrial buildings into a city in miniature for the Regional Department of Agriculture in Seville. The streets, fountains, square, gates, and urban landmarks were masterfully used to integrate the restored buildings with the new ones designed on the same scale and dimensions. Avoiding monotony, which the architect must have regarded as a personal enemy, the buildings stand differentiated in isolation or in groups of two or three: the stone and glass office block that skillfully makes its function obvious, the three modest identical pavilions in the square, and the series of long warehouse buildings. Each volume was given an identity of its own through an exuberant variety of vaults and overhead lights. Since the ensemble was completed in 1991, González Cordón has been quite prolific. In 1995, together with Carlos García Vázquez he completed the port authority building and workshops in the Mazagón marina in Huelva. With the formal ease that characterizes the work of its architects, the ensemble links together a collection of volumes enveloped in canopies, lattices, and brise-soleils that are justified by the luminosity of the site.

Seville's joie de vivre stems first from its delightful climate and then from man's skill at finding ways to enjoy life to the full. The centuries-old *casa patio*, or courtyard house, has always been the basic ingredient in this recipe for life that is now described as ecological. It might prove interesting to delve more deeply into how this recipe has absorbed the distributive requirements of housing in the twentieth century.

Santa Justa railway station, south terminal of the AVE high-speed train, Seville, 1988–1991, Cruz / Ortiz.

La Maestranza theater, Seville, 1986–1991, Marín de Terán / Del Pozo.

Catalana Occidente building, Seville, 1987–1991, J. Ramón Sierra / Ricardo Sierra.

The need to build high-rise blocks to maximize the profitability of the land—four, six, or more apartments, one on top of the other, reached by elevators—imposes a certain type of block and house. One of the problems that contemporary Andalusian architects have faced is reconciling the idea of the courtyard house, naturally linked to the ground, and the block-with-elevator—an instrument that actually separates the dwelling from the ground. All the Seville architects featured in these pages began studying in the seventies the house-courtyard relationship found in Seville, reflecting the features of the Seville courtyard or patio in doctoral theses, architectural guides, studies on the urban party wall, or typological surveys. Compass geometry, the plastic nature of party walls, the opening of closures, the inhabited flat roofs, and the popular *corrala* apartments built around an open court were all taken on board by these architects. Taking advantage of these traditions, they came up with the formulas needed to make the courtyard house compatible with the block-with-elevator. By combining stairs and open walkways with large, common patios or small courtyards separated from the ground, they put together the mixed formulas that were suitable for the times.

In the 40 houses built in Mairena del Aljarafe, Gonzalo Díaz Recaséns and Ignacio Capilla were determined to make the tradition of the Seville house set around a courtyard compatible with the forms of contemporary life and the architectural types that suit it—row housing in this case. The subsidized housing estate built in San Bernardo by José Luis Daroca and the residential estate built in Jerez de la Frontera by Daroca and José Antonio Carbajal are also good examples of the handling of access spaces between street and courtyard and of the skill and taste for difficult domestic geometries that is already a genre in Seville.

In the return journey between Seville and Central Europe that we believe characterizes the work of Seville architects, Antonio Cruz and Antonio Ortiz used the Nordic L-shaped ground plan to build two small districts in Arabic style with narrow streets and white walls in Sancti Petri. In the houses they designed in 1986 and finished building in 1989 in the district of Carabanchel, they exported to Madrid a Sevillian sense of housing that is recognizable in the exterior space—more a courtyard than a terrace—given to each apartment. The details, like a canopy or molding, supported by the wise choice of brick, also contributed to give a faint Andalusian look and feel to Madrid's periphery.

With the precision of a good craftsman that he applies to the constructive details of all his work, ranging from walls down to locks and hinges, Guillermo Vázquez Consuegra has built works that have become increasingly more abstract. In his social housing on Calle Ramón y Cajal, as well as in the Cádiz and Almendralejo estates built in 1992, he produced the effects of abstract expressionism by bending sheet metal or rendered brick planes into smooth curves and using windows that flow through their

This page, from left to right and from top to bottom:
Red Eléctrica regional center, Isla de la Cartuja, Seville, 1989–1992, Bayón.

Central theater, Isla de la Cartuja, Seville, 1991–1992, Ayala.

Televisión Española Center in Andalusia, Seville, 1990–1993, Ayala.

Alamillo bridge and viaduct, Seville, 1990–1992, Calatrava.

Rehabilitation of the monumental complex of La Cartuja (15–19th c.), Seville, 1987–1995, Vázquez Consuegra.

Opposite page:
Navigation Pavilion, Isla de la Cartuja, Seville, 1989–1992, Vázquez Consuegra.

repeated or curved forms. The inclusion of courtyards and accesses, however, continued to be in the Seville tradition.

As in contemporary Seville house design, transformed tradition reappears time and again in buildings designed for public use. In the 1991 Santa Justa railway station project, Cruz and Ortiz successfully solved a large-scale work with a professional maturity derived from a long, sustained process of personal definition. In the well-known Doña María Coronel building, they had already stated their preference for a nonabstract architecture that was more concerned with the acceptance and solution of particular problems than with stylistic debates. The Santa Justa building is certainly modern—in the sense that its functional nature and constructive, structural, and decorative solutions are all modern—but it belongs to a modernity in which the techniques used are actually conventional and traditional. That is why it is neither avant-garde nor experimental: it falls into the naturalist tradition of architects whose intention is simply to describe things as they are. The materials are exposed but not exhibited, and the building is adorned by developing the construction to indicate the use of spaces that are direct, discreet, and obvious: the entrance hall with its benches, its height, and its clock, the stairs from which the trains are visible, and the platforms designed like motionless trains.

In the stadium built in 1994 for the Madrid regional government (see page 154), Cruz and Ortiz did not waste the opportunity to develop a more

abstract type of architecture than the actual nature of the commission required: a powerful sloping plane with a strong cantilever gathers the spectators on one side of the bean-shaped perimeter. Despite unbalancing the public view of the athletes, this emphatic decision managed to concentrate the spectators in the best orientation and the density of the services in one location, with the subsequent working economies. A wall closes off these services before the sloping plane with a systematic window striping whose somewhat abstract look links it up with the curve. The outcome is a sober, flat contraption that rises out of the dry, barren landscape to the east of Madrid, dotted with a few bare hills (some of which are natural and others built out of waste dumps), in the form of a bean or ornamental comb, a *peineta*, as it was christened by the people of Madrid, perhaps as a tribute to its attractive charm.

The work of these two architects has been prolific, sober, and serious ever since. Two examples that are worth mentioning are the headquarters of the Seville provincial government and the Chipiona port buildings, both from 1995. Since the regionalist bias of the Calle Hombre de Piedra housing block, their work has become increasingly abstract and modern, as if international acclaim required them to use a different language. The design for a bridge over the Maas in Holland, and the Basel train station, a competition they won in 1996, are their first steps in what is known as global architecture.

At the Expo grounds, Vázquez Consuegra—an architect who had incor-porated the expressionism of single perforated walls and long roofs and pergolas in the Seville tradition into the Rolando house, and the expres-sionism of curved walls and horizontal bands into his blocks of apart-ments—turned the Navigation Pavilion into an architectural exercise full of direct, powerful meaning. He saw the Universal Exposition as an event that required a special architecture capable of expressing such general and ambitious questions as a historical moment in time, a city's presence and ability to communicate, or the meaning of architecture as something that must necessarily and fortunately be produced and displayed through the subjective work of a talented architect. The building brims over with movement and spatiality in the development of its ramps and staircases, the height of its ceilings, and the curved lines of its roofs. It is an imme-diate building in the metaphorical style of the timber rib cages built by carpenters on the shore. It has a slender tower with monumental aspira-tions and an interior route that leads up to a panoramic terrace above. In the mid-nineties, Vázquez Consuegra was keen to take on large-scale projects awarded through competitions, like the Museo de la Ilustración (Museum of the Enlightenment) in Valencia, executed from 1997 to 2000; the Archives of Castilla-La Mancha in Toledo, built in 1997; the National Museum of Marine Archaeology, in Cartagena, dating from 1998; and, above all, the 1997 plan for the Vigo promenade, where he redesigned the area where city and port come together (see page 150).

Other architects, both Spanish and foreign, also designed buildings linked to the Seville Expo. Although some of these pavilions were dismantled, such as those designed by Tadao Ando (Japan) and Grimshaw (United

Airport terminal,
Seville, 1987–1991,
Moneo.

Port facilities,
Chipiona, Cádiz, 1994–1995,
Cruz / Ortiz.

Social housing
in the district of La Paz,
Cádiz, 1986–1991,
Vázquez Consuegra.

Opposite page:
Bus station,
Granada, 1994–1995,
Torres Martínez.

Social housing estate,
Los Palacios
(Seville), 1989–1996,
García Márquez / Ignacio
Rubiño / Luis Rubiño.

Kingdom), others remain, contributing their variety and difference to the city. These include the pavilions designed by the Monark group (Finland), Vigieur and Jodry (France), Makovecz (Hungary), Nemec and Stempel (Czechoslovakia), Cruz Ovalle and del Sol (Chile), and Calatrava (Kuwait). They are the thoughts and responses that other cities brought to Seville to honor its memory. Some of the top-rated architects in Spain were also called on to execute other designs, including Sáenz de Oiza (Torretriana building), Feduchi, Vázquez de Castro (World Trade Center), Carvajal, Martorell, Bohigas, Mackay, Cano Lasso (Spanish pavilion), and Moneo.

The revamped city airport, which the locals, with their delightful obsession with words, call the *Puerta del Aire* (Gateway to the Air), was extended by Rafael Moneo with a new terminal that expresses his view on local traditions. Having decided not to compete with the naturally technological image of the plane, the architect designed the airport with a traditional look: a gigantic, low-cost Andalusian *cortijo* with a huge hall that he filled with Ottoman-inspired columns as a way of criticizing the kind of "naive regionalism" that, in Seville, always leaned toward the use of the horseshoe arch.

Several communications buildings were also designed around this time. The Television Center completed in Málaga in 1996 by Díaz Recaséns is reminiscent of the one we saw in Seville, although in Málaga the tower stands as a counterpoint to a series of vaulted container buildings. In Granada, the bus station, built around the same time by Francisco Torres, uses sections to express functionality: huge areas of movement are lit from above, thus making elevations irrelevant.

As this section draws to a close, certain conclusions can be drawn. Seville architects unanimously work within their local tradition. The construction techniques they use are the traditional ones: structures with brick facing, rather than rendering or conventional concrete structures. Their typological choices are personal variations on the same themes, such as the courtyard and the flat roof. The compositional and ornamental decisions they take reinforce these types through the use of a local language intimately linked to them. There is no trace of exhibitionism in these architectures. Equally, there are no dizzying heights of research, and if there are, they are only to see how modernity can be absorbed. Contemporary architecture in Seville is compact, homogeneous, and serious.

Let us take one last look at these traits in works that, owing to the nature of the commission and the age of the architects, have remained on the sidelines of the constructive mainstream of Expo '92 and explain the continuity of the principles studied. Jasone Ayerbe and Javier Ruiz Recco built a series of small squares and street corners designed to tidy up a periphery of the city affected by infrastructure work with an architecture of lines and planes rooted in abstraction and offset by the realistic precision of the materials. In 1986, Antonio Ampliato and José María Jiménez designed an ensemble of twelve houses in Santiponce, Seville. This disciplined work took the form of an arrangement of concise white parallelepipeds enclosing the distributions of a modern, conventional, cleverly organized house on a stone plinth.

Railway station, Córdoba, 1990–1994, Asensio / Benítez / Gabriel Rebollo / Ángel Rebollo.

In 1992, Ignacio Rubiño, Pura García, and Luis Rubiño were responsible for the latest in a long line of modifications made to the ancient Convento de los Mínimos, one that seemed to take its minimal-sounding name to heart as they converted it for its new use as the Sanlúcar de Barrameda cultural center in Cádiz. In the best Andalusian tradition, the white outer walls continue to offer protection to discreet clean spaces within. The same architects displayed similar simplicity in the cultural center in Huevar del Aljarafe, Seville, and in the 136 state-subsidized apartments built in Los Palacios, also in Seville, completed in 1996. The minimal ground plans that effectively resolve the different programs for two-, three-, and four-bedroom apartments basically hinge the principles of distribution on the use of two courtyards: a central one, designed as a roofless room for access purposes, and a rear one, designed as a service feature. The beautiful effect created by the simple volumes in this ensemble mirrors their interior arrangement. To use a bullfighting simile once again, Sevillians show us that the important thing is to position your feet correctly.

As with Barcelona, the brilliance of the city of Seville has tended to overshadow the rest of Andalusia, where, notwithstanding, certain names have managed to shine. Such is the case of Miguel Centellas and Francisco Martínez Manso in Almería, or Rafael Soler and Francisco Martínez in Granada. The former made their mark in 1989 with the simple, white volume of the Vícar school that is capable of withstanding the region's intense sun; the latter did so in 1990, with the precision and strength of the brickwork used for 124 conventional, sober, and powerful apartments in the Almanjayar district of Seville.

In Jerez de la Frontera, Ramón González de la Peña built a fire station by deploying a series of geometrical volumes, among which the tower stands out with its rhombus ground plan and the finishing touch of an elliptic shrine that establishes a dialogue with the city.

Finally, in Córdoba, the new railway station was built by José Miguel Asensio, Jorge Benítez, and Gabriel and Ángel Rebollo as a transparent box held up by simple brick and concrete legs under which the trains travel through tunnels. When the passengers alight from the train they are welcomed by the Sierra Morena mountain range.

In the late eighties, Spain's triple-headed strategy for 1992 included the celebration of the Olympic games in Barcelona, Expo '92 in Seville, and the Cultural Capital of Europe in Madrid. Things did not work out quite as well as planned, however. It may have been the crisis that forced the cutting back of one of these events, or it may have been the inherent emptiness of the idea of a cultural capital. Whatever the case, the truth is that Madrid's role in the plan fizzled out almost completely. A number of good concerts and exhibitions—which would have been held in any case—and two events—which had been scheduled to take place on the sidelines of the 1992 celebrations (although they were fundamental)—were all that came of the cultural capital idea. These two events were the reopening of the Reina Sofía National Museum of Art, designed by Antonio Fernández Alba, with a splendid collection—albeit with some important absences— of Spanish contemporary painting, and Moneo's museum for the Thyssen collection, which opened to the public in October of that year.

As a result, unlike Seville or Barcelona, Madrid was left with no tangible reminder of 1992. There was to be no resounding improvement in its insufficient transport infrastructures, or urban gain, or river, or port, or airport, or opening up of the city to anywhere at all. *Madrid*, in the sense in which the word is used in Spain by anyone from outside the city, i.e., the central authority, simply did not spend money on Madrid, on the city or its inhabitants.

This assertion does not mean, however, that architects were inactive. Some built important works inside and outside the city, while others continued working in a field of activity that had been particularly significant in the course of the last forty years—social housing, of which more later.

Another point that must be stressed here is the effect of the lack of work in the city itself, which reinforced the idealistic, enlightened, and distinct-ly nonlocal bias of its architects. The architects without tenure whom we saw in the context of the seventies consolidated their position in the School of Architecture and dragged students in their wake into lecturing posts. As a result, they consolidated the institution in its role as an instrument that passes on its legacy of knowledge. The younger architects in Madrid, now actually born in rather than emigrated to the city, followed in the footsteps of Cano Lasso, de la Sota, Sáenz de Oiza, and Moneo (who also has followers in other latitudes), inheriting the open-minded nature of their elders. To work in Barcelona, Seville, or Galicia, it was assumed that an architect had to be close to the region in order to be able to interpret it, but this was not the case in Madrid. The city's nature, however, has always prevailed in the end, creating a common tone and feel.

Some of the most widely read journals, such as *El Croquis*, *Arquitectura Viva*, and *A&V Monografías*, published anything of interest that was being built—not just in Spain—as a visible sign of the nonlocal interests of Madrid architects. In 1991, the journal published by the Architects' Chamber of Madrid, *Arquitectura*, edited by Fernando Porras and Federico

Soriano, moved into a more theoretical phase in line with these interests. When its publication was interrupted, the dispersal of its editorial board resulted in the appearance of a number of independent publications, such as *Bau* (Architects' Chamber of Castile), *Fisuras*, *Exit*, and *Circo*. These journals were all slightly different in nature but similar in an almost marginal, outsider feel that was very much in the contemporary aesthetic taste, publishing less conventional up-to-date texts and works. The government itself, once it had devolved powers to the self-governing regions, kept up a constant stream of up-to-date exhibitions alongside those organized by museums and the cultural sections of banks.

Of the influential figures on the Madrid scene, Sáenz de Oiza, with an infinitely youthful vigor and influence, continued to work on ever tougher projects built in the midst of the controversy he so enjoyed. One such was the housing estate on the M-30 ring road, for which he won the competition with a design that used an exaggerated layout in the late urban expressionist style that all of his opponents had rejected, turning need into virtue in the construction of an extremely powerful ghetto where marginalized sectors of the population were rehoused. Until his death in 1996, Alejandro de la Sota was also an extremely important architect whose influence continued to increase as his reputation grew among the younger generation.

Lacking work in their own city, architects Julio Cano Lasso and José Antonio Corrales went to other regions to build. In his auditoriums, Cano Lasso manifested his love of profound volumes. In the Spanish Pavilion in Seville, for instance, he produced a building that is admired for its sober and elegant presence in the midst of fatuous exhibitionism. In the Galicia Auditorium in Santiago de Compostela, the volumes were toned down by the inclusion of Galician themes: the water and the glass of the bay windows. In La Coruña, Corrales built a School of Fine Arts with the same rationalist approach that runs through all of his output, using white tones and horizontal lines to put together a building that draws its formal inspiration from its preassigned position on a slope. In 1996, he also completed a Wood Research Center in Toledo where he once again demonstrated a confident handling of modern techniques and styles and an effective use of modern resources.

Rafael Moneo received the Pritzker Prize in 1996, an award that is tantamount to a Nobel prize in architecture. That same year he won the competition to design and build the cathedral in Los Angeles, California, and the following year he became a member of the prestigious Spanish Academy of Fine Arts. A defining trait of Moneo's work is his precise and ideologically unprejudiced philosophy of "place" in the widest possible sense of the word. This is evident in Stockholm, where the fragmented environment and the importance of roofs in the island-dotted landscape determined his museum; in San Sebastián, where he understood that the Kursaal center could not simply act as an extension of the urban layout, but had to serve as an element that competed against and withstood the strength of the sea, as if it were the last rocks torn out of the mountainside; in Palma de Mallorca, where he reacted to the sight of a once beautiful landscape now spoiled by boldly reproducing original nature

Kursaal auditorium
and congress center,
San Sebastián, 1990–2000,
Moneo.

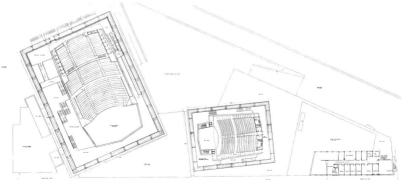

and building a mirror of water; in Madrid, where he solved the urban chaos and complexity of a modern train station program in Atocha by accumulating volumes and forms of different styles and turning disorder into variety; in the auditorium of Barcelona, on which he worked from 1987 to 1999, and in the airport of Seville, where he avoided competing with the technological image of flying machines.

Juan Navarro Baldeweg is another of the influential figures working from Madrid. In the conference center in Salamanca, he gave proof of his masterly skill in certain forms used: concrete domes and other weightless ceilings, suspended between cracks of light inside pure boxes; delicate material contrasts, which are the result of a labor of research that is always attractive to the onlooker. Navarro Baldeweg gave other signs of this light, airy architecture in the Villanueva de la Cañada cultural center of 1992 and in the Mahón Law Courts building of 1997.

Manuel de las Casas, Ignacio de las Casas, and Jaime Lorenzo designed huge housing complexes in which rigor prevailed as the dominant feature of the distribution and composition; but these architects were also delicate when the occasion so required, as in the case of the Castile-La Mancha Pavilion built for the Seville Expo. The constructional technique they used in this silent, neutral building involved mounting sections made up almost exclusively of two materials—steel and laminated wood—which gave rise to one of the most inherently modern pieces on the exhibition grounds. The argument is reinforced if, to these dismantling characteristics, we add the fiction of wood that acts as stone in the way it is cut or the abstract, almost white state it acquires inside.

Another architect working on the production of a limpid architecture is Mariano Bayón—he and Navarro Baldeweg can both be regarded as disciples of de la Sota—who has an extensive portfolio but is, nevertheless, less popular than the other architects mentioned above. In the head offices he built for Red Eléctrica, the Seville electricity company, he also worked with simple volumes, seductive materials, and light solutions.

As we have already pointed out, Víctor López Cotelo and Carlos Puente were de la Sota's most direct disciples, although in the Zaragoza library they leant more toward Scandinavian influences that distanced them from their mentor. It was almost as if, after seeing libraries like the ones designed by Asplund or Aalto, they thought this kind of environment better suited to guaranteeing public reading than any other. This assertion may be a little too categorical; not so the success of this work, which became totally absorbed in its own exotic interior atmosphere in a world set quite apart from the predominant brickwork of Zaragoza. From 1984 to 1993, the same architects worked on the rehabilitation of the Renaissance Casa de las Conchas (House of Shells) building in Salamanca for use as a library. This work seamlessly brought together the old and the new, fragmenting the layout and adapting each part to its position. The unity of the ensemble was preserved through an interpretation of the notions of cloister and silence that suit a library so well. Carlos Puente was also responsible for the Ciempozuelos cultural center built in 1996 and the Camarma cemetery completed in 1997. These works achieved a

Cultural center, Villanueva de la Cañada (Madrid), 1992–1997, Navarro Baldeweg.

Opposite page, from left to right and from top to bottom: Gaspar house, Zahora (Cádiz), 1990–1991, Campo Baeza.

Public Library of Aragón, Zaragoza, 1984–1989, López Cotelo / Puente / García.

Cultural center, Ciempozuelos (Madrid), 1994–1995, Puente.

Botanical Garden, Madrid, 1991–1993, Ángel Fernández Alba.

Office building on Plaza de las Once Colmenas, Tres Cantos (Madrid), 1990–1992, Andrés Perea.

lightness of appearance with no other apparent effort than an informed use of materials. It is significant that small towns in the province of Madrid appreciated the concept of modernity that this architecture displays.

Alberto Campo Baeza brings to a close, albeit temporarily, the list of architects who have followed in de la Sota's footsteps, although he also displays a strong affinity with Coderch, as witnessed in the state school and the Gaspar house in Cádiz, where the white purity of the interiors is a direct consequence of an asceticism sought through simplification. Within the Madrid school, Campo Baeza—an independent, almost solitary architect—stands out for a personal line and an easy style that few can lay claim to.

Together with the architects we have seen above, who came after Moneo and who followed on where de la Sota left off, there have been others who, with the same training and the same convictions, added to their architecture elements borrowed from other approaches. Ángel Fernández Alba, who has both early Nordic influences and a love of American pop styles, is a good example of this tendency. As a result of this approach, the constructional solutions he used in the greenhouse in Madrid's Botanical Garden—the glass "waterfalls"—are not as straightforward as they might have been and, in fact, seek an expressive richness in their crooked lines and points of encounter that makes them that much more complex.

Another example is Andrés Perea, who takes an expressionist line in his work. In his most recent designs, such as the office building in Tres Cantos,

Madrid, or the La Coruña electricity company building, he has demonstrated his skill at slashing a regular volume with narrow, wavy cracks, where walkways and stairs enveloped in glass and white reflecting sheets produce an effect of tense working efficiency. The spatiality and fluidity of these spaces reach their zenith in the parish church in Tres Cantos.

The oeuvre of Jerónimo Junquera and Estanislao Pérez Pita, who have also built huge social housing complexes, encompasses programs as wide-ranging as the construction of the Parla Town Hall or the restoration of the National Library. These architects, who might be described as eclectic due to their varied responses, display in their work a love of significance, power, and emphasis that differentiates them from the other architects mentioned above. In 1996, they completed the Caja Madrid office building and calculation center in Las Rozas, where the sheer size of the commission enabled them to deploy an image of power to their full satisfaction.

When Javier Vellés, a first-class watercolor artist, paints a landscape, he forgoes interpretations and metaphors; the froth of waves breaking on rocks is nothing more than water turned into spray. Similarly, when he designs a building, he uses a direct approach. When his studio, which he shares with María Casariego, Fabriciano Posada, and Mercedes Anadón,

Caja Madrid offices and calculation center, Las Rozas (Madrid), 1991–1995, Junquera / Pérez Pita.

Consolidation of the rock cliff face, Melilla, 1990–1995, Vellés / Casariego / Posada.

School of Social Sciences, University of Navarre, Pamplona, 1994–1996, Vicens / Ramos.

was given the task of restoring the chapel of San Isidro, they limited their work to literally reconstructing the original chapel—quite a feat in itself—without attempting to interpret or adapt or unashamedly reproduce the gilding, marbles, and imitation gold leaf of the baroque space as it used to be. Likewise, when he built the huge trade fair and exhibition hall in Jerez de la Frontera, he solved the problem of its large dimensions by resorting to the expressive sobriety of concrete and brick in an exercise in repetition. In Melilla, he built a 27-meter-high parabolic arch. The technique he used was totally contemporary and based on budgetary constraints, but its argument and nature were preclassical in tone. The commission to consolidate the rock cliff face seemed to become the work of creating a doorway to a mythological cavern. In the case of Vellés, drawing and painting continue to act as a vehicle for understanding and communication.

From the mid-nineties onward, the younger generations of Madrid architects mostly began to turn to architectures that interpreted modernity as a particular way of expressing new techniques and using new materials—although there have been a few exceptions, such as Burillo and Lorenzo, whom we shall look at later. This clear-cut line of architecture draws inspiration from other architects besides de la Sota. In addition to Carvajal and Cano Lasso, who have exerted an influence that is acknowledged in

Opposite page:
Trade fair and exhibition hall, Jerez de la Frontera (Cádiz), 1985–1992, Vellés / Casariego / Posada / Anadón / Soto.

Fine Arts wing of the Cáceres Museum, Cáceres, 1991, Aranguren / González Gallegos.

Los Zumacales sports center, Simancas (Valladolid), 1990–1991, Ábalos / Herreros.

Housing estate on the M-30 ring road, Madrid, 1989–1993, Ábalos / Herreros.

the works that follow, the living architect who has wielded the greatest influence on the work of this new generation is Navarro Baldeweg, whose excellent lessons are clearly reflected in the styles adopted by the Madrid architects who bring this section to a close.

In 1996, Ignacio Vicens and Antonio Ramos completed the School of Social Sciences in Pamplona. Smooth, clean concrete surfaces were used to shape the emphatic abstract parallelepipeds on the outside and white prismatic cavities inside, just as the original design had set out. In the office building on Calle Alcalá Galiano in Madrid, Enrique Álvarez Sala, Carlos Rubio Carvajal, and César Ruiz Larrea demonstrated their skill at converting an overly simple and elementary program into a sequence of piled-up spaces suggesting transparent industriousness. The sports center built in San Sebastián de los Reyes in 1995 by Sol Madridejos and Juan Carlos Sancho is another example of fine architecture in which pure volumes and white lights are used to brilliant effect.

The modern tension produced in the observer by materials such as smooth or molded steel sheets and glass is not the only effect that interests Iñaki Ábalos and Juan Herreros. Their predilection for materials associated with the most modern techniques and clean, distinct lines bears witness to an

interest in an architecture rooted in Central Europe that has a long tradition in Madrid. In their recent projects, including the Simancas sports center in Valladolid, and the RENFE offices and the police headquarters building in Madrid, the abstraction of the materials seems to steer them into a direct relationship with the air, light, and sky, ignoring the clumsier environment that surrounds them: nature is made amorphous by the hand of man. In a similar vein, the designs drawn up by Mateo Corrales and Enrique Becerril give rise to neat, clear-cut volumes that defy gravity: distinct lines and planes that form serenely elegant spaces.

In their restoration of the Cáceres museum, María José Aranguren and José González Gallegos took an analytical and neoplastic approach to the planes that they put together by following constructional evidence. The outcome is a sober, serious, and effective architecture.

In the Garay factory in Oñate, Guipúzcoa, Beatriz Matos and Alberto Martínez Castillo successfully applied a perspicacious, precise understanding of the nature of materials, such as folded steel sheets, to turn a conventional industrial roofing scheme into a geometrical work made up of beautiful, stern volumes. The factory is thus sheltered by a shining curve that looks quite natural in the green, snowy landscape of Guipúzcoa.

A totally different landscape, one characterized by the geometrical pattern formed by the olive groves of Jaén, provided the backdrop for the prison designed by Juan Mera, Jesús San Vicente, and Blanca Lleó, made up of pavilions and closed courtyards drawn up on orthogonal lines and enclosed by a citadel-like wall. Together with Javier Maroto, Blanca Lleó won the competition for the design of the Lorca Town Hall, for which she fashioned a powerfully spatial architecture through an imaginative and precise handling of rooms, stairs, or ceilings and tense and tactile materials. The same understanding of the role played by interior spaces and their parts—the black marble wall that works as a mirror is an example—can be seen in the rehabilitation of the Law Courts in Soria undertaken by Javier Maroto, Ricardo Antón, María Fraile, and Mariano Magister. In the houses and facilities designed together with Álvaro Soto, Maroto has clearly shown his predilection for a style achieved with sophisticated sensitivity and irony, as witnessed by a series of minor works, including the ice rink in Majadahonda, Madrid, completed in 1996. The solution to the problem of how to keep a cool atmosphere in the ice rink led to a simple architecture made of laminated sheets and glass that produces light, airy spaces perfectly in keeping with the concerns of the time.

The Castilian city of Zamora, which features several examples of the best modern architecture produced in Spain over recent years, saw the completion of the trade fair grounds in 1997, the winning entry in a competition designed by María Fraile and Javier Revillo. In this austere setting, the architects erected a straightforward, neat glass box that rises over the plowed fields with a transparent air that replicates the mists that hang over the Duero River. Emilio Tuñón and Luis Moreno Mansilla provided a counterpoint to its neomodern style—a unanimous inclination among young Madrid architects—with their Archaeological Museum in Zamora, completed in 1996, a work characterized by powerful yet constrained forms. Into a plot closed off by a set of buildings and a variety of topographical accidents they inserted a rectangular ground plan that is highly effective when judged against the stark volume of the nearby church. The *promenades architecturales*, overhead lights, and double heights typical of modern architecture were used here with the smooth fluency of something long known. The building was sensitively closed off by compact ashlar walls that skillfully define its scale, and crowned by a flat roof whose geometric precision remains a low-key feature when seen from the higher parts of the city and directs the gaze of the observer toward the river and the Castilian horizon.

Also outside Madrid, Federico Soriano and Dolores Palacios won the competition for the Bilbao congress and music hall with a "ghost ship" design executed from 1994 to 2000. The architects used this Wagnerian image and the city's nostalgia for its former days of naval glory to liken attendance at the opera to a journey on board a boat.

Although the works we have just reviewed satisfy the traditional conditions of austerity that Madrid's geographical and cultural environment still inspires, they are, nonetheless, extremely varied. This variety, which Madrid shares with other cities like Barcelona, is evidenced in the works of the most recent internationalized generations. One name that immedi-

Ice rink, Majadahonda (Madrid), 1995–1996, Soto / Maroto.

Zamora Museum, 1989–1995, Moreno Mansilla / Tuñón.

Zamora Trade Fair grounds, 1993–1996, Fraile / Revillo.

ately comes to mind as an example of this situation is Alejandro Zaera, who, though he cannot be regarded as being from Madrid as far as home and cultural influences are concerned, produces designs that are certainly in tune with the interests of its younger architects and may even represent them better than anyone else.

Having looked at the buildings that have been influential for their style, we can proceed to the works that have been produced as a direct outcome of the city's requirements. In Madrid, a city that has been absorbing immigrants since the Civil War, a great deal of experience has been built up in the construction of social housing. As some critics have pointed out, this is perhaps the most important collective contribution made to this field in recent years.[57] The success of these works lies in a series of easily identifiable characteristics and circumstances. The first of these concerns the extensive contemporary appraisal of the works built by Madrid architects back in the fifties. Organizations such as the Regiones Devastadas (Devastated Regions), the Instituto Nacional de Colonización (National Settlement Institute), or the Instituto Nacional de la Vivienda (National Housing Institute)—names that take us back to the times of Franco—commissioned designs from the likes of Sáenz de Oiza and Romany, Ferrán and Mangada, Vázquez de Castro and Íñiguez de Onzoño, and a long list of other professionals who were strongly committed to the idea of architecture as a social service. All of these architects took up the rationalist experience of the prewar period—which had never reached Spain and consequently had a certain novelty value—to erect their houses along the lines of those exemplary models. Thus, when architectural thought in the rest of Europe was becoming more sophisticated in its quest for new experiences, social housing architecture in Spain remained, or rather moved into, modern classicism. Proof of this can be found in the housing estate in Entrevías in which Sáenz de Oiza and Romany developed J. J. P. Oud's ideas of minimal dimension.

Even before the architects of the generations between Manuel de las Casas and Javier Frechilla could begin to guess how much work awaited them in this field, they were fascinated by the idea of social housing (they still remember interminable slide sessions of their travels through Holland, attired in jeans and clogs). And even before Aldo Rossi and Rafael Moneo came along to talk about this particular typology, their repeated viewing of the Viennese *Höfe*, the German *Siedlungen*, or the Fuencarral or Caño Roto experiences in Spain had already instilled in them an idea of what could be obtained from a 12-meter-deep plot, from an H-shaped ground plan or a block. They had sharpened their weapons for a battle that intuition told them was around the corner and that they were eager to fight.

It worked to their advantage that the social service approach that shaped their obsessions, in an era when it was shameful to talk about architecture as art, led them to forgo any concern for composition of facades, which were called vertical outside walls, and to focus their efforts on strict distributions and tight budgets. The result was an architecture that almost solely and exclusively used brick in the local building tradition, the most tested types, and a formal soberness that was restful to look at and effective in a totally chaotic periphery. Indeed, this was the weakness that

Passenger terminal,
Yokohama port (Japan),
1995–2000,
Zaera / Moussavi.

Housing in Madrid Sur,
Madrid, 1992–1994,
Martínez Lapeña / Torres Tur.

Euskalduna congress hall
and music center,
Bilbao, 1994–2000,
Soriano / Palacios Díaz.

Opposite page:
Promenade and aquarium,
Vilagarcía de Arousa
(Pontevedra), 1983–1987,
Portela.

reared its head most frequently: well-designed houses were erected over chaotic and often dense urban layouts.

All of the above can still be seen in the works built by the younger generation of Madrid architects. The housing estate on the M-30 ring road designed by Ábalos and Herreros, or the one built by Jesús Hernández Matamoros and Mateo Corrales, or the work produced by the studio made up of Areán, Casariego, and Vaquero, which we will be looking at over the next few pages, are all good examples.

The completely new neighborhood of Valdebernardo must be singled out as one of the largest-scale operations of recent years. Designed by José María Ezquiaga and his collaborators using a repetitive system of closed blocks on a grid layout, it was completed in 1997. This work enabled the architects to experiment with a variety of contrasting solutions: strict ground plans were offset with complex solutions like duplex apartments, dry volumes or soft facades. In stark contrast to this sober repertoire stands the solution adopted by Torres Tur and Martínez Lapeña in their design for the residential estate of San José, which was completed the year before. This estate displays a geometry of ordered planes set in a helicoidal pattern, an unprejudiced composition that highlights the Mediterranean roots of its architects. The result is an architecture that is formally consistent with a long building tradition and has quite rightly been dubbed "eclectic rationalism" by Antón Capitel. It displays an attitude toward the periphery that is possibly the most strictly Madrid-based input of this period but that has been brilliantly adopted in other cities since.

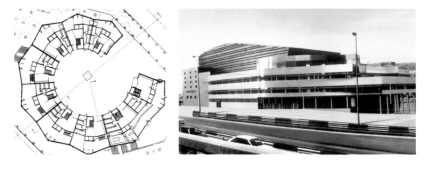

At a time when all the signs seemed to indicate that Spain had been left exhausted by the efforts made in Barcelona and Seville in 1992 and was quite incapable of tackling anything else for some time, Galicia appeared on the scene. Once again, as if he were trying to demonstrate the essential truth of the division of time in the holy year and the earthly power of his call, St. James the Apostle opened the roads to Galicia. Pilgrims made their way to Santiago de Compostela and brought back pictures and news of the new buildings dotting the landscape. Exhibitions and journals regaled us with details of "Galicia in the holy year." Critics would like us to think that it marked the start of a new golden age, locating the architecture that is currently being built in the region within movements or trends that point to the foundations of a school. They agree on who the big names are, on Portela's challenge and on Gallego's response.[58] The patently obvious personal approach of these two architects gives serious weight to this dichotomy, but critics actually get much closer to the mark when they pull the dichotomy apart, revealing the common roots and results of their architecture, and compare and contrast these with the third approach adopted by the youngest architects of the region who have turned away from parochial inspiration in order to create more international forms. This same approach can also be detected in Gallego's most recent works.

Before proceeding with this attempt to establish a Galician school, it would be convenient to clarify the question of these personal architectures and the importance attributed to the International Seminar organized by the Tendenza in Santiago de Compostela in 1976—an importance that was real enough, given the intense relationship between architecture and place described by Rossi in his writings, a message that Galician nationalist sentiment understood perfectly. The fact that it was illustrated with pictures of their own region—the Poor Clares—seemed to endorse the impression that the author's words were specifically intended for a Galician audience. In Santiago de Compostela, in 1976, Baltar, Gallego, Portela, and others felt sure that Rossi's message was targeted at them. Like other architects in other regions within Spain, they went on to build some of the best interpretations of the Tendenza culture, as described in previous chapters. In the early nineties, however, the revival of other influences such as the Galician culture of Alejandro de la Sota and the irresistible proximity of Alvaro Siza have to be stressed. This signifies a return to the dominant culture of the modern movement in the twentieth century.

But let us first look at the architects themselves. César Portela's main virtue is the personal conviction and continuity that allow one to say that he has achieved his own style. Everyone acknowledges his work. He, more than anyone else, has revived the use of granite, the house made up of elementary volumes, the pavilions and shoreline platforms that produce, with rhythmic monotony, fine works like the aquarium in Vilagarcía de Arousa, or the Azuma Bridge in Japan.

Gallego's most ambitious and successful work is probably the Museum of Fine Arts in La Coruña, in which lights, distances, and wisely chosen materials take their place among the historical remains with the gentle and consciously didactic effectiveness that the brief required. A balanced approach and a clear geographical awareness enable this architect always to tailor his solutions to the traditions and techniques used.

Speaking of materials, this seems the right time to point out that this is one of the most unifying aspects of contemporary Galician architecture. The important role played by granite in Portela's work was mentioned earlier; something similar might be said about his use of glass in bay windows and skylights and about his predilection for brightly colored frames. Granite and glass, used in different ways, are materials that underscore the nature of this region, its quarries and its climate. These materials, which reappear in all the works studied here, are used by the architects as a safe bet rather than as an obligation. Compositional and constructional solutions involving the use of granite and glass in stark volumes are highly effective in Galicia's gentle and humid landscape. They are used in abundance in works such as the sports centers designed by Pedro Llano and Baltar, Bartolomé and Almuíña, in the School of Administration built by Carlos Meijide or the civic center in Burela designed by Xosé Manuel Casabella. Iago Seara's work is also in the same vein. In the rehabilitation of the Valedor do Pobo headquarters in Santiago de Compostela, he transferred to the interiors the strategy of volumes and materials described above, in order to conjure up an atmosphere of warm, solid calmness with granites, woods, and lights that fitted the function quite aptly

In the Fisheries Training School in Arousa designed by Pascuala Campos, using the classical university cloister model that suited the occasion, the building's uses were distributed with an almost innocent direct effectiveness and the whole enveloped in a powerful play of smooth-walled volumes built with heavy through stone. The apertures punctuate the walls with such easy fluency that the heavy or monotonous impact of the use of stone is avoided. The building radiates power and lightness, nimbleness and discipline at one and the same time. It is in this ability to combine contradictory values that the true excellence of the design lies.

In contrast with what critics see as the promising unanimity of the lines described above, José Bar Boo—an architect who precedes all of the professionals mentioned above—continued to fly the flag of an expressionism, also very Galician, in the new Law Courts built in La Coruña. Glass and stone are still present, but here they are used to enclose interiors with organic circulation patterns, sustained by columns like totem poles.

Other architects have moved in the sphere of a different modernity, one that is more neomodern than living tradition. They have not differed from the architects mentioned above in their approach to materials or their philosophy of light. In fact, there is a gentle continuity between the architects we are going to mention now and others like Gallego or Seara. However, they do display a desire to move in a direction that draws less on the local background for inspiration, perhaps claiming that the interests and specific problems of architecture do not necessarily have to be affected by vernacular tradition, particularly since nowadays history and tradition are authentically universal. Such is the case of Noguerol, Blanco,

School of Philology, Santiago de Compostela (La Coruña), 1988–1991, Noguerol / Díez.

Museum of Fine Arts, La Coruña, 1988–1995, Gallego.

School of Economics, Vigo (Pontevedra), 1989–1995, Penela.

Fisheries Training School, Vilagarcía de Arousa (Pontevedra), 1990–1992, Pascuala Campos.

and Irisarri. In the School of Philology in Santiago de Compostela, Alberto Noguerol and Pilar Díez opened up the cloister ground plan—which Pascuala Campos closed with such discipline—and shifted the interior planes and centers of the curved roofing. The result is an optimistic, self-assured architecture around which the users should feel eager to move. Similar feelings are prompted by the School of Economics in Vigo, designed by Alfonso Penela, where equivalent patterns and strategies were used to open up the building. In this case, the location of the building in a less developed area led to an even looser composition in which the successful roofing scheme plays a starring role. The health center in Villamarín, Orense, by Jesús Irisarri is an appropriate choice to bring this brilliant chapter of recent Galician architecture to a close. Here, a vocabulary of granite outer walls and white inner walls, soft skylights and gentle roofs, encloses the relaxed spaces of a small-scale program in an ancient setting.

Celestino García Braña took full advantage of the opportunity offered by the hostels for pilgrims set up for the Jacobean holy year to build a number

of small works that fit into the gentle Galician topography with exquisite modesty. In Tricastela, the two pavilions of bedrooms, whose forms make no attempt to hide their modern leanings, link up with the surrounding buildings through the use of one material, slate, and with the site by means of well-judged distances. In 1993, in Ribadixo, Melide (La Coruña), the wood used for structures and walls and the stone used for floors and pathways are the means of linking the building with the environment.

While the works we have examined so far all feature the same sweet values related to the region and its traditions, regardless of their use, the port of Vigo shows the industrial face of Galicia. As a result of the competition held in 1993 and the effective work undertaken by the politician Francisco López, Vigo is now solving some of its port's urban problems with an architecture spearheaded by the Seville architect Guillermo Vázquez Consuegra.

The Basque country, a region with an architectural tradition as rich as it is long, was hit harder than most by the industrial and economic recession. It was only through the institutional agreements reached in the mid-nineties that Bilbao received the impetus needed for infrastructure and development operations of the kind seen in cities like Seville or Barcelona and regions like Galicia under the aegis of commemorative events.

Brilliant proof of the above are the two works built in Bilbao by foreign architects: the Museum of Contemporary Art erected by the Basque regional government in collaboration with the Guggenheim, following a design by the California architect Frank Gehry, and the Metro underground system drawn up by the British architect Norman Foster. The Guggenheim Museum—the most powerful and ambitious work undertaken by Gehry to date—is a magnificent design that has been able to interpret the place where it is sited and to endow this obsolete industrial section of the estuary, which is still full of formal strength, with renewed urban meaning. The project ignored social considerations and rules on territorial sharing out of public investment and stuck to its role as a monument as its only functional justification. In this sense it is an old-fashioned piece of architecture where the architect freely designed a monumental building for a public authority that wanted to shine. Paradoxically, the Guggenheim will end up being the great Spanish work for the twenty-first century. In contrast to the formal heights reached by the museum, the underground is a restrained work strictly tailored to its purpose.

The vitality of Navarre and the Basque country can also be seen in countless small-scale works that meet social needs, such as local health centers. A close look at the architecture found in these parts of Spain confirms a tendency that is visible in all Spanish architecture of this period: the decisive victory in the early nineties of that trend known as neomodern, over all others—disciplinary or postdisciplinary—that may have had their chance of success at an earlier moment in time, as we have seen in previous chapters. In Pamplona and San Sebastián, the studios that still cling tenaciously to concepts like type and discipline qualify or enrich their approach without betraying it.

Recreation of the seafront, Vigo (Pontevedra), begun 1997, Vázquez Consuegra.

In his building for the School of Architecture in San Sebastián, Miguel Garay produced a highly "divided" work in which the different parts, designed separately according to the architect's "traditional style," were put together by a process of addition in line with a much more up-to-date idea. In their most recent works, such as the changing rooms in the Pamplona swimming club, Manuel Íñiguez and Alberto Ustarroz enlivened their architecture with the relaxed import of foreign themes: the Top-Kapi kitchens come to mind in this case. What defines this work is not the move toward more "modern" positions but the classicist interpretation of architecture that has resulted in the most profound and, at the same time, the lightest work of all their oeuvre.

An architect who once had much in common with the Basques mentioned above but has since grown apart from them is José Ignacio Linazasoro. The distance separating them is not merely a question of geography—Linazasoro lectures in Madrid, whereas Garay, Íñiguez, and Ustarroz do so in San Sebastián—but of attitude. This distance is an interesting way of illustrating the question of style and manner raised above. The value of the San Sebastián professors lies in their loyalty to a manner of understanding architecture that is didactic and rigorous, all the more necessary today given that it is not at all frequent. In their case, style is displayed as a faithfulness to a manner of undertaking architecture. In the case of Linazasoro, however, style is defined by a lack of faithfulness to any specific manner. His approaches could be described in much the same terms as those of painters, by dividing his output into eras or periods: hence his Tendenza period, his disciplinary period and, currently, his neomodern period. The same style, however, runs through all of his work, as reflected by an unvarying attitude toward architecture. That is why the UNED Open University lacks the experimental touch that tends to characterize the neomodern approach, a category in which we could not classify this work. The modern elements that appear in its design—canopies, *fenêtres en longueur*, slender piles, and a rigorous, sensible approach—have the same style as the windows and roofs of his Mendigorría buildings, for instance. Both in the library, almost a perfect cube, and in the functional comblike ground plan of the university office building, the distributive order is governed by knowledge and discipline.

In the next generations of Basque architects it seems that the most common approach to architecture is the modern, with personal variations. Roberto Ercilla has already built up an extensive portfolio of work from his studio in Vitoria. The powerful presence of the new Internal Revenue headquarters built in collaboration with Miguel Ángel Campo and José Luis Catón is particularly outstanding. Its solid image seems at once to be inspired by and guarantor of its function. Ercilla and Campo were also responsible for the Armentia house, which underscores its modern, solid approach by flaunting a series of tastefully executed concrete and iron elements. Javier Mozas takes a more neoplastic approach to his work, and both his building for Azol-Gas and the Vitoria sports center, which he built with Pablo López Lacalle, Fernando Gallego, and Iñaki Aristondo, prove his ability to deal confidently with industrial images.

Patxi Mangado's work also keeps to this modern approach to architecture, as witnessed by the Marco Real wineries in Olite, Navarre, built in 1991, where he worked with subtle cleanness to particular effect. In 1990, in the Iturrama Health Center in Pamplona, he collaborated with Alfonso Alzugaray and Maite Apezteguía in the construction of a small volume that holds its own against much bigger buildings owing to its precision. Around 1997, with works like the Pamplona industrial building, where he fluently wielded dominant formal resources and materials, or the prizewinning Zuasti Golf Club, he demonstrated a precocious maturity.

In the Azpilagaña Health Center, in Pamplona, Jesús Leache and Eduardo de Miguel skillfully overcame the almost insurmountable difficulty of building a health center on a tiny plot between high, densely populated blocks of flats. They did so by reducing the volume, placing part of the program in the basement and enveloping the visible part in a simple, well-built brick wall. The resulting small volume receives light from the courtyards that perforate it as controlled, private spaces.

Azpilagaña health center, Pamplona, 1989–1993, De Miguel / Leache.

Pamplona swimming club, 1992–1993, Íñiguez / Ustarroz.

Azol-Gas office and warehouse building, Vitoria, 1992–1993, Mozas.

Zuasti Golf Club, Zuasti (Navarre), 1993–1995, Mangado.

The work done in the area of health facilities in Navarre is quite notable. To the examples already mentioned we should add the health center in Olite. Here, Fernando Tabuenca and Ignacio San Juan carried out a brilliant exercise in urban solutions and environmental answers without forgoing modern, relaxed spaces with a healthy look and feel. These architects belong to a modernity that is not the one practiced by the neomodern architects—who above all stick close to what was called the orthodoxy of the modern movement. Instead, they are part of the much wider modernity interpreted by Rafael Moneo, in whose studio Tabuenca worked earlier in his career.

The Autonomous Community of Valencia, a Mediterranean region with an ancient culture and a dynamic business environment, has much to offer in different artistic fields such as music, its composers embracing the whole spectrum from minimal to baroque styles and covering the most advanced positions in Spain. Nonetheless, it has never managed to stand out in the field of architecture. The city of Valencia, the region's capital, does not lead the way in architecture as happens in other regions. What is the reason for this dispersion? Could it be that this society, so efficient in business matters, disdains making an effort when it comes to its physical environment? Its School of Architecture, a contemporary of others that have already become consolidated, offers a panorama of division and fragmentation that prevents it from ideologically spearheading the quest for its own identity. The works illustrated below demonstrate, in my view, a dormant power. If, as I believe, a different line of thought can only emerge from the contradictions entailed by the hybrid nature of its architecture and their resolution, a line of thought that is capable of producing works with a new look and feel to them, Valencia's architecture and culture in general must be standing on the threshold of a very different proposition. With this in mind, some initiatives under way will only assume their full significance when completed. Apart from the slow-moving, now rather old project to recover the channel of the Turia River, the Nou University campus and the Sagunto ensemble should also be mentioned here.

In works built during the past decade, three different approaches can be distinguished in the region of Valencia. To simplify matters, we could describe them as being those taken by the technical architects, the essentialist architects, and the disciplinary architects. As representative of the technical architects, we can mention the works designed by José María Lozano, Jorge Bosch, and José Luis Gisbert, and those by Miguel Ángel Campo and María Jesús Rodríguez. The Technological Institute in Paterna,

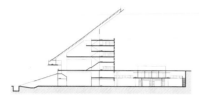

Madrid Autonomous Community sports stadium (section and partial view), Madrid, 1989–1994, Cruz / Ortiz.

Santo Domingo subsidized housing estate, Alicante, 1991–1992, Dolores Alonso.

Opposite page: UNED Library, Open University (partial view and axonometric drawing), Ciudad Universitaria, Madrid, 1989–1994, Linazasoro.

Regional government building, Alicante, 1992–1996, García-Solera Vera / Payá.

designed and built by the first of these teams, displays a confidence and mastery of materials: glass, folded plates, metal profiles, continuous pavings, and "functionalist" distributions and spatial arrangements are consistent with the name of the building they constructed. The same goes for the sports center built by Campo and Rodríguez in Villarreal. Both works bear a Nordic stamp, a special concern for industrial culture. The Inelcom plant in Jativa was built in 1995. By running through the whole machinist repertoire of folded plates, slender-profile stairs, and abstractly composed facades, Carmelo Gradolí, Luis Francisco Herrero, and Arturo Sanz managed to create a building that is far from boring.

The essentialist architects, who admit to the architectural influence of de la Sota, Cabrero, Siza, or Coderch, form a compact group in Alicante. Although Carmen Rivera, Javier García-Solera, and Dolores Alonso had previously only shown their style in small works—health centers or detached houses—Alonso recently designed a work that adds scale and power to her portfolio. The double brick blocks of the Santo Domingo subsidized housing estate rise over a number of rural constructions with a neat mass that is qualified on the outside by strokes of horizontal window bands.

The disciplinary line goes back further in Valencia. We already saw it when looking at the work of Salvadores and Portaceli, among others. Portaceli, who had been refining his architecture in large works and housing estates, was given the most significant opportunity of his career with the commission to rehabilitate the Roman theater of Sagunto, a project on which he worked in collaboration with Giorgio Grassi. Only the talent of these two architects, a precise understanding of the relationship between history and architecture (based to a certain extent on the nonhistorical nature of architecture), and the architect-developer's capacity for suffering made this work possible. Throughout 1992 and 1993, the Sagunto theater was plunged into a controversy whose positive side was that it forced the architects to reflect—under extreme conditions—on certain fundamental aspects of their work. Today, this theater, the only ancient theater with a roofed stage, transports us back to the Roman world in a way that no other arena does, making it in a way the most Roman theater of them all.

The office building for the regional railway authority was built in 1996 by Carlos Salvadores. The building's colors, derived from intense red brick surfaces and white planes, reinforce the interpretation of a ground plan that also divides up the program into two different uses: administrative

Rehabilitation
of the Roman theater,
Sagunto (Valencia),
1985–1993,
Grassi / Portaceli.

offices and management modules. The building takes advantage of this distinction and bases its composition on the contrast between straight and curved lines, some of which venture into areas that would have been classified as organicist some years earlier.

Distant and secure in his Swiss studio and in demand the world over, Santiago Calatrava continued to produce white structures with bone references in Spain. He created whale bellies in the Alcoy subsoil, Jurassic skeletons in the bridges he designed for Bilbao, Valencia, or Barcelona, bridges that were on occasion rather excessive, like the ones in Seville (see page 132) or Mérida (where he spanned a river forded by livestock and people). Whatever the case, he always had extraordinary success among the administrations. Tenerife is a case in point, where he began by setting up a shell to house the municipal trade fair grounds and continued as a favorite architect called on for occasions of note.

The future course of the undoubtedly important transformation wrought on Spain's geography by the new political organization of the state is a matter for geopolitical science. The territorial divisions, the relationship between cities and their areas of influence, and even the distances in time are already unquestionably very different from those of pre-eighties Spain. The classification into center and periphery, so useful to explain architecture in the first pages of this book, is no longer valid. Today, as we have seen, powerful, vital cities and regions are found in what was previously the long-suffering and distant periphery. On the other hand, some of the areas of the country with a strong cultural tradition, whether physically far from or near to the center, are far removed from the hustle and bustle of publications and information circuits. These are what we could call the remote or isolated regions.

Extremadura and the two Castiles have become the poorest regions, owing to the gap left by emigrating professionals. Good builders, for instance, have moved to the big cities in search of better wages, leaving their home region with no one to ply the trade. The ancient, popular architecture that needed little money but much skill is no longer possible. The nursery school built in Badajoz by Julián Prieto takes constructive modesty to its very limits and shows how white enclosing walls built at the right height and gentle sloping roofs can envelop the simple spaces needed by children. Also in Badajoz, Begoña Galeano built a small volume for the Regional Department of Agriculture whose image was enhanced through the skillful use of limes and indigos. Jorge López Álvarez and Rodolfo

Open block of
64 subsidized apartments,
Badajoz, 1987–1992,
Carrasco López / López
Álvarez / Prieto Fernández.

Nursery school,
Badajoz, 1986–1989,
Prieto Fernández.

Carrasco worked with the architects mentioned above and with Elíseo Pérez Álvarez on an open block of 64 subsidized apartments where they demonstrated an unsurpassed ability to understand the conditions of the place and to improve on them with a cheerful, varied architecture. In 1996, Justo García completed the provincial offices of the INEM (National Employment Institute) in Cáceres. The functional rooms inside, delimited by the pure and simple planes of materials that exhibit their texture and color (wood and glass, blacks and blues), are all contained in a composition of simple prisms. Flat facades share out their surfaces between glass and stone, following a strict modulation punctuated from time to time by the odd metallic sparkle.

The architect from Extremadura with the most solid career today is probably Gerardo Ayala, who obeyed the law of poverty and emigrated from his home region to build elsewhere. We have already seen his design for the Central Theater in Seville. His studio also drew up the design for the Spanish Television Center in Andalusia, constructed in Seville between 1990 and 1993. The sober volumes of this building display an excellent understanding of de la Sota's approach to architecture.

In the olden days, Castile was one of the most populated regions in Spain. Today, it is a half-empty land. In the hard-wearing inland areas, it seems that the most likely architecture is always one of simple volumes, enclosing walls, whitewashed surfaces, and strict apertures. This is how Gabriel Gallegos and Juan Carlos Sanz see it. Their tiny school unit in Pozal de Gallinas, Valladolid, was a more than worthy attempt to express this. In Alcázar de San Juan, where bright indigos are traditionally used to paint outer doors and other rural carpentry and powerful whitewashed walls enclose buildings, Antonio Areán, Juan Casariego, and José Ángel Vaquero turned the relationship on its head to solve a facade of small dimensions with an abstract composition of apertures and strong colors. Together with Juan Vicente, the same architects employed similar arguments in the Guijuelo sports center, where they used earthy structural materials (now brick) in contrast to white detailing, and precise constructional elements like windows, corners, and handrails.

Asturias and Cantabria, two regions located between the Cantabrian mountains and the sea, share the same geography, climate, and recession, although the economic base of Asturias is industry and mining while that of Cantabria is livestock raising and services. This perhaps shows through in the architecture built in the two regions. The regions' status as far from the country's cultural centers is accepted as a fact of life, and the architecture built, of a modern kind, takes into account the wet climate that is such an important determining factor. Let us take a look at a few examples. For the Asturias Regional Treasury Department, brothers Manuel and Enrique Hernández Sande and Enrique Perea built a powerful building on the basis of the winning design in a competition. It is the already classic office-landscape building that envelops a functional distribution in stone and steel clothing—the materials thought to be the most fitting to denote an official building. In 1992, in Meruelo, Santander, Pedro Arbea built a small health center. Formally restrained, its distribution is direct and effective and its choice of materials accurate. Sandstone and brick contrast

with white walls and ceilings, creating a simple, double-height interior in which columns lined with gresite show their graceful proportions.

Despite its small size and apparently marginal position, Murcia is a region that often produces a surprising architecture. Very rarely does the visitor to any city receive such a striking impression as the one produced in Alcantarilla by the blocks of 85 apartments built by Enrique Carbonell, Vicente Martínez Gadea, Antonio Álvarez, and Miguel Moreno. Two powerful half-red, half-white cubes dotted with an apparently disorderly sequence of windows of different shapes and sizes are arranged on either side of an arcaded square. Each solid parallelepiped volume encloses an irregular courtyard, the result of broken geometries, behind a smooth surface. The same geometric design governs stairs, elevators, corridors, and apartments, of which there is an endless variety of types. All of them are of a good, indeed a very good, standard, offering a variety and wealth of spaces that is difficult to achieve in subsidized housing.

In 1989, José María Torres Nadal drew up the design for the state library in Murcia, which was completed six years later. The building solved the basic requirements of the program with functional effectiveness: movement routes, extensive areas for reading, and rigorous lighting. Once again, as in so many famous libraries, light was the driving force behind the architecture. This time, faced with the need to perforate successive slabs to introduce light from the top to the bottom level, the architect came up with a peculiar skylight solution based on the use of elements that he called "urns" to channel and reflect light through the different stories. The design, which involved an extremely rigorous and arduous research exercise, shows surprising results on the outside, where a chromatic interplay of porticos was resolutely superimposed over a simple volume.

Paradoxically, although the region of Aragon has always held a central position within Spain, it is now isolated, in the middle of a no-man's land between the periphery of Barcelona and Madrid, emptied by the emigra-

Regional Treasury
Department,
Oviedo, 1989–1992,
M. Hernández Sande /
E. Hernández Sande /
Perea Caveda.

State library,
Murcia, 1988–1994,
Torres Nadal.

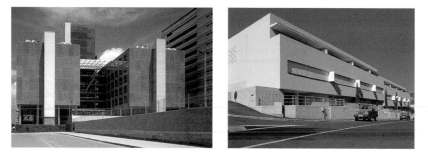

Regional government
building,
Las Palmas de Gran Canaria,
1990–1997,
González García.

Social housing block,
La Laguna (Tenerife), 1988,
Sosa / Gutiérrez.

tion of its inhabitants to the big cities. In the School of Health Sciences in
Zaragoza, Basilio Tobías performed the task in hand with constructional
restraint and an understanding both of the district of the city where the
building is located and of the functional needs of a medical building.
Brown brick—a noble material rooted in local tradition—and well-cast
concrete, mainly used for the canopies, enclose rooms where modern
resources such as double-height spaces or sloping ceilings are aptly used.
Also in Zaragoza, the adaptation of the Aljafería palace, one of the
crowning glories of Spanish-Islamic architecture, for use as the regional
parliament of Aragon was a risk-filled, courageous exercise accomplished
by Mariano Pemán Gavín and Luis Franco Lahoz with a shrewd sense of
the relationship between old and new based on the approach proposed
by the master Carlo Scarpa, but in a starker, harder version. Two other
architects who are as much from Aragon as they are from Madrid also
work along the same lines. We have already seen works by Luis Burillo
and Jaime Lorenzo earlier on in this book. Here they reappear with the
Latorre Theater, where they used the textures of the materials, light, and
color to particular effect.

With a cultural personality very much marked by their status as a
Mediterranean archipelago through which different civilizations have
passed, the Balearic Islands have experienced a process of intense
construction prompted by tourism. Among a series of excessive and
abusive works, a few high-quality pieces by architects Coderch, Sáenz
de Oiza, and Moneo have brightened the architectural landscape. At
present, enhanced quality control is making an impact on large-scale
public works such as the restoration of the city walls in Palma de Mallorca
and a number of works by young architects, such as the Son Ferriol
school.

Two architects who have already appeared in connection with Barcelona—Elías Torres, an architect from Ibiza, and José Antonio Martínez
Lapeña—have built works in the Balearic Islands marked by deep-seated
local inspiration and quality. At the foot of the hefty buttresses of the
cathedral in Palma de Mallorca, under the gaze of Gaudí and Jujol, they
restored the old walls with walkways and gardens. With a diversity of
elements—concrete blocks for the pavements, spur stones and stone wells,
pergolas, awnings, and benches—they have built up wide pathways that
present rich wall and floor textures and play with the air that fills the sails,
its shadows, lights, and colors. Climbing plants and palm trees were
planted in the garden. Rather than cramping the style of the architects,
the imposing cathedral structure sparked off their fantasy.

Maritime jet-foil station,
Santa Cruz de Tenerife,
1986–1991,
Martínez / Pérez Amaral /
Corona.

Industrial premises,
Arico, Poris de Abona,
Tenerife, 1988–1991,
García Barba.

Antonio Forteza and Francisco Pizá erected a school in Son Ferriol, Palma de Mallorca, with a series of ceilings and embankments. The ground was molded into planes that were arranged into successive heights, leaving the classrooms and other multipurpose spaces under them, setting up flowing movement in one direction that takes us from one to the other, up and down ramps or stairs, comprising diverse alternative routes to walk through and over the school. The different areas were closed off with multiple forms and conventional materials arranged in safe constructional solutions with a modern air about them.

In Ca les Munares, Mercé Berengué and Miguel Roldán built an extremely delicate ensemble of houses. The structure was designed along perfect, suitable orthogonal lines atop which the walls were arranged following a different orthogonal pattern. This use of varying orthogonal designs created an elegant work that blends the ancient and the modern.

In 1996, Salvador Roig and Javier Pallejá completed a suite of dwellings in Ibiza. The ensemble was divided up into two blocks due to the shape and topography of the plot. In the upper part, a small tower was tailored to the slope, its volume toned down through gentle planes. The lower corpus, built above the swimming pool, was made up of a row of two-story houses. The use of a nonorthogonal geometric pattern ensures that the right amount of light reaches the whitewashed houses and divides the volume, adapting it to the place in an imaginative fashion that does not draw on clichés.

We have chosen to bring this review of the isolated regions to an end with the Canary Islands not simply because, geographically speaking, they are the farthest away from the mainland center. The truth is that the infinite wealth of landscapes that differ from island to island and from valley to valley on each island, or perhaps the status of the islands' ports as stopover points on maritime routes between all continents, have given rise to a very particular kind of architecture in the Canary Islands.

Now that we have reached this point, it is easy to conclude that the architecture built in Spain over the last three or four years has achieved a surprising degree of unanimity in a manner that some have described as neomodern, though its quality and slight variability in nuance enable us to avoid using the word "monotony." The influence exerted by the work of Coderch and de la Sota on the younger generations is the most refined explanation for this situation. Nevertheless, certain original stances can be detected in the Canary Islands.

The state-subsidized ensemble of 35 apartments designed by María Luisa González and built in Montañeta de San Mateo attempts to merge fully into the place. Stones, woods, and colors are arranged on rudimentary farm terracing following the random order of the topography. The ground plans of the apartments skillfully embrace modern clichés: fluid interiors with double-height spaces and a well-judged relationship with the nature found in this mild climate.

On the island of Tenerife, José Antonio Sosa and Virgilio Gutiérrez designed and built the 33 subsidized housing units in La Laguna with the patent, orthodox influence of modern Central European architecture. Such influences are an early tradition in these parts. A couple of industrial buildings are also exemplary. In the maritime jet-foil station in Puerto de Santa Cruz, Eustaquio Martínez, Antonio Corona, and Arsenio Pérez Amaral used concrete to construct a building capable of withstanding the sea, a building whose shadows are its best feature. An industrial facility for dairy products presented Federico García Barba with an excellent opportunity to create an architecture stripped of ornamentation—an architecture that relies on the toughness of the materials used and the nakedness of the exposed facilities.

Also in Tenerife, Felipe Artengo, Fernando Martín Menis, and José María Rodríguez Pastrana have slowly created a strongly expressionist language and style. The volcanic landscape of sharp-edged, dark rocks, in contrast to the fleshy, exuberant vegetation, prompted them to create an architecture made up of stark rubblework, rough concretes, and eloquent apertures and roofs. In short, a hearty sort of architecture. They were not self-taught. After their professional training at the Barcelona School of Architecture, they inherited an interpretation of architecture from their elders: Javier Díaz-Llanos, Vicente Saavedra, Francisco Artengo, and José Ángel Domínguez Anadón. The young architects on the island are also embracing this Tenerife manner. By exploring the tectonic possibilities of materials, in works such as the Ana Bautista sports pavilion in Santa Cruz de Tenerife or the San Agustín student residence hall in La Laguna, as well as in a wide range of urban buildings, they have achieved a varied and independent formal repertoire that looks to the valleys and the island rocks with a sense of humor and a playfulness that infects the observer.

Left:
Ana Bautista sports pavilion, Santa Cruz de Tenerife, 1988–1993, Artengo / Martín Menis / Rodríguez Pastrana.

Below and right:
Museum of the Enlightenment, Valencia, 1997–2000, Vázquez Consuegra.

Altamira Museum, Santillana del Mar (Santander), 1994–2000, Navarro Baldeweg.

Scottish Parliament, Edinburgh, 1999, Miralles.

A Final Word

Before embarking upon a conclusion, we should take a last look at the architecture that is being proposed in the final moments of this century.

In the summer of 2000, the Spanish pavilion at the Venice Biennial, erected by Spain's commissioner, Alberto Campo, was awarded the prize for the best pavilion. It displayed the work of more than thirty architects, almost all of whom were in their thirties, and was a demonstration of the vitality with which Spanish architects are facing up to the coming century. But it would be unjust to consider only the young as being masters of the future, and—to prove it—these days are witnessing the inauguration of what may well be the best proposals by some of the architects who fill the previous pages: Vázquez Consuegra with his Museum of the Enlightenment, 1997–2000, in Valencia, and Navarro Baldeweg with his Altamira Museum, 1994–2000, in Santillana del Mar, Santander, provide clear evidence of this.

However, the summer also brought with it the sad news of the deaths of Francisco Javier Sáenz de Oiza and Enric Miralles. Miralles died while working on major commissions which—had he lived to see them completed—would have reflected his talent and added still further to his prestige. But his work should not be regarded as inconclusive or ended short of its maturity. The time which he was given more than enabled him to demonstrate both his understanding of architecture and his attitude toward life, an attitude full of vitality and commitment toward the era he lived in, which was perhaps his greatest contribution. Together with the death of Sáenz de Oiza, *maestro* of the era portrayed in these pages, we have lost two vital links in the history of the modern in Spain. Yet the modern continues in the work of their disciples, thereby creating another story yet to be told.

CONCLUSION: AN ERA, A STYLE, A FEELING

As we approach the end of this book, it becomes necessary to answer some of the questions we posed at the beginning. Is it possible to talk of a Spanish architecture? Is there anything in the works we have looked at that differs from what is seen beyond Spain's borders? Or perhaps the question should be more ambitious: can we talk of a school, or even of a style?

As early as the mid-twenties there were examples of modern architecture in Spain, which we have called "the modern" in this book. However, these examples were few and far between—isolated gestures due to the efforts of isolated artists. The tuberculosis clinic designed by Sert, Torres Clavé, and Subirana dates from 1934. The Zarzuela racetrack designed by the engineer Torroja and the architects Arniches and Domínguez, and the Frontón Recoletos *pelota* court, also by Torroja though this time with the architect Zuazo, both masterpieces in their own right, date from the following year. It is therefore possible to state that the modern had already taken root in Spain before the Civil War. However, the backlash to the modern had also appeared in triumphal vein, as in the New Ministries which Zuazo himself designed in those years for the Socialist minister Indalecio Prieto (completed by Franco's government after the Civil War without introducing any variations to the original design) and which corresponded stylistically to the monumental proposals of the governments in power not only in Italy and Germany but also in the French Republic.

Wars do not only destroy people and buildings; they also sever traditions, institutions, and cultural processes. This is why after the Civil War—when the majority of the architects who had worked in the thirties were either dead or in exile or simply demoralized—it was necessary to reconstruct the very idea of architecture from the foundations upward. And it can be claimed—as we do in these pages—that contemporary Spanish architecture had its precise origin around 1950, when the modern idea triumphed once and for all.

How does the story of modern Spanish architecture fit into the general, universal history of modernity? Cautiously. In the mid-eighties, when Spanish architecture was "discovered" by international critics, the dominant feeling was one of surprise. "Where had these people suddenly appeared from?" seemed to be the thought of both architects and critics. What they really discovered was not how good Spanish architecture was but rather how much they liked it, that is, how similar it was to what they wanted to do. Because although Spanish architecture had been traveling alone, it had been doing so on a path parallel to the one taken in a group by the architectures of Italy, America, France, England, or Germany . . . because these countries had also been through a war, or because there was only one road possible, or because there was in fact no isolation. Or for all of these reasons.

We have journeyed through a small part of history, through half a century of architecture, with the purpose of establishing the identity of Spanish architecture, of the "Spanish modern," and how it came to be. We started with the relaunch of the discipline following the harsh aftermath of the Civil War, when moral requirements and closed dialogues typified the attitudes of architects. This was the moment when the modern was definitively founded in a specific way that derived from Spain's isolation. It was the moment when architects identified abstraction as the only functional language.

Then came the years of political protest, which gave rise to an architecture of protest that found its expression in formal terms. This was a time when architects sought a way to express themselves as a group, through the Escola, organicism, "teams." Years of exposed concrete, of exposed materials in general.

With the political transition there came an era of reading and absorbing diverse critical influences, and of showing renewed interest in tradition, both disciplinary and local, and in the recovery of forgotten authors and knowledge.

Then political normality was achieved, followed at the beginning by substantial building activity that produced work of a high quality, devoid of avant-garde displays. The longing for realism and rationalism triumphed. The closed dialogue of the forties and fifties opened up and became global. Not only did international circles honor the Spanish by publishing their work, but they also invited them to teach and build abroad. Borders dissolved.

At the end of the twentieth century, even though Spanish architecture continues to offer standardized samples of all the international styles—as it has been doing for quite some time—it also shows a substantial level of uniformity. But if we are to talk about style, we ought to begin by taking a closer look at the two interpretations of the word "style" that interest us here. The first interprets it as the personal approach of an artist, with style defined as an attribute of each person. The second considers style to be the feature of an era—Gothic, for example, or romanticism. In other words, we could talk of the personal and of the school approach as synonyms for the two interpretations of style. And we could come to the conclusion that a school is neither more nor less than the accumulation and mutual influence of the approaches of several contemporary or successive artists. We would then recognize, if not a school, then a style in Spanish architecture, the sum of the personal styles of the various architects who took part in this dialogue. When working out their own particular discourses, architects showed a substantial interest in the discourses of their peers. Some stood out because they worked out a style of their own, thereby substantially influencing the others, and there were many important recuperations. This is what happened in the sixties with figures such as Sostres, Moya, or Cabrero, who recuperated the present through disciplinary analysis, and it happened again at the end of the eighties with the exhibition on Jujol. These recuperations, and the variable intensities of authors such as the ever-present Coderch, de la Sota, or Sáenz de Oiza, show that this was not a linear process, that there was no clear and unanimous path, but rather exploratory efforts in different directions, the sum of which made this history.

Coderch took many photographs of popular and historical works of architecture, which he then showed to his contemporaries and friends and which formed the basis of debates. His way of looking directly at things is inferred from his photographs of architecture and other topics—of bullfighting, one of his great passions—and his photomontages of popular architecture show clearly how he reinterpreted it, selecting and juxtaposing what interested him, to develop a personal approach. His first works are surely the most poetic, the most personal, and, more importantly for the topic at hand, the ones that contributed most powerfully to establishing a style. But in all of his work there is a nimbleness, an apparent ease in the solution, that makes it clear and direct, and that we know to be the result of an absorbing effort and passion for architecture, a hand-to-hand fight with his own excitable sensitivity to force it—the source of his capacity to look, understand, and design—to humbly disappear in the face of the reality and the objective and social importance of the task at hand.

Through all these years, only one other architect has had an influence comparable to that of Coderch: Alejandro de la Sota. In the same way that the former's work stemmed from the exploration of popular tradition, the latter fought to break away from tradition and turned to technique as his main source of inspiration. In the forties, de la Sota proved his sensitivity to the vernacular in the settlements he built; he acquired a mastery of clay and lime, of earth colors and popular forms, simplified at one and the same time to both ascetic and refined tastes, in line with the dictates of a postwar climate. Perhaps because continuing to work with the same materials as ever, whose conventions of use and composition were well known to say the least, forced him into a mannerist game of respect-transgression that was only resolved with a show of sensitivity, he decided—in the mid-fifties and embracing the principles of modernity— to work with new materials: iron and cement-fiber plates and tubes . . . light materials devoid of aesthetic and academic constraints. Materials and approaches whose conventions had yet to be invented. Spain's isolation and cultural backwardness—which in those years was beginning to be overcome—were not an obstacle to executing this kind of architecture; on the contrary, they allowed de la Sota to explore certain territories that the pioneers of the modern movement had prematurely abandoned before they had been fully exploited.

Toward 1965, terms connected with the "social mission" of building dominated the thoughts of teachers and students in the schools. The idea of architecture as a "service" was the guideline adopted not only by people but also by institutions. In those years the schools of architecture were among the university faculties most involved in political demonstration. Architects linked to clandestine political parties held the management posts of the professional associations and carried out a policy of opposition which, though removed from the circles of power, was made effective through their reputation.

In Madrid, in addition to Fernández del Amo, who was the first to take it upon himself to defend these principles from the standpoint of his progressive Catholicism, there were other architects who upheld this role of left-wing morality to their colleagues: Antonio Fernández Alba through his work and his lectures at the Madrid School of Architecture, where he was the most theoretical professor in those years, or Ferrán and Mangada in the field of urban planning. But the most representative and effective voice was without doubt that of the Catalan architect Oriol Bohigas and, alongside him, Federico Correa, providing the counterpoint with his careful forms.

The counterpoint of form to the ethical demands of social issues had a champion in Madrid in the person of Sáenz de Oiza, at this point through the organicism of his Torres Blancas building. He became a point of reference due, more than anything else, to his constant nonconformity and rebelliousness which turned into a dominant stylistic feature. But the biggest rebels were without doubt the members of the PER studio. With the militant activity in Marxist parties of some, and the provocative irony of the others, they adopted an uninhibited and on occasions scandalous attitude that allowed them to leave their imprint in a medium that they criticized with destructive zeal.

In 1965 *Revista de Occidente* published Juan Benet's work *La inspiración y el estilo* (Inspiration and Style). The book was carefully read not only by the writers and poets to whom it was addressed, but also by architects who understood how applicable the approaches and theses expounded by the author were to the theoretical problems faced by their profession and to the art of construction. When Benet brought face to face such mutually opposing convictions as "each work of art has a moral obligation" and "every artistic task is autonomous, so to speak, rather than arbitrary," thereby establishing the relative weight and noncontradictory relationship of both, it was almost as if he was revealing the architects' obsessions. An illustration of the above would be Luis Peña Ganchegui who, taking his inspiration from popular architecture on the coast of the Basque country (to use the writer's own terminology), he used his understanding of this architecture and its conditions—social, climatic, etc.—to endow himself with a "style" in the truest sense of the word, which he used to build the houses we have seen. As a result of both his houses and his style, he became a model for the whole of Spain of how to make architecture far away from Madrid and Barcelona.

It was around this time that Rafael Moneo came onto the scene. On the threshold of the seventies, it was as if he had arrived to interpret the moment. The rapid and simultaneous dissemination of the latest foreign texts and architectures—those of Tafuri, Venturi, and Rossi—found the right debating partner in Moneo. He and his work have always been presented as eclectic. In this context, the concept of eclecticism should be understood as an attitude rather than a style. An attitude defined largely by universal curiosity, which leads him to be present in every controversy, to get involved in every question, responding to Aldo Rossi with his Bankinter building and with his writings, and to the regionalist and postmodernist movements in Seville, and to American culture with the Kursaal auditorium. His involvement in every issue shows through in his work, where it is possible to identify several of the interests that he has pursued simultaneously. In order to establish the principal line of approach, he is constantly obliged to make a double effort of understanding comprised of the design process and the didactic role that his architecture has to fulfill. It is in this effort of "sensitive intelligence"—as María Zambrano would say—that his style and, at the same time, his inspiration is born.

The counterpoint to this cultured interpretation of architecture was provided not only by the tenacity of de la Sota but also by that of Alvaro Siza, another *maestro* from the Iberian peninsula, who was decisive not only in Portugal but also in Spain, where he was introduced by Nuno Portas and Oriol Bohigas. The forging of Siza's style through a personal interpretation of Alvar Aalto adapted to the former's land and time con-tributed toward confirming the Spanish dialogue around the modern.

This process of thought has produced an emotional "way" of executing architecture, a "way" that has always been deeply felt. On occasions with dramatic feeling, as in the case of Sáenz de Oiza, Alonso, or Viaplana. On others with a playful feeling. De la Sota used to say: "Architecture raises a laugh, life doesn't." With a sense of play and humor in Tusquets, Molezún, or Pastrana. With a sense of risk in Miralles and of distance in Peña, in Cruz and Ortiz, or in Bonell. With a sense of sobriety in Sostres, Llinás, or Campo Baeza.

A process in which there was always an intense appetite for knowledge. In Correa's expression, quoted by his disciples: "What I'm interested in is understanding something." In the effort of understanding and the didactic demands of the work designed by Moneo, or in the extension of knowledge in Bohigas. And an artistic sense in Navarro Baldeweg, the Torres, and the Sierras. And from the very beginning in Cabrero and Coderch.

The future is uncertain, and only time will tell how it will affect architecture and bring the period we are living in to a close. Today, we can only finish this book by remembering Coderch, when he said that to do architecture you need an intelligent client and a good architect. At the heart of the matter is an oft-repeated truth: the success of Spanish architects in this period is the result of Spanish society's interest in seeing itself represented by good architecture.

We have reached the end, and in return for some answers we have found ourselves face to face with some new questions: Which works of merit from this period have not been included in this book? We trust that they are neither sufficient nor obvious enough to detract from the purpose of this work, which was a general knowledge of the subject. How many will survive the test of time? Some of the buildings we have seen have almost disappeared or have been substantially transformed; others, on the other hand, have been restored. Many of the works published here will be destroyed or will lose their appeal, but in the years when they were built, and at the time of writing, they awoke interest. With them, a state of modernity was finally achieved.

NOTES

1

Although Baudelaire first mentioned "l'héroïsme de la vie moderne" in 1845, it was not until 1863, in his article "Le peintre de la vie moderne," that he developed the concept of *modernité* to which we refer here.

2

The regenerationist drive propelling cultural life in Spain between 1898 and 1917 was embodied by the Generation of '98 and by the Catalanists. In politics, this school of thought triggered an optimistic drive to overcome the agrarian structure of the country. Opinion on the issue was divided into two viewpoints: the modern and conservative posture of Antonio Maura y Montaner and the progressive and socialist one of José Canalejas y Méndez, who was supported by part of the bourgeoisie. The assassination of Canalejas in 1912 disillusioned many of his followers and helped radicalize the issue, leading later to what came to be termed "invertebrate Spain" (Ortega y Gasset).

3

In political terms, however, the most committed architect was Josep Puig i Cadafalch, a disciple of Domènech. Although also Catalanist, Gaudí's disciples, Josep María Jujol and Joan Rafols, displayed a pure and unblemished Catholicism that enabled them to continue holding their academic posts at the School of Architecture, from where they kept the Catalanist flame alive in the forties.

4

The flowering of Domènech's and Gaudí's architecture was made possible, from the middle of the nineteenth century onward, by the demolition of Barcelona's city walls and the implementation of the Cerdà Plan, which proved to be an unsurpassed tool for city growth.

5

In the first months of 1989, *Quaderns* published its issue no. 179–180, which acted as a catalogue for the Jujol exhibition organized by Josep Llinás. Many authors contributed to this issue.

6

Noucentisme (novecentism) attempted to overcome the irrationality it detected in styles such as art nouveau or liberty. Based on some of the premises set down by Puig i Cadafalch, it was represented in Barcelona by Francesc Folguera Grassi, Rafael Masó Valentí, and Josep María Pericàs. They were followed by the Brunelleschians, such as Nicolás Rubió i Tuduri and Ramón Reventos, who established the bases of a posture that emphasized greater formal simplicity and rational analysis, as exemplified by Ramón Durán i Reynals. In the north, the rationalist analysis of the Gothic carried out by Vicente Lampérez (a follower of Viollet-le-Duc) gave rise to the proposals made by Leonardo Rucabado, Javier Riancho, and Eugenio Fernández Quintanilla in Cantabria, and Manuel María Smith Ibarra in the Basque country. Despite incorporating aspects of modern technology into their programs, these architects stayed within the bounds of stylistic revivals and traditions without venturing into the field of formal research that characterized the modern movement: the interest in the machine. It is interesting to observe that this Catalan *renaixença* manifested itself in architecture more clearly than in any other art form. At the beginning of the twentieth century, two geniuses, Gaudí and Picasso, coincided in Barcelona, although they never actually met. Picasso, like so many artists of the time—Juan Gris, María Blanchard, Joan Miró, Julio González, Pablo Gargallo, Salvador Dalí—had to emigrate: Spain was not ready for modernity.

7

GATCPAC, the Grup d'Arquitectes i Tècnics Catalans per al Progrés de l'Arquitectura Contemporània (Group of Catalan Artists and Technicians for Progress in the Building Arts), was the Catalan section of the Spanish GATEPAC,

a group founded in 1930 in Zaragoza to design an architecture which met the rationalist postulates of the Bauhaus and Le Corbusier. Before the Civil War cut short its initiatives, it expressed its aims and views in the magazine *AC*.
8
In Spain, the initiatives to import new tendencies were marginal and prey to immediate attack from critics. Barcelona saw the presentation of cubism at the Dalmau Gallery in 1912. In Madrid, it was not until 1925 that the Salón de los Artistas Ibéricos organized the first show of contemporary local artists committed to the spirit of their time, coinciding with the construction of the Pavón cinema theater, designed by Anasagasti, which is generally considered to be the first rationalist work in the capital. This building was soon followed by a series of works that were more clearly inscribed within rationalism, such as the Rincón de Goya municipal hall in Zaragoza, designed by García Mercadal, dating from 1927; the expressionist designs executed by Fernández-Shaw; and a group of definitively modern works, such as the San Sebastián sailing club by Aizpurúa and Labayen, from 1929, the residential building on Calle Muntaner in Barcelona by Sert and Yllescas, from 1930, and the Tuberculosis Clinic also in Barcelona by Sert, Subirana, and Torres Clavé, from 1934. These, however, were isolated events.

A special case that merits particular mention—one that established a productive relationship between art and architecture and which survived the Spanish Civil War—is that of the Canary Islands, which probably resulted from the islands' fertile contact with Atlantic Europe. In Tenerife, Eduardo Westerdahl established the magazine *Gaceta del Arte* in 1932, which voiced the ideas of the island's contemporary elite and showcased the precocious rationalist works of its architects. The most influential architect in Las Palmas prior to the Civil War was Miguel Martín Fernández de la Torre. In Tenerife, the most outstanding architect of the thirties was Enrique Marrero Regalado, who had made a name for himself with clearly rationalist works such as the Siboney building, in Santander, before he left the peninsula. For an in-depth study of Spanish architecture prior to the Civil War, see Oriol Bohigas's *Arquitectura española de la Segunda República* (Barcelona: Tusquets Editor, 1970).
9
Torres Clavé died on the Catalan front fighting for the revolution; Sert, his former partner, took advantage of a commission in Paris to avoid returning to Barcelona; Aizpurúa, a leader of the Spanish Falangist movement in San Sebastián, was executed by a firing squad; Lacasa and Sánchez Arcas went into exile in Moscow; Zuazo was deported to the Canary Islands, from which he would eventually return; Mercadal was never fully reinstated; and others who survived on the winning side, like Gutiérrez Soto, abandoned the tension and investigation of the modern. A detailed list of architects who went into exile as a result of the Civil War can be found in Raúl Rispa, ed., *Architectural Guide: Spain, 1920–1999* (Basel and Boston: Birkhäuser, 1998).
10
In Madrid, as early as 1940, a group of Falangist intellectuals led by Eugenio d'Ors, conscious of the existing cultural void, backed from their informal literary meetings at the Café Gijón and the Lion d'Or such initiatives as the Academia Breve de Crítica de Arte (Brief Academy of Art Criticism) with a view to recovering artistic thought linked to modernity. One of the results of these efforts was the inauguration by Biosca, another Catalan and a friend of the former, of the Salón de los Once, through which the art produced in Catalonia—always more open to change than the capital—was showcased. In Barcelona, in the Layetana Gallery, the first Salón de Octubre was held in 1948, with works by Antoni Tàpies and Modesto Cuixart who, together with Joan-Josep Tharrats, Joan Ponç, Arnau Puig, Juan Eduardo Cirlot, and Joan Brossa, founded the Dau al Set group. Art thus gradually gained ground until the celebration of the very important Hispano-American Biennial of 1951, which can be seen as the closing event of this period and the first episode of the period that we are about to study. All of this

brought about the recovery of the most valuable and modern work produced prior to the Civil War. Surrealism, so important to the prewar European avant-garde and particularly to Spaniards, would become the point of departure not only of the Dau al Set group but also of other artists, such as the Canary Islands members of the LADAC group or Ángel Ferrant. It also made an appearance in the works of certain architects, such as in Coderch's Ugalde house, de la Sota's settlement of Esquivel, or in the oil paintings produced by Aburto and Cabrero for the feverish design of the Monument to the Counter-Reformation. In Barcelona, this surrealist vein coexisted with rationalist designs.

11

From J. M. Rovira's article "Hora es de abandonar el silencio . . . ," in *La arquitectura de los años cincuenta en Barcelona,* catalogue of the exhibition organized by the General Directorate for Housing and Architecture (MOPU) and the Barcelona School of Architecture (Barcelona, 1987), p. 202.

12

The official *Boletín de la Dirección General de Arquitectura* published one of Francisco Cabrero's texts featuring the conclusive phrase: "In Italy I have seen a different thing." This expression, which the author used to explain the impression Italian architecture of the thirties made on him during a trip immediately after the Spanish Civil War, was intelligently valued by Antón Capitel many years later on the occasion of the exhibition entitled "Arquitectura para después de una guerra," organized in 1977 by Lluis Domènech, Roser Amadó, Carlos Sambricio, and Capitel himself. The exhibition, which first opened in Barcelona and then traveled to Madrid, was a courageous attempt to elucidate a recent, and politically incandescent, past, but above all it was the fruit of the interpretation of the period made by the architects Domènech, Amadó, and Capitel and the historian Sambricio, all of whom were actively working at the end of the seventies. Their recovery of the decade of the forties, thirty years later, was an act of historical correction, of restoration, we could say.

13

The Spanish philosopher and writer Miguel de Unamuno was the representative par excellence of a school of thought in which profound love of Christ and rebellious atheism coincided in a violently personal and painful interpretation of Catholicism. In line with this blasphemous school, Oteiza sculpted thirteen apostles rather than twelve, which he identified with Unamuno, whom he admired, and the crew of a *trainera,* a small fishing boat with twelve rowers typical of northern Spain. In a second blasphemy, Oteiza explained the expressionist dramatism of his sculptures by recalling the rural images of pig slaughtering.

14

Organized by the Summer University of Santander. This was established during the Republic and renamed the Menéndez y Pelayo International University (UIMP) after the war. In the beginning, the UIMP was merely a language school for foreigners, but by the fifties it had attained scientific level.

15

He was appointed to the post by Joaquín Ruiz-Jiménez, a representative of the group of Christian Democrats in Franco's government who, during the time he resisted his Falangist adversaries, paved the way for an enthusiastic though fragile cultural opening from his post as Minister of National Education. This opening was the consequence of the new relations established with the United States, a country that regarded the Soviet Union as its new enemy and therefore admitted the Franco regime, a sworn enemy of the reds, among its allies. The entry of Spain into UNESCO in 1952 put an end to the autarchy of the forties.

16

To illustrate the importance of this, consider the fact that Correa and Bohigas only met—in 1954—after one of Sartoris's conferences. Federico Correa recounts that Oriol Bohigas left the hall in an impassioned and convinced state, quoting the lecturer: "Easel painting is dead." Certainly, Correa and Milà knew of the existence of Bohigas, who had criticized their contribution to the Salón del Hogar Moderno (Modern Home Exhibit) organized by the FAD in an article published by Serra d'Or, in which, on the other hand, Bohigas had praised Gili's stylistically functionalist montage. On the basis of these disagreements they founded an effective, complementary friendship, and this despite the fact, as Oscar Tusquets puts it, that Oriol never managed to teach Federico to speak Catalan, nor Federico to teach Oriol to dress well.

17
Català-Roca's photographs have been widely published. In particular, we can refer to the catalogue of the exhibition "La arquitectura de los años cincuenta en Barcelona," which had access to the photographer's archive and consequently featured an extensive and well-selected collection of photographs of Barcelona architecture. See note 11.

18
Revista Nacional de Arquitectura, no. 182, p. 26.

19
To gain an in-depth view of Sostres's work, see the monographic issue no. 4 of *2C, La construcción de la ciudad*.

20
Josep María Sostres, "El funcionalismo y la nueva plástica," *Boletín de la Dirección General de Arquitectura*, no. 15 (July 1950). Later included in "Opiniones sobre arquitectura," *Arquitecturas*, no. 10, published in Murcia. The catalogue quoted in note 11 features an article by Josep María Rovira in which he amply and correctly analyzes Sostres's position within the contemporary Barcelona controversy.

21
2C, La construcción de la ciudad, no. 4.

22
This adventure has been studied in detail by Esteban Terradas Muntañola in his doctoral thesis, submitted to the Barcelona School of Architecture in 1993.

23
Ibid., p. 238.

24
Robert Bufrau and Agustín Obiol, "El diseño estructural en Barcelona durante el periodo 1950–1963," in the exhibition catalogue *La arquitectura de los años cincuenta en Barcelona*, p. 231. See note 11.

25
The classicizing style did not appear, either in its Escorialesque or its plateresque version, in the Basque country. Instead, a Basque tradition, which had already made its presence felt before 1936, was reinforced.

26
Elías Mas Serra's book *50 años de arquitectura en Euskadi* (Vitoria: Gobierno Vasco, Departamento de Urbanismo, Vivienda y Medio Ambiente, 1990), published by the Basque government, is a very complete catalogue of Basque architecture.

27
The maritime provinces, no doubt due to their tradition of white villages, were the best spared. During the forties, each province had a small group of architects who were skillful at interpreting the imperatives of the local tradition. Fernando de la Cuadra in Cádiz, Víctor Escribano and José Rebollo in Córdoba, Francisco Prieto Moreno in Granada, Francisco Sedano Arce in Huelva, Ramón Pajares Pardo in Jaén, José González Edo in Málaga, and Juan Talavera in Seville were some of the architects who represented this posture. Simultaneously, in the Seville of the forties there was a large group of architects who exercised an architecture rooted in rationalism. Outstanding among them were the Medina Benjumea brothers—Rodrigo and Felipe—Luis de Sala, Alfonso Toro, Balbontín de Orta, and Rafael Arévalo.

28

Carlos Flores, *Arquitectura española contemporánea* (Madrid: Editorial Aguilar, 1959). Lluis Domènech, ed., *Arquitectura española contemporánea* (Barcelona: Editorial Blume, 1968), with texts by Oriol Bohigas, Vittorio Gregotti, and Alexandre Cirici i Pellicer.

29

Following the first conference, held in Madrid, a second was held in Barcelona, for which a small committee was set up comprised of Bohigas, Correa, Carvajal, and Fisac, among others. The third, organized by Peña Ganchegui, was held in San Sebastián, with successive iterations taking place in Córdoba, Málaga, Tarragona, Segovia . . .

30

The architects from Barcelona played a major role in the links forged with foreign architects. In the first place, there was Correa, who attended the CIAM courses and congresses from 1952 onward; in the second, Bohigas, who participated in the famous Team X congress in Otterlo, where he met Louis Kahn. In 1968 another event took place: the Design Congress in Aspen, whose main theme was "Europe versus America." Federico Correa was responsible for presenting the situation in Europe, an event that bears witness to the role he played in the debate at the time. Correa thus headed the Iberian group formed by Bohigas, Fernández Alba, Nuno Portas, Salgado, André Ricart, Blanc, Miguel Milà, and Prieto Moreno, to name but a few. There he established an early friendship with Peter Eisenman.

31

Nueva Forma was published from 1966 to 1977. Initially, under the direction of Garbino A. Carriedo, it appeared under the name of *El Inmueble*. Juan Daniel Fullaondo took over its direction from the nineteenth issue onward.

32

In order to gauge the importance attached to Alvar Aalto's work in those early years in Madrid, it would suffice to look at the texts published in *Arquitectura* and the article written by Moneo for *Arquitecturas bis* upon the death of the master, entitled "El rey ha muerto . . ." (The king has died . . .).

33

In reference to the Propylaea, the great gates at the entrance to the Acropolis.

34

Alejandro de la Sota, "Sobre Chillida," *Arquitectura*, no. 180, published by the Architects' Chamber of Madrid.

35

Arquitectura, no. 118 (1968), published by the Architects' Chamber of Madrid.

36

The work of Erwin Broner was reviewed in a monographic issue of the journal *D'A*, published by the Architects' Chamber of the Balearic Islands under the direction of Federico Climent.

37

The architecture of these islands was studied by Elías Torres in the book *Guía de la arquitectura de Ibiza y Formentera* (Barcelona: COAC [Architects' Chamber of Catalonia], 1981).

38

Rodríguez designed works like the Molinoblanco estate in Torrevieja and performed an outstanding town planning role in conjunction with A. Soldevilla and Julio García Lanza.

39

For further information on the work of these architects, see Miguel Martín Fernández de la Torre, *Arquitecturas para la gran ciudad* (Las Palmas de Gran Canaria: Centro Atlántico de Arte Moderno, 1995), and M. I. Navarro and A. Ruiz, *Marrero Regalado (1897–1956). La arquitectura como escenografía* (Santa Cruz de Tenerife: COACa [Architects' Chamber of the Canary Islands], 1992).

40

As Ignasi de Solà-Morales explains in his book *Contemporary Spanish Architecture: An Eclectic Panorama* (New York: Rizzoli, 1986), the term "architecture" was used in the plural and further reinforced with the epithet "bis." These expressions can be interpreted as signifying that a single, orthodox architecture was not recognized, thereby admitting the publication, revision, or mere evocation of all kinds of past and present architecture.

41

At the time, Rosa Regàs, who later became a great novelist and journalist, worked in the world of publishing. In Barcelona and Cadaqués she participated in a wide variety of intellectual adventures—see, for example, the seductive images that remain of her chess games with Marcel Duchamp. In addition to the people already mentioned, the editorial committee included Helio Piñón, who represented the new generations, Luis Peña Ganchegui and Rafael Moneo, who represented the architects from outside Barcelona, art critic Tomás Lloréns, designer Enric Satué, and architect and town planner Manuel de Solà-Morales.

42

A group of young architects from Barcelona—such as Carlos Martí Aris, Chico de Cotijoch, Armesto, Iago Bonet, and Teilacker—and from other regions—such as Antonio Barrionuevo, Paco Torres, and César Portela, to name but a few—gathered around the figure of Tarragó. They organized fruitful seminars and meetings with members of the Tendenza from Switzerland, Italy, and other countries in cities such as Santiago de Compostela, Seville, Barcelona, Naples. The diachronic and versatile production of this group lives on today.

43

In keeping with the other journals quoted here, the title of this magazine was also symbolic, albeit less clearly so. The literal translation of the title is "The street of the city," but Carrer de la Ciutat was also the name of the street where the historical headquarters of the Communist Party of Catalonia was located. A fine coincidence. Its first issue was published in November 1977 and its board of directors was made up of Xavier Blanquer, Luis Burillo, Beatriz Colomina, Enric Granell, José Manuel Pérez Latorre, Helio Piñón, Santiago Planas, Francesco Properetti, José Quetglas, José María Rovira, and Txatxo Savater.

44

Such was the case with the most active series, the Colección de Arquitectura y Crítica, directed by Ignasi de Solà-Morales and published by Gustavo Gili.

45

Rafael Moneo, "28 arquitectos no numerarios," *Arquitecturas bis*, no. 23–24 (1978).

46

Antón Capitel, *Arquitectura española—años 50–años 60* (Madrid: MOPU, Dirección General de Arquitectura, 1986).

47

Oriol Bohigas, "Actualidad de la arquitectura catalana," *Arquitecturas bis*, no. 13–14 (1976).

48

Helio Piñón, "Actitudes teóricas en la reciente arquitectura de Barcelona," *Arquitecturas bis*, no. 13–14 (1976).

49

Bohigas, "Actualidad de la arquitectura catalana." See note 47.

50

Eduard Bru and José Luis Mateo, *Arquitectura española contemporánea* (Barcelona: Gustavo Gili, 1984).

51

Separata was a sophisticated Seville publishing venture in which poets, philologists, painters, and a certain number of architects participated. Only four issues were ever published: Winter 1978 and Spring, Summer, and Autumn 1979.

52
Solà-Morales, *Contemporary Spanish Architecture*. See note 40.
53
Rafael Moneo in "Arquitecturas para Barcelona: la escuela, la vivienda y el resto verde," *Arquitecturas bis*, no. 28–29 (May 1979).
54
Lluis Clotet, "A Barcelone pour une architecture de l'évocation," *Archithese*, no. 35–36.
55
Arquitectura neoclásica en el País Vasco, exhibition catalogue (Vitoria: Gobierno Vasco, Departamento de Cultura y Turismo, 1991).
56
The book *Cincuenta años de arquitectura en Murcia*, written by José María Hervás and published in 1982 by the COAM (Architects' Chamber of Murcia), presents works executed over the past 50 years.
57
Antón Capitel, "Tradición y cambio en la arquitectura y la ciudad de Madrid," and Ignasi de Solà-Morales, "Madrid es la capital de España," in *Tradición y cambio en la arquitectura de seis ciudades europeas* (Madrid: Centro Cultural Conde Duque, 1992).
58
The architecture produced in Galicia in 1993 was rigorously published in *AV*, no. 41 (1993).

SELECTED BIBLIOGRAPHY

This bibliography includes some of the most relevant works on Spanish architecture and architects currently available in the market. The following abbreviations are used: COA: Colegio Oficial de Arquitectos (Architects' Chamber). Hence, COAAoc: de Andalucía Occidental (of Western Andalusia); COAAor: de Andalucía Oriental (of Eastern Andalusia); COAAs: de Asturias; COAB: de Baleares (of the Balearic Islands); COAC: de Cataluña (of Catalonia); COACV: de la Comunidad Valenciana (of Valencia); COAG: de Galicia; COAM: de Madrid; COAMu: de Murcia; COAVN: Vasco Navarro (of the Basque Country and Navarre). CSCAE: Consejo Superior de Colegios de Arquitectos de España (Spanish Council of Architects' Chambers). ETSA: Escuela Técnica Superior de Arquitectura (School of Architecture). Hence, ETSAB: of Barcelona; ETSAM: of Madrid; ETSAV: of El Vallés. MOPT: Ministerio de Obras Públicas y Transportes (Spanish Ministry of Public Works and Transport). MOPTMA: Ministerio de Obras Públicas, Transportes y Medio Ambiente (Spanish Ministry of Public Works, Transport, and the Environment). MOPU: Ministerio de Obras Públicas y Urbanismo (Spanish Ministry of Public Works and Town Planning). UIMP: Universidad Internacional Menéndez Pelayo (Menéndez Pelayo International University).

Abitare, no. 246 (Milan, 1986). Monograph on Spain.

Alas Casariego Arquitectos, 1955–1995. Madrid: MOPTMA, 1995.

"Alberto Campo Baeza." *Documentos de Arquitectura*, no. 2 (Almería, 1987).

"Alberto Noguerol, Pilar Díez." *Documentos de Arquitectura*, no. 31 (Almería, 1995).

"Alejandro de la Sota." *Quaderns d'Arquitectura i Urbanisme*, no. 152 (Barcelona, 1982).

Alonso Pereira, J. R. *Asturias. 50 años de arquitectura*. Oviedo: COAAs, 1990.

Antoni Bonet Castellana 1913–1989. Barcelona: COAC / Madrid: Ministerio de Fomento, 1996.

Architectural Review, no. 1071 (London, 1986). Monograph on Spain.

Areán, A., J. M. Vaquero, and J. Casariego Córdoba. *Madrid. Arquitecturas perdidas 1927–1986*. Madrid: Pronaos, 1995.

Arqués, M. *Miguel Fisac*. Madrid: Pronaos, 1996.

Arquitectura, no. 236 (Madrid, 1982). Several articles on Rafael Moneo.

Arquitectura a Catalunya. L'era democràtica 1977–1996. Barcelona: Generalitat de Catalunya, Departament de Cultura, 1996.

"Arquitectura espanyola." *Quaderns d'Arquitectura i Urbanisme*, no. 156 (Barcelona, 1983).

L'arquitectura i l'art dels anys 50 a Madrid. Barcelona: Fundació La Caixa, 1996.

Arquitectura para después de una guerra, 1939–1949. Barcelona: COAC, 1977.

Artengo, F., et al. *Artengo. Menis. Pastrana. Obras y proyectos en Canarias*. Stuttgart: Architektur-Gallerie / Santa Cruz de Tenerife: Gobierno Autónomo Canario, 1993.

Ayala, G. *Gerardo Ayala*. Madrid: Munilla-Lería, 1994.

Baldellou, M. A. (coord.). *J. M. García de Paredes, arquitecto, 1924–1990*. Madrid: COAM, 1992.

Baldellou, M. A. *Lugar, memoria y proyecto. Galicia 1974–1994*. Madrid: Electa España, 1995.

Baldellou, M. A., and A. Capitel. *Summa artis. Historia general del arte. XL. Arquitectura española del siglo XX*. Madrid: Espasa Calpe, 1995.

"Barcelona Olímpica." *A&V Monografías de Arquitectura y Vivienda*, no. 37 (Madrid, 1992).

Barreiro, P. *Casas baratas. La vivienda social en Madrid, 1900–1939*. Madrid: COAM, 1992.

Bayón, M. *Mariano Bayón*. Stuttgart: Architektur-Galerie am Weissenhof, 1992.

Benet, J. *La inspiración y el estilo*. Madrid: Revista de Occidente, 1966; Alfaguara, 1999.

Bienal de Arquitectura Española (selection committee: L. Peña Ganchegui, I. de Solà-Morales, L. Fernández-Galiano, J. P. Kleihues, A. Colquhoun, G. Grassi, M. Waisman, P. Buchanan, and J. Benet). *I Bienal de Arquitectura Española. 1991*. Madrid: MOPTMA, CSCAE, UIMP, 1991.

— (selection committee: B. Carreras, J. Duró, F. Candela, F. de A. Cabrero, J. A. Corrales, and L. Peña Ganchegui). *Muestra de Arquitectura Española 1991–1993*. Madrid: MOPTMA, CSCAE, UIMP, 1994.

— (selection committee: P. Casariego, J. L. Íñiguez de Onzoño, J. Llinás, F. Nanclares, G. Vázquez Consuegra, M. de la Dehesa, I. León, and J. Maruri). *II Bienal de Arquitectura Española 1991–1992*. Madrid: MOPTMA, CSCAE, UIMP, 1993.

— (selection committee: J. Frechilla, B. Carreras, J. Duró, E. Lluch, E. Bonell, A. Campo Baeza, J. M. Gallego, and F. J. Mangado). *III Bienal de Arquitectura Española. 3rd Biennial of Spanish Architecture*. Madrid: MOPTMA, CSCAE, UIMP, 1991.

— (selection committee: C. Narbona, J. Duró, E. Lluch, M. D. Gil, R. Vázquez Molezún, J. L. Mateo, J. M. Botey, and J. Molinero). *I Muestra de 10 años de Arquitectura Española 1980–1990*. Madrid: MOPTMA, CSCAE, UIMP, 1991.

— (selection committee: C. Ferrater (dir.), A. Cruz, R. Ercilla, J. Garcés, J. Herreros, G. Mingo, I. León, L. Fernández-Galiano, and J. Ibáñez). *Cuarta Bienal de Arquitectura Española 1995–1996*. Madrid: Ministerio de Fomento, CSCAE, UIMP, Universidad de Alcalá, 1997.

— (selection committee: C. Portela, G. Mingo, I. León, J. Ibáñez, R. Sanabria, L. Burillo, J. L. Trillo de Leyva, J. M. Torres Nadal, V. Verdú, and F. Chaslin). *V Bienal de Arquitectura Española, 1997–1998: El Lugar Público*. Madrid: Ministerio de Fomento, CSCAE, UIMP, Universidad de Alcalá, 1999.

Bienal Iberoamericana de Arquitectura e Ingeniería Civil (jury: A. Adao de Fonseca et al.). *I Bienal Iberoamericana de Arquitectura e Ingeniería Civil*. Madrid: Bienal Iberoamericana de Arquitectura e Ingeniería Civil / Electa España, 1998.

— *II Bienal Iberoamericana de Arquitectura e Ingeniería Civil*. Seville: Tanais Ediciones / Madrid: Bienal Iberoamericana de Arquitectura e Ingeniería Civil, 2000.

Bohigas, O. *Barcelona, entre el Pla Cerdà i el barraquisme*. Barcelona: Ediciones 62, 1963.

— *Contra una arquitectura adjetivada*. Barcelona: Seix Barral, 1969.

— *Garcés y Sòria*. Barcelona: Gili, 1988.

— *Modernidad en la arquitectura de la España republicana.* Rev. ed. Barcelona: Tusquets, 1998.

Bohigas, O., P. Buchanan, and V. Magnago Lampugnani. *Barcelona, arquitectura y ciudad, 1980–1992.* Barcelona: Gili, 1990.

Botia, L. (ed.). *Fernando Higueras.* Madrid: Xarait, 1987.

Brú, E., and J. L. Mateo. *Arquitectura española contemporánea.* Barcelona: Gili, 1987.

Buchanan, P. (intro.). *Bonell & Gil.* Seville: Tanais Ediciones, 2001.

Buchanan, P., and J. Quetglas. *Lapeña / Torres.* Barcelona: Gili, 1990.

Cabrero Torres-Quevedo, F. de Asís. *Cuatro libros de arquitectura.* Madrid: COAM, 1992.

Campo Baeza, A. *Campo Baeza.* Madrid: Munilla-Lería, 1996.

Campos, C., and J. M. Vidal. *Arquitectura del Mediterráneo. Comunidad Valenciana.* Valencia: COACV, 1990.

Cano Lasso, 1949–1995. Madrid: MOPTMA, 1995.

Capitel, A. *Arquitectura española años 50–años 80.* Madrid: Dirección General de Arquitectura, MOPU, 1986.

Capitel, A., F. Chueca, J. M. Hernández León, G. Ruiz Cabrero, and C. Sambricio. *Arquitectura de Madrid, siglo XX.* Seville: Tanais Ediciones / Madrid: Fundación Camuñas, 1999.

Capitel, A. (dir.), L. Fernández-Galiano, P. Moleón, et al. *Twentieth-Century Architecture: Spain.* Exhibition catalogue. Frankfurt: Deutsches Architektur-Museum / Seville: Tanais Ediciones / Madrid: Sociedad Estatal Hanover 2000, 2000.

Capitel, A., J. L. Mateo, V. Pérez Escolano, J. D. Fullaondo, et al. *Architecture espagnole: Trente oeuvres. Années 50–années 80.* Madrid: MOPU, 1985.

Capitel, A., and J. Ortega. *Coderch, 1945–1976.* Madrid: Xarait, 1978.

Capitel, A., and I. de Solà-Morales. *Contemporary Spanish Architecture: An Eclectic Panorama.* New York: Rizzoli, 1986.

Capitel, A., W. Wang, J. M. Ezquiaga, J. P. Kleihues, M. Pechinski, P. Feduchi, I. de Solà-Morales, and G. Ruiz Cabrero. *Tradición y cambio en la arquitectura de seis ciudades europeas.* Madrid: Consorcio para Madrid Capital Europea de la Cultura 1992, 1993.

Carlos Ferrater. Barcelona: COAC, 1995.

Casas, M., et al. *Arquitectura de regiones devastadas.* Madrid: MOPU, 1989.

"Casas españolas." *A&V Monografías de Arquitectura y Vivienda,* no. 60 (Madrid, 1996).

"César Portela." *Documentos de Arquitectura,* no. 16 (Almería, 1991).

Cirici, A. *La estética del franquismo.* Barcelona: Gili, 1977.

Climent, J. (intro.). *Francisco Cabrero, arquitecto 1939–1978.* Madrid: Xarait, 1979.

Coderch, J. A. *Conversaciones con Enric Sòria.* Murcia: Colegio de Aparejadores de Murcia, 1997.

— "No son genios lo que necesitamos ahora." *Arquitectura,* no. 38 (Madrid, 1962).

"Coderch." *Arquitectura,* no. 268 (Madrid, 1987).

Coderch de Sentmenat. Madrid: Museo Español de Arte Contemporáneo, 1980.

Cohn, D. (intro.). *Manuel Gallego.* Basel: Birkhäuser, 1998.

Cohn, D. *Young Spanish Architects.* Basel: Birkhäuser, 2000.

Controspazio, no. 4 (Rome, July-August 1979). Monograph on Spanish architecture during the seventies.

Corrales y Molezún. Madrid: Xarait, 1983.

Corrales y Molezún. Madrid: CSCAE, 1984.

Corredor, J. *Antoni de Moragas Gallisà.* Barcelona: Gili, 1989.

Cruells, B. *Ricardo Bofill.* Barcelona: Gili, 1992.

Curtis, William J. R. *Modern Architecture since 1900.* London: Phaidon, 1996.

Els darrers cent anys. Arquitectura i ciutat. Barcelona: Generalitat de Catalunya, 1988.

DBZ, no. 6 (Gutersloh,1992). Monograph on Spain.

Diez años de planeamiento urbanístico en España 1979–1989. Madrid: MOPU, 1989.

DoCoMoMo Ibérico. *Arquitectura del Movimiento Moderno. Registro DoCoMoMo Ibérico.* Barcelona: Fundación Mies van der Rohe / DoCoMoMo, 1996.

Domènech, L. *Arquitectura de siempre. Los años cuarenta en España.* Barcelona: Tusquets, 1978.

— *Arquitectura española contemporánea.* Barcelona: Blume, 1974.

Domínguez Ortiz, A., A. Bonet Correa, G. Pérez Villalta, E. Mosquera Adell, M. T. Pérez Cano, M. Martín, F. J. Rodríguez Baberán, and V. Pérez Escolano. *1492–1992. Transformaciones de cinco siglos de arquitectura en Andalucía.* Seville: COAAoc, 1992.

"Dossier Juan Navarro Baldeweg." *L'Architecture d'Aujourd'hui,* no. 83 (Paris, 1992).

Drew, P. *La realidad del espacio. La arquitectura de Martorell / Bohigas / Mackay / Puigdomènech.* Barcelona: Gili, 1993.

"Eduardo Torroja." *Informes de la Construcción,* no. 137 (Madrid, 1962).

"Eduardo Torroja." *Nueva Forma,* no. 32 (Madrid, 1968).

"Elías Torres & Martínez Lapeña 1988–1993." *El Croquis,* no. 61 (Madrid, 1993).

Erwin Broner. Ciudadano-arquitecto-pintor. Ibiza 1934–1971. Ibiza: COAB, 1980–1981.

"Erwin Broner 1898–1971." *d'A,* no. 11–12 (Ibiza, 1994).

"Espagne, Madrid, Barcelone." *L'Architecture d'Aujourd'hui,* no. 149 (Paris, 1970). Monograph.

"Especial Expo92. Análisis crítico de arquitectura y diseño." *DiseñoInterior,* no. 15 (Madrid, 1992).

Félix Candela, Arquitecto. Madrid: MOPTMA, 1994.

Fernández Alba, Antonio. *La crisis de la arquitectura española: 1939–1972.* Madrid: Edicusa, 1972.

— "25 años de arquitectura española 1939–1964." *Arquitectura,* no. 64 (Madrid, 1964).

Fernández del Amo, J. L. *Palabra y obra.* Madrid: COAM, 1995.

Fernández del Amo, arquitectura 1942–1982. Madrid: Ministerio de Cultura, 1983.

Fernández-Galiano, L. (intro.). *Francisco Mangado.* Barcelona: Gili, 1994.

Fernández-Galiano, L., J. Isasi, and A. Lopera. *La quimera moderna. Los poblados dirigidos en la arquitectura de los 50.* Madrid: Hermann Blume, 1989.

Fernández-Isla, J. M. (coord.). *J. Carvajal, arquitecto.* Madrid: Fundación COAM, 1994.

Fernando Higueras. Arquitecturas. Madrid: COAM, 1997.

Flores, C. *Arquitectura española contemporánea.* Madrid: Aguilar, 1989. (1st ed. 1961.)

Fochs, C. (ed.). *J. A. Coderch de Sentmenat: 1913–1984.* Barcelona: Gili, 1989, 1995.

Frampton, K. *Studies in Tectonic Culture: The Poetics of Construction in Nineteenth and Twentieth Century Architecture.* Chicago: Graham Foundation for Advanced Studies in the Fine Arts / Cambridge, MA: MIT Press, 1995.

Frampton, K. (intro.), A. Campo Baeza, and C. Poisay. *Young Spanish Architecture.* Madrid: COAM, UPC de Madrid, 1985.

Frampton, K., A. Capitel, V. Pérez Escolano, and I. de Solà-Morales. *Building in a New Spain.* Chicago: Art Institute / Barcelona: Gili, 1992.

Frampton, K., A. C. Webster, A. Tischhauser, and S. Calatrava (foreword). *Calatrava Bridges.* 2nd ed. Basel: Birkhäuser, 1996.

Francesc Mitjans, arquitecte. Barcelona: COAC, 1996.

"Francisco Cabrero." *Arquitectos*, no. 118 (Madrid, 1990).

"Francisco Javier Sáenz de Oiza 1947–1988." *El Croquis*, no. 32–33 (Madrid, 1988).

Freixa, J. *Josep Lluis Sert*. Barcelona: Gili, 1995.

Fullaondo, J. D. *Antonio Fernández Alba, 1957–1967, arquitecto*. Madrid: Alfaguara, 1968.

— *Las arquitecturas de Bilbao. A la búsqueda del tiempo perdido (sobre todo ecléctico)*. Bilbao: COAVN, 1993.

— "Asís Cabrero y la arquitectura de los 40." *Nueva Forma*, no. 76 (Madrid, 1976).

— *La bicicleta aproximativa. Conversaciones en torno a Francisco J. Sáenz de Oiza*. Madrid: Kain, 1991.

— "Emilio Pérez Piñeiro 1935–1972." *Nueva Forma*, no. 78–79 (Madrid, 1972).

— "La Escuela de Madrid." *Arquitectura*, no. 118 (Madrid, 1968).

— "Interpretación de la obra de Antonio Vázquez de Castro." *Nueva Forma*, no. 14 (Madrid, 1967).

— *Miguel Fisac*. Madrid: Ministerio de Educación y Cultura, 1972.

Fullaondo, Juan D., and M. T. Muñoz. *Historia de la arquitectura española contemporánea*. Vol. I. Madrid: Kain Editorial, 1993.

— *Historia de la arquitectura española contemporánea*. Vol. II. Madrid: Munilla-Lería, 1995.

— *Historia de la arquitectura española contemporánea*. Vol. III. Madrid: Molly Editorial, 1997.

"Galicia Jacobea." *A&V Monografías de Arquitectura y Vivienda*, no. 41 (Madrid, 1993).

García Barba, F. "La arquitectura artesanal de Saavedra y Díaz-Llanos." *Basa*, no. 10 (Santa Cruz de Tenerife, 1989).

Hernández Pezzi, C. *José María García de Paredes*. Málaga: COAAor, 1992.

Hervás, J. M. *Cincuenta años de arquitectura en Murcia*. Murcia: COAMu, 1982.

Insausti, P., T. Llopis, and V. Pérez Escolano. *Arquitectura valenciana. La década de los ochenta*. Valencia: IVAM, 1992.

"J. A. Coderch." *A+U*, no. 62 (Tokyo, 1976).

"J. A. Corrales—R. Vázquez Molezún." *Documentos de Arquitectura*, no. 33 (Almería, 1996).

Jarauta, F. "J. M. Torres Nadal." *Quaderns d'Arquitectura i Urbanisme*, no. 197 (Barcelona, 1992).

"Jerónimo Junquera—Estanislao Pérez Pita." *Documentos de Arquitectura*, no. 30 (Almería, 1995).

J. L. Fernández del Amo. Madrid: Museo Centro Nacional de Arte Reina Sofía, 1995.

Jordá, C. (dir.). *20 x 20. Siglo XX. Veinte obras de arquitectura moderna*. Valencia: Generalitat Valenciana / COACV, 1997.

"José Antonio Martínez Lapeña—Elías Torres Tur." *Documentos de Arquitectura*, no. 3 (Almería, 1988).

"José María García de Paredes." *Documentos de Arquitectura*, no. 22 (Almería, 1992).

"José María Sostres." *2C. Construcción de la ciudad*, no. 4 (Barcelona, 1975).

"José R. Sierra, Ricardo Sierra." *Documentos de Arquitectura*, no. 27 (Almería, 1993).

"Juan Navarro Baldeweg, 1982–1992." *El Croquis*, no. 54 (Madrid, 1992).

"Juan Navarro Baldeweg, 1992–1995." *El Croquis*, no. 73 [II] (Madrid, 1995).

Julio Cano Lasso. Madrid: CSCAE, 1992.

Julio Cano Lasso, arquitecto. Madrid: Xarait, 1985.

Julio Cano Lasso–Estudio Cano Lasso. Madrid: Munilla-Lería, 1995.

Lahuerta, J. J. "Razionalismo e architettura in Spagna negli anni trenta." *L'Europa dei razionalisti*. Milan: Electa, 1989.

Lahuerta, J. J., and A. Pizza (eds.). *Alejandro de la Sota, arquitecto*. Barcelona: C.R.C. Galería de Arquitectura, 1985.

Levene, R., F. Márquez Cecilia, and A. Ruiz Barbarín. *Arquitectura española contemporánea 1975–1990*. 2 vols. Madrid: El Croquis Editorial, 1989.

Linazasoro, J. I. *Escritos. 1976–1989*. Madrid: COAM, 1989.

Llano, P. de. *Alejandro de la Sota. O nacemento dunha arquitectura*. Pontevedra: Diputación de Pontevedra, 1995.

Llinás, J., and A. de la Sota (intro.). *Josep Llinás*. New York: Whitney Library of Design, 1997.

Lloréns, T., and H. Piñón. "La arquitectura del franquismo." *Arquitecturas bis*, no. 26 (Barcelona, 1979).

López Sardá, M. L. (curator). *Arquitecturas de representación. España de Oriente a Occidente*. Madrid: Ministerio de Asuntos Exteriores, MOPTMA, Fundación COAM, 1995.

Manifiesto de La Alhambra. Granada: 1953.

Manrique, César. *Lanzarote. Arquitectura inédita*. Arrecife: Cabildo Insular de Lanzarote, 1988.

"Manuel e Ignacio de las Casas." *El Croquis*, no. 15–16 (Madrid, 1984).

"Manuel e Ignacio de las Casas." *Documentos de Arquitectura*, no. 15 (Almería, 1990).

Marchán, S. *Linazasoro*. Barcelona: Gili, 1989.

Martorell, J. M., O. Bohigas, D. Mackay, and A. Puigdomènech. *La Villa Olímpica: Arquitectura. Parques. Puerto deportivo*. Barcelona: Gili, 1991.

Mas Serra, E. *50 años de arquitectura en Euskadi*. Vitoria: Gobierno Vasco, Consejería de Obras Públicas, 1990.

Maure, L. *Zuazo, arquitecto*. Madrid: COAM, 1987.

"Miguel Fisac." *Documentos de Arquitectura*, no. 10 (Almería, 1989).

Miguel Fisac. Medalla de Oro de la Arquitectura 1994. Madrid: CSCAE / Ministerio de Fomento, 1997.

Miguel Martín. Arquitecturas para la gran ciudad. Las Palmas de Gran Canaria: Centro Atlántico de Arte Moderno, 1995.

Moleón, P., and K. Frampton (intro.). *Angel Fernández Alba*. Madrid: Fundación Argentaria, 1995.

Molinari, L. *Calatrava*. Barcelona: Gili, 1999.

Moneo, R. (ed.). *Alejandro de la Sota*. Cambridge, MA: Harvard University, 1987.

Moneo, R. *Contra la indiferencia como norma. Anyway*. Santiago de Chile: Ediciones ARQ, Universidad Católica de Chile, Escuela de Arquitectura, 1995.

— Introduction to *Cruz / Ortiz*. New York: Princeton Architectural Press, 1996.

— "La llamada Escuela de Barcelona." *Arquitectura*, no. 121 (Madrid, 1969).

— "Madrid: los últimos 25 años." *Hogar y Arquitectura*, no. 75 (Madrid, 1968).

— *Sobre el concepto de tipo en arquitectura*. Madrid: ETSAM, 1991.

— "28 arquitectos no numerarios." *Arquitecturas bis*, no. 23–24 (Barcelona, 1978).

Montaner, J. M. *Después del movimiento moderno. Arquitectura de la segunda mitad del siglo XX*. Barcelona: Gili, 1993.

— *La modernidad superada. Arquitectura, arte y pensamiento del siglo XX*. Barcelona: Gili, 1997.

Monteys, X. (coord.). *La arquitectura de los años cincuenta en Barcelona*. Madrid: Dirección General de la Vivienda y la Arquitectura, MOPU / Barcelona: ETSAV, 1987.

Morales, M. C. *La arquitectura de Miguel Fisac*. Ciudad Real: COA de Ciudad Real, 1979.

Mosquera, E., and M. T. Pérez Cano. *La vanguardia imposible. Quince visiones de arquitectura contemporánea andaluza*. Seville: Junta de Andalucía, 1990.

Moya González, L. *Barrios de promoción oficial. Madrid 1939–1976*. Madrid: COAM, 1983.

Navarro Baldeweg, J. *La habitación vacante*. Valencia: PreTextos, 1999.
— *Juan Navarro Baldeweg*. Catalogue. Valencia: IVAM, 1999.
— *Juan Navarro Baldeweg*. Corte Madera, CA: Gingko Press, 2001.
Nigst, P. (ed.). *Rafael Moneo: Bauen für die Stadt*. Stuttgart: Gerd Hatje, 1993.
El Noucentisme. Un projecte de modernitat. Barcelona: Generalitat de Catalunya, 1994.
La obra de E. Torroja. Madrid: Instituto de España, 1977.
La obra de Luis Gutiérrez Soto. Madrid: COAM, 1988.
Ortiz-Echagüe, C. *La arquitectura española actual*. Madrid: Rialp, 1965.
— "40 años de arquitectura española." *Binario*, no. 25 (Madrid, 1960).
"Oscar Tusquets." *A&V Monografías de Arquitectura y Vivienda*, no. 27 (Madrid, 1991).
Palerm, Juan M., et al. *Arquitectura y urbanismo en Canarias, 1968–1988*. Las Palmas de Gran Canaria: ETSA, 1989.
Peña, R., and M. Sangalli (eds.). *Luis Peña Ganchegui. Arquitecturas 1958–1994*. San Sebastián: Universidad del País Vasco, 1994.
Peña Amaro, A., et al. *Rafael de La Hoz, arquitecto*. Córdoba: COAAocc, 1991.
Pérez Escolano, V. "Una década prodigiosa." In *1978–1988. Andalucía: diez años de cultura*. Seville: Junta de Andalucía, Consejería de Cultura, 1988.
Pérez Escolano, V., M. T. Pérez Cano, E. Mosquera, and J. R. Moreno. *50 años de arquitectura en Andalucía. 1936–1986*. Seville: Junta de Andalucía, Consejería de Obras Públicas, 1986.
Pérez Escolano, V., J. R. Sierra, and F. Torres. *Arquitectura pública en Andalucía*. Seville: Junta de Andalucía, Consejería de Obras Públicas, 1994.
Pérez Escolano, V., and I. de Solà-Morales. *España: Arquitecturas de hoy*. Madrid: MOPT, 1992.
Pérez Lastra, José R. *Vaquero Palacios, arquitecto*. Oviedo: COAAs, 1992.
Pérez Parrilla, Sergio T. *La arquitectura racionalista en Canarias. 1927–1939*. Las Palmas: Cabildo Insular de Gran Canaria, 1977.
Piñón, H. *Arquitecturas de las neovanguardias*. Barcelona: Gili, 1984.
— "Tres décadas en la obra de José Antonio Coderch." *Arquitecturas bis*, no. 11 (Barcelona, 1976).
Piñón, H., and F. Català-Roca. *Arquitectura moderna en Barcelona (1951–1976)*. Barcelona: Edicions UPC / ETSAB, 1996.
Pisapia, P. (curator). *Dieci anni di architettura spagnola*. Milan: Electa, 1998.
Pizza, A. *Alberto Campo Baeza*. Barcelona: Gili, 1999.
Poisay, Ch., and R. B. Hassine (eds.). *Architecture en Espagne. 1974–1984*. Exhibition catalogue. Paris: 1985.
Polano, S. *Santiago Calatrava. Opera completa*. Milan: Electa, 1996.
Quaderns d'Arquitectura i Urbanisme, no. 179–180 (Barcelona, 1989). Monograph on Jujol.
Quetglas, J. "4—10—4—5." In *Juan Navarro Baldeweg Conferencia*. Bolzano: Galleria Arge Kunst, 1994.
— *Der Gäserne Schrecken. Imágenes del Pabellón de Alemania*. Montreal: 1991.
— "Al margen de una imposible Escuela de Barcelona." *Jano Arquitectura*, no. 48 (Barcelona, 1977).
Quetglas, J., F. Alonso, J. M. López-Peláez et al. *Conversaciones en torno a Alejandro de la Sota*. Madrid: Departamento de Proyectos de la ETSAM, 1996.
"Rafael Moneo." *A+U*, no. 227 (Tokyo, 1989).

"Rafael Moneo." *El Croquis*, no. 20 (Madrid, 1985).
"Rafael Moneo 1986–1992." *A&V Monografías de Arquitectura y Vivienda*, no. 36 (Madrid, 1992).
"Rafael Moneo 1990–1994." *El Croquis*, no. 64 (Madrid, 1994).
Rispa, R., and M. J. Aguaza (eds.), F. Dal Co (intro.), J. Pellón, V. Pérez Escolano, and S. Polano. *Expo'92 Seville. Architecture and Design*. New York: Abbeville, 1992.
Rispa, R. (ed.), I. de Solá-Morales, A. Capitel, G. Ruiz Cabrero, V. Pérez Escolano, P. de Llano, J. Cenicacelaya, and P. Buchanan (selection committee). *Architectural Guide. Spain 1920–1999*. New York: Birkhäuser, 1998. Book format version of the *Register of Spanish Architecture, phase I*, Ministerio de Fomento, G. Mingo and G. Vázquez Consuegra (scientific dirs.)
Rodríguez Cheda, J. B. *Alejandro de la Sota.Construcción, idea y arquitectura*. La Coruña: COAG, 1994.
"Roser Amadó—Luis Domènech 1976–1989." *Documentos de Arquitectura*, no. 7 (Almería, 1988).
Rossi, A. *The Architecture of the City*. Cambridge, MA: MIT Press, 1982.
Ruiz, J. *Barba Corsini, arquitectura 1953–1994*. Barcelona: Galería H20, 1995.
Rykwert, J. (intro.), and X. Güell (ed.). *Arquitectura española contemporánea. La década de los 80*. Barcelona: Gili, 1990.
Sáenz de Oiza, F. J., A. Capitel, and J. Sáenz Guerra. *Francisco Javier Sáenz de Oiza, arquitecto*. Madrid: Pronaos / Ministerio de Fomento, 1996.
Sambricio, C., F. Roch, and R. López de Lucio. *La vivienda en Madrid en la década de los 50: El Plan de Urgencia Social*. Madrid: Ministerio de Fomento, Ayuntamiento de Madrid, Electa España, 1999.
Schneider, F. *Grundrißatlas Wohnungsbau. Floor Plans Atlas: Housing*. Basel: Birkhäuser, 1994.
"Sevilla Expo." *A&V Monografías de Arquitecura y Vivienda*, no. 34–35 (Madrid, 1992).
"Sevilla 1992." *A&V Monografías de Arquitectura y Vivienda*, no. 20 (Madrid, 1989).
Silvetti, J. "Architecture's Outside, Juan Navarro Baldeweg." *Assemblage*, no. 34 (Cambridge, MA, 1998).
Siza, A. (intro.). *Vázquez Consuegra*. Seville: Tanais Ediciones, in press.
"Sobre la arquitectura de Alberto Campo Baeza." *Arquitectura*, no. 305 (Madrid, 1996).
Sobrino, J. *Arquitectura industrial en España (1830–1990)*. Madrid: Cátedra, 1996.
Solà-Morales, I. de. "Un'altra tradizione moderna. Dalla rottura dell'anno trenta al progetto urbano moderno." *Lotus International*, no. 64 (Milan, 1990).
— "L'arquitectura a Catalunya. 1939–1970." In E. Jardí, *L'art català contemporani*. Barcelona: Aymá, 1972.
— "La arquitectura de la vivienda en los años de la autarquía (1939–1953)." *Arquitectura*, no. 199 (Madrid, 1976).
— "Arquitectura española: Balbuceos y silencios." In Bozal and Lloréns (eds.), *España. Vanguardia artística y realidad social, 1936–1976*. Barcelona: Gili, 1976.
— *Bach / Mora Arquitectos*. Barcelona: Gili, 1996.
— *Differences. Topographies of Contemporary Architecture*. Cambridge, MA: MIT Press, 1996.
— *Eclecticismo y vanguardia. El caso de la arquitectura moderna en Catalunya*. Barcelona: Gili, 1980.
Solana, E. *El patrimonio de la arquitectura moderna en la ciudad de Las Palmas de Gran Canaria 1922–1960*. International Conference on the Conservation of Historic Quarters, 1994.
Sòria, E. *Coderch*. Barcelona: Blume, 1979.
Sostres, J. M. "El funcionalismo y la nueva plástica." *Boletín de la Dirección General de Arquitectura*, no. 15 (Madrid, 1950).

— *Opiniones sobre arquitectura*. Murcia: COAMu, 1983.

Sota, A. de la. *Alejandro de la Sota*. Madrid: Pronaos, 1989.

The Structures of Eduardo Torroja. New York: F. W. Dodge, 1958.

"Studio PER." *El Croquis*, no. 11–12 (Madrid, 1983).

"Studio PER." *El Croquis*, no. 23 (Madrid, 1986).

Tagliabue, B. (ed.). *Enric Miralles. Mixed Talks*. London: Academy, 1995.

— *Enric Miralles. Obras y proyectos*. Madrid: Electa España, 1996.

Terán, F. de. *Historia del urbanismo en España III, siglos XIX y XX*. Madrid: Cátedra, 1999.

Tischhauser, A., and S. von Moos. *Calatrava Public Buildings*. Basel: Birkhäuser, 1998.

Torroja Miret, E., et al. *Eduardo Torroja. Su obra científica*. Madrid: Asociación de Miembros del Instituto Eduardo Torroja / Ministerio de Fomento, 1999.

Tzonis, A., and L. Lefaivre (eds.). *Santiago Calatrava's Creative Process*. 2 vols. Basel: Birkhäuser, 2000.

Uría, L. (intro.). *Antonio Fernández Alba. Arquitectura 1957–1980*. Madrid: Xarait, 1980.

Urrutia, A. *Arquitectura española. Siglo XX*. Madrid: Cátedra, 1997.

"Vázquez de Castro—Íñiguez de Onzoño." *Nueva Forma*, no. 102–103 (Madrid, 1974).

Venturi, R. *Complexity and Contradiction in Architecture*. New York: Museum of Modern Art, 1966.

Viaplana, A., and H. Piñón. *Viaplana, Piñón*. Barcelona: COAC, 1996.

Werk, Bauen + Wohnen, no. 9 (Zurich, 1984). Monograph on Spain.

Winter, K. (ed.). *Moneo. Byggsander och projekt 1973–1993*. Stockholm: Arkitekturmuseet, 1993.

"Xosé Bar Boo, arquitecto." *Obradoiro*, no. 17 (Santiago de Compostela, 1990).

Zabalbeascoa, A. *Miralles Tagliabue. Time architecture, Arquitecturas del tiempo*. Barcelona: Gili, 1999.

— *The New Spanish Architecture*. New York: Rizzoli, 1993.

Zaera, A. (intro.). *Abalos & Herreros*. Barcelona: Gili, 1993.

Zodiac, no. 15 (Milan, 1965). Monograph on Spanish architecture during the sixties.

INDEX

Page numbers in italics indicate illustrations.

ILL USTRATION CREDITS

Ábalos & Herreros 143c; Ábalos & Herreros - L. Asín 143d; Alas Casariego - C. Casariego 49b; Alonso de Santos 104b; Alonso Vera 154b; Amadó / Domènech 123a; Amadó / Domenéch / Puig 97a; AMP arquitectos 114c; Aranguren / González Gallegos 143b; Archivo Coderch - F. Catalá Roca 24; Archivo Ruiz Cabrero 58f, 63a, 162; Archivo Ruiz Cabrero - F. Catalá Roca 32b, 34-35, 35a, 58d, 58e; Ayala 132b; Ayala - J. Soto 132c Bach / Mora 100b; Bar Boo - Foto Magar 62b; Barrionuevo 111; Bayón - H. Suzuki 132a; Bellosillo 107c; Benítez / Rebollo, G. / Rebollo, A. - F. Alda 136; Bofill - J. Sarrà 118a; Bofill Taller de Arquitectura 58a; Bonell - cb foto 83b; Bonell - L. Casals 98-99; Bonell - H. Suzuki 118c; Bru - J. Bernardó 118b; Bru - M. Laguillo 125d; Burillo / Lorenzo 107b Cabrero 8, 16b, 18b, 54a, 54b; Cabrero - Férriz fotógrafo industrial 74c; Campo Baeza 107h; Campo Baeza - H. Suzuki 141a; Campos - L. Alonso-Lamberti 149c; Cano Lasso 51a; Carrasco López 157a; Casas, M. / Casas, I. - L. Casals 107g; Casas, M. / Casas, I. - Portillo 74a; Clotet / Paricio - L. Casals 97b; Clotet / Tusquets 58c, 83d; COAAs 37a; COAC 25, 27a, 28a, 32a; Coderch 14-15; Corrales 21a, 22-23b; Corrales / Vázquez Molezún 22-23a, 51b; Corrales / Vázquez Molezún - J. Gorospe 21b; Correa / Milà 33b; Cotelo / Puente 104a; Cruz / Ortiz, S.L. 88-89, 89, 154a; Cruz / Ortiz - D. Malagamba 130, 134b, 154b De Miguel / Leache - L. Casals 152; Díaz Llanos / Saavedra 63b; Díaz Llanos / Saavedra - E. Pintos 64a; Díaz Recaséns 110a; Domènech / Puig / Sanmartí / Sabater 56 Fernández Alba, Ángel - Lluís Casals 107e; Fernández Alba, Ángel - R. Halme 141d; Fernández Alba, Antonio 46-47, 47b; Fernández del Amo - *Kindel* 17a, 18a; Ferrater - L. Casals 127b; Fisac - *Kindel* 16a, 19, 40-41; Foreign Office Architects, Ltd. 146a; Fraile / Revillo 144-145; Frechilla / López-Peláez / Sánchez 102b; Fundación César Manrique 64d; Gallego 87a Gallego - P. Gallego 149b; Gallego - J. Rodríguez 113b; Garay / Linazasoro - G. Mezzacasa 86; Garcés / Soria - L. Casals 96a; García Barba - A. Delgado 161b; García de Paredes 76a; García de Paredes - A. Schommer 49a; García de Paredes - L. Casals 76b; García de Paredes - Pando Fotógrafos 39a; García Márquez / Rubiño, I. / Rubiño, L. - D. Malagamba 135b; García-Solera Vera 155b; García-Solera Vera - P. Balaguer / González Cordón 110b, 129b; González, Mª Luisa - L. Casals 160a Higueras 47c, 64b, 64c; HSP Arquitectos, S.L. - D. Malagamba 158; Inza 48a; Iñiguez / Ustarroz 153a; Junquera / Pérez Pita 102c; Junquera / Pérez Pita - Baltanás / Sánchez 142a Linazasoro 155c; Linazasoro - J. Azurmendi 155a; Llinás - cb foto 83c; Llinás - H. Susuki 125a; Llinás - L. Jansana 125b, 125c; A. López 47a; López Cotelo / Puente 107d; López Cotelo - G. Ruiz Cabrero 141b; J. M. López-Peláez 52-53, 54c, 74d Mangado 153c; Marín de Terán 131a; Martínez / Pérez Amaral / Corona - J. Nerea 161a; Martínez Lapeña / Torres Tur 98b, 123b, 146b; Martínez Lapeña / Torres Tur - L. Casals 124a; Martínez Lapeña / Torres Tur - L. Jansana 98a; Mateo / Moliner 124c; MBM arquitectes - cb foto 83a; Miralles / Pinòs 127c; Miralles / Tagliabue 126a, 163b; Moneo 62a, 134a, 75a, 75b, 139; Moneo - L. Casals Moneo - L. Jimenez 48b; 90; Moneo - D. Malagamba 138-139; Moneo / Solà-Morales, M. - L. Casals 121a; Moreno Mansilla / Tuñón - L. Asín 145; Mozas - *a+t* / C. San Millán 153b; Museo Thyssen-Bornemisza Cbta. Navarro Baldeweg - J. Bretón 163a; Navarro Baldeweg - J. M. Churtichaga 76c, 140; Navarro Baldeweg - L. Casals 107a; Navarro Baldeweg - D. Malagamba 116-117; Noguerol / Díez - J. Azurmendi 149a; Oteiza 17c Penela - M. García Vicente 148-149; Peña Ganchegui 66-67, 39b; Perea - J. Azurmendi 141e; Piñón / Viaplana - F. Catalá Roca 94; Portaceli 156a, 156b; Portela 113a, 147; Prieto Fernández 157b; C. Puente - Baltanás / Sánchez 141c Registro de Arquitectura de España, Ministerio de Fomento / Tanais 28b, 29, 33a, 44, 50a, 50b, 132e; Registro de Arquitectura de España, Ministerio de Fomento / Tanais - Arxiu González-Torán 35b; Registro de Arquitectura de España, Ministerio de Fomento / Tanais - F. Catalá Roca 27b; Rodrigo / Cantallops - Maspons + Ubiña 57; Ruisánchez / Vendrell - M. Roselló 127a; G. Ruiz Cabrero 102a; Ruiz Cabrero - M. Moreno 76d S. E. Hanover 2000, S. A. 37c, 71; S. E. Hanover 2000, S. A. - F. Catalá Roca 36; Sáenz de Oiza 45a, 72; Sáenz de Oiza - Archivo Ruiz Cabrero 45b; Sáenz de Oiza / Laorga 17b; Salvadores / Portaceli - P. Balaguer / L. Vicen 114b; Sierra, J. R. / Sierra, R. 131b; Sierra, J. R. / Sierra, R. - L. Casals 129a; Soriano / Palacios Díaz 146c; Sosa / Gutiérrez - E. Pintos 160b; Sota 20, 70; Sota - Freixa, Ferrán 12; Soto / Maroto 144; Sunyer / Badía - H. Susuki 126b Tanais 129c; Tanais - A. Elías 30, 34; Tanais - R. Cuevas 132d; Torres - J. Granada 135a; Torres Nadal - J. de la Cruz 159; Tusquets, Díaz & Assoc. 80a, 80b, 80c, 80d, 80e, 81a, 81b, 96b, 121b Vázquez Consuegra 150b, 162-163; Vázquez Consuegra - R. Morais de Souza 133; Vázquez Consuegra - D. Malagamba 132f, 134c, 150a, 150c; Vázquez Consuegra - H. Suzuki 108; Vázquez Consuegra - L. Casals 87b; Vellés 74b, 107f, 142b; Vellés - J. Moreno 143a; S. Vergano 58b; Viaplana / Piñón 124b; Viaplana / Piñón - F. Catalá Roca 100a; L. Vicen 114a; Vicens / Ramos - D. Malagamba 142c